Chinese Pottery

(Volume

Ming and Ch'ing Porcelain

R. L. Hobson

Alpha Editions

This edition published in 2024

ISBN : 9789367241592

Design and Setting By
Alpha Editions
www.alphaedis.com
Email - info@alphaedis.com

Contents

VOL. II

CHAPTER I

明

THE MING   DYNASTY, 1368–1644 A.D.

As we have already discussed, so far as our imperfect knowledge permits, the various potteries which are scattered over the length and breadth of China, we can now concentrate our attention on the rising importance of Ching-tê Chên. From the beginning of the Ming dynasty, Ching-tê Chên may be said to have become the ceramic metropolis of the empire, all the other potteries sinking to provincial status. So far as Western collections, at any rate, are concerned, it is not too much to say that 90 per cent. of the post-Yüan porcelains were made in this great pottery town.

What happened there in the stormy years which saw the overthrow of the Mongol dynasty and the rise of the native Ming is unknown to us, and, indeed, it is scarcely likely to have been of much interest. The Imperial factories were closed, and did not open till 1369, or, according to some accounts, 1398.[1] If we follow the *Ching-tê Chên T'ao lu*, which, as its name implies, should be well informed on the history of the place, a factory was built in 1369 at the foot of the Jewel Hill to supply Imperial porcelain (*kuan tz'ŭ*), and in the reign of Hung Wu (1368–1398) there were at least twenty kilns in various parts of the town working in the Imperial service. They included kilns for the large dragon bowls, kilns for blue (or green) ware (*ch'ing yao*), "wind and fire" kilns, seggar kilns for making the cases for the fine porcelain, and *lan kuang* kilns, which Julien renders *fours à flammes étendues*. The last expression implies that the heat was raised in these kilns by means of a kind of bellows (*kuang*) which admitted air to the furnace, and Bushell's rendering, "blue and yellow enamel furnaces," ignores an essential part of both the characters[3] used in the original.

From this time onward there is no lack of information on the nature of the Imperial wares made during the various reigns, but it must be remembered that the Chinese descriptions are in almost every case confined to the Imperial porcelains, and we are left to assume that the productions of the numerous private kilns followed the same lines, though in the earlier periods, at any rate, we are told that they were inferior in quality and finish.

The Hung Wu 洪 武 palace porcelain, as described in the *T'ao lu*, was of fine, unctuous clay and potted thin. The ware was left for a whole year to dry, then put upon the lathe and turned thin, and then glazed and fired. If there was any fault in the glaze, the piece was ground down on the lathe, reglazed and refired. "Consequently the glaze was lustrous (*jung*) like massed lard." These phrases are now so trite that one is tempted to regard them as mere Chinese conventionalities, but there is no doubt that the material used in the Ming period (which, as we shall see presently, gave out in the later reigns) was of peculiar excellence. The raw edge of the base rim of early specimens does, in fact, reveal a beautiful white body of exceedingly fine grain and smooth texture, so fat and unctuous that one might almost expect to squeeze moisture out of it.

The best ware, we are told, was white, but other kinds are mentioned. A short contemporary notice in the *Ko ku yao lun*,[4] written in 1387, says, "Of modern wares (made at Ching-tê Chên) the good examples with white colour and lustrous are very highly valued. There are, besides, *ch'ing*[5] (blue or green) and black (*hei*) wares with gilding, including wine pots and wine cups of great charm." Such pieces may exist in Western collections, but they remain unidentified, and though there are several specimens with the Hung Wu mark to be seen in museums, few have the appearance of Ming porcelain at all. There is, however, a dish in the British Museum which certainly belongs to the Ming dynasty, even if it is a century later than the mark implies. The body is refined and white, though the finish is rather rough, with pits and raised spots here and there in the glaze and grit adhering to the foot rim; but it is painted with a free touch in a bright blue, recalling the Mohammedan blue in colour, the central subject a landscape, and the sides and rim divided into panels of floral and formal ornament. It must be allowed that the style of the painting is advanced for this early period, including as it does white designs reserved in blue ground as well as the ordinary blue painting on a white ground.

Yung Lo 永樂 (1403–1424)

The usual formulæ are employed by the *T'ao lu* in describing the Imperial ware of this reign. It was made of plastic clay and refined material, and though, as a rule, the porcelain was thick, there were some exceedingly thin varieties known as *t'o t'ai*[6] or "bodiless" porcelains. Besides the plain white specimens, there were others engraved with a point[7] or coated with vivid red (*hsien hung*). The *Po wu yao lan*,[8] reputed a high authority on Ming porcelains and written in the third decade of the seventeenth century, adds "blue and white" to the list and gives further details of the wares. The passage is worth quoting in full, and runs as follows: "In the reign of Yung Lo were made the cups which fit in the palm of the hand,[9] with broad mouth, contracted waist, sandy (*sha*) foot, and polished base. Inside were drawn two lions rolling balls. Inside, too, in seal characters, was written *Ta Ming Yung Lo nien chih*[10] in six characters, or sometimes in four[11] only, as fine as grains of rice. These are the highest class. Those with mandarin ducks, or floral decoration inside, are all second quality. The cups are decorated outside with blue ornaments of a very deep colour, and their shape and make are very refined and beautiful and in a traditional style. Their price, too, is very high. As for the modern imitations, they are coarse in style and make, with foot and base burnt (brown), and though their form has some resemblance (to the old), they are not worthy of admiration."

As may be imagined, Yung Lo porcelain is not common to-day, and the few specimens which exist in our collections are not enough to make us realise the full import of these descriptions. There are, however, several types which bear closely on the subject, some being actually of the period and others in the Yung Lo style. A fair sample of the ordinary body and glaze of the time is seen in the white porcelain bricks of which the lower story of the famous Nanking pagoda was built. Several of these are in the British Museum, and they show a white compact body of close but granular fracture; the glazed face is a pure, solid-looking white, and the unglazed sides show a smooth, fine-grained ware which has assumed a pinkish red tinge in the firing. The coarser porcelains of the period would, no doubt, have similar characteristics in body and glaze. The finer wares are exemplified by the white bowls, of wonderful thinness and transparency, with decoration engraved in the body or traced in delicate white slip under the glaze and scarcely visible except as a transparency. Considering the fragility of these delicate wares and the distant date of the Yung Lo period, it is surprising how many are to be seen in Western collections. Indeed, it is hard to believe that more than a very few of these can be genuine Yung Lo productions, and as we know that the fine white "egg shell" porcelain was made throughout the Ming period and copied with great skill in the earlier reigns of the last dynasty, it is not necessary to assume that every bowl of the Yung Lo type dates back to the first decades of the fifteenth century.

Fig. 1

Fig. 2

Plate 59.—White Eggshell Porcelain Bowl with Imperial dragons faintly traced in white slip under the glaze.

Mark of the Yung Lo period (1403–1424) incised in the centre in archaic characters. 1. Exterior. 2. Interior view.

Diameter 8¾ inches.

British Museum.

It is wellnigh impossible to reproduce adequately these white porcelains, but Plate 59 illustrates the well-known example in the Franks Collection, which has long been accepted as a genuine Yung Lo specimen. It represents the *ya shou pei* in form, with wide mouth and small foot—the contracted waist of the *Po wu yao lan*; the foot rim is bare at the edge, but not otherwise sandy, and the base is glazed over, which may be the sense in which the word "polished"[12] is used in the *Po wu yao lan*. The ware is so thin and transparent that it seems to consist of glaze alone, as though the body had been pared away to vanishing point before the glaze was applied—in short, it is *t'o t'ai* or "bodiless." When held to the light it has a greenish transparency and the colour of melting snow, and there is revealed on the sides a delicate but exquisitely drawn design of five-clawed Imperial dragons in white slip (not etched, as has too often been stated), showing up like the water-mark in paper. On the bottom inside is the date-mark of the period etched with a point in four archaic characters (see vol. i, p. 213). A more refined and delicate ceramic work could hardly be imagined.

Close to this bowl in the Franks Collection there are two smaller bowls or, rather, cups which in many ways answer more nearly the description of the *ya shou pei*,[13] though they are thick in substance and of coarser make. They have straight spreading sides, wide at the mouth, with foliate rim, and contracted at the foot. The foot rim is bare of glaze, but the base is covered. They are of an impure white ware with surface rather pitted, and inside is a lotus design traced in white slip under the glaze and repeated in radiating compartments. These are perhaps a product of the private factories. The same form is observed among the blue and white porcelain in two small cups, which are painted in blue with a landscape on the exterior and with bands of curled scrolls inside and the Yung Lo mark in four characters. The base is unglazed, and though they are undoubtedly intended to represent a Yung Lo type, these not uncommon bowls can hardly be older than the last dynasty. Another blue and white bowl in the Franks Collection has the Yung Lo mark and the scroll decoration inside, and on the exterior a long poem by Su Shih, covering most of the surface. It is painted in a grey blue, and the ware, though coarse, has the appearance of Ming manufacture, perhaps one of the late Ming copies which are mentioned without honour in the *Po wu yao lan*. It is, however, of the ordinary rounded form.[14]

Hsiang Yüan-p'ien illustrates in his Album one Yung Lo specimen, a low cylindrical bowl of the "bodiless" kind, "thin as paper," with a very delicate dragon and phœnix design, which is seen when the bowl is held to the light and carefully inspected. This style of ornament is described as *an hua* (secret decoration), but it is not stated whether, in this case, it was engraved in the paste or traced in white slip.

The mention of "fresh red" (*hsien hung*), which seems to have been used on the Yung Lo porcelain as well as in the succeeding Hsüan Tê period, brings to mind a familiar type of small bowl with slight designs in blue inside, often a figure of a boy at play, the exterior being coated with a fine coral red, over which are lotus scrolls in gold. There are several in the British Museum, and one, with a sixteenth-century silver mount, was exhibited at the Burlington Fine Arts Club in 1910.[15] The term *hsien hung* is certainly used for an underglaze copper red on the Hsüan Tê porcelain, and it is doubtful whether it can have been loosely applied to an overglaze iron red on the earlier ware.

For the bowls to which I refer have an iron red decoration, though it is sometimes wonderfully translucent and, being heavily fluxed, looks like a red glaze instead of merely an overglaze enamel (see Plate 74). Several of these red bowls have the Yung Lo mark, others have merely marks of commendation or good wish. Their form is characteristic of the Ming period, and the base is sometimes convex at the bottom, sometimes concave. They vary considerably in quality, the red in some cases being a translucent and rather pale coral tint, and in others a thick, opaque brick red. Probably they vary in date as well, the former type being the earlier and better. It is exemplified by an interesting specimen in the Franks Collection marked *tan kuei* (red cassia), which indicates its destination as a present to a literary aspirant, the red cassia being a symbol of literary success. This piece has, moreover, a stamped leather box of European—probably Venetian—make, which is not later than the sixteenth century. This, if any of these bowls, belongs to the Yung Lo period, but it will be seen presently that the iron red was used as an inferior but more workable substitute for the underglaze red in the later Ming reigns, and, it must be added, these bowls are strangely numerous for a fifteenth-century porcelain. That they are a Yung Lo type, however, there is little doubt, for this red and gold decoration (*kinrande* of the Japanese) is the adopted style which won for the clever Kioto potter, Zengoro Hozen, the art name *Ei raku*, i.e. Yung Lo in Japanese.

CHAPTER II

HSÜAN TÊ 宣德 (1426–1435)

In this short reign, which Chinese writers regard as the most brilliant period of their porcelain industry, the number of kilns occupied with the Imperial orders had increased to fifty-eight, the majority of them being outside the Imperial factory and distributed among the private factories. According to the *T'ao lu*,[16] the clay used at this time was red and the ware like cinnabar, a statement which is difficult to reconcile with the glowing description of the jade-like white altar cups and other exquisite objects for which the reign was celebrated. It is, of course, possible that a dark coloured body was employed in some of the wares, as was done at other periods, or it may be that the words are hyperbolically used to describe a porcelain of which the exposed parts of the body assumed a red colour in the firing. This latter peculiarity is noticeable on specimens of later Ming porcelain, particularly the blue and white of the Chia Ching period. But in any case a red biscuit cannot have been invariable or even characteristic of the period, for no mention is made of such a feature in the *Po wu yao lan*, which gives by far the fullest account of the Hsüan Tê porcelain.

The description in the *Po wu yao lan*,[17] which seems to have been generally accepted, and certainly was largely borrowed by subsequent Chinese works, may be freely rendered as follows:

"Among the wares of the Hsüan Tê period there are stem-cups[18] decorated with red fish. For these they used a powder made of red precious stones from the West to paint the fish forms, and from the body there rose up in relief in the firing the precious brilliance of the fresh red ravishing the eye. The brown and blackish colours which resulted from imperfect firing of the red are inferior. There were also blue decorated wares, such as stem-cups with dragon pine and plum designs, wine stem-cups with figure subjects[19] and lotus designs, small cinnabar pots and large bowls in colour red like the sun, but with white mouth rim, pickle pots and small pots with basket covers and handles in the form of bamboo joints, all of which things were unknown in ancient times. Again, there were beautiful objects of a useful kind, all small and cleverly made with finely and accurately drawn designs. The incense vases, trays and dishes[20] were made in large numbers, and belong to a common class. The flat-sided jars with basket covers, and the ornamented round pots with flanged[21] mouth for preserving honey, are very beautiful and mostly decorated in colours (*wu ts'ai*). The white cups, which have the character *t'an* (altar) engraved inside the bowl, are what are known as 'altar cups.' The material of these things is refined and the ware thick, and the form beautiful enough to be used as elegant vases in the true scholar's room. There are besides white cups for tea with rounded body,[22] convex[23] base, thread-like foot, bright and lustrous like jade, and with very finely engraved[24] dragon and phœnix designs which are scarcely inferior to the altar cups. At the bottom the characters *ta ming hsüan tê nien chih*[25] are secretly engraved in the paste, and the texture of the glaze is uneven, like orange peel.[26] How can even Ting porcelain compare with these? Truly they are the most excellent porcelains of this reign, and unfortunately there have not been many to be seen since then. Again, there are the beautiful barrel-shaped seats, some with openwork ground, the designs filled in with colours (*wu ts'ai*), gorgeous as cloud brocades, others with solid ground filled in with colours in engraved floral designs, so beautiful and brilliant as to dazzle the eye; both sorts have a deep green (*ch'ing*) background. Others have blue (*lan*) ground, filled in with designs in colours (*wu ts'ai*), like ornament carved in cobalt blue (*shih ch'ing*, lit. stone blue). There is also blue decoration on a white ground and crackled grounds like ice. The form and ornament of these various types do not seem to have been known before this period."

Fig. 1

Fig. 2

Plate 60.—Reputed Hsüan Tê Porcelain.

Fig. 1.—Flask with blue decoration, reputed to be Hsüan Tê period. Height 3¼ inches. *British Museum*.

Fig. 2.—Brush Rest. (?) Chang Ch'ien on a log raft; partly biscuit. Inscribed with a stanza of verse and the Hsüan Tê mark. Length 6 inches.

Grandidier Collection.

Fig. 1

Fig. 2

Plate 61.—Porcelain with *san ts'ai* glazes on the biscuit.

Fig. 1.—Wine Jar with pierced casing, the Taoist Immortals paying court to the God of Longevity, turquoise blue ground. Fifteenth century. Height 11½ inches. *Eumorfopoulos Collection.*

Fig. 2.—Screen with design in relief, horsemen on a mountain path, dark blue ground. About 1500. Height 14 inches. *Benson Collection.*

It will be seen from the above that the Hsüan Tê porcelains included a fine white, blue and white and polychrome painted wares, underglaze red painted wares, and crackle. The last mentioned is further specified in the *Ch'ing pi tsang* as having "eel's blood lines,"[27] and almost rivalling the Kuan and Ju wares. The ware was thick and strong, and the glaze had the peculiar undulating appearance (variously compared to chicken skin, orange peel, millet grains, or a wind ruffled surface) which was deliberately produced on the eighteenth century porcelains.

Another surface peculiarity shared by the Hsüan Tê and Yung Lo wares was "palm eye" (*tsung yen*) markings, which Bushell explains as holes in the glaze due to air bubbles. It is hard to see how these can have been other than a defect. Probably both these and the orange peel effects were purely fortuitous at this time.

Of the various types which we have enumerated, the white wares need little comment. The glaze was no doubt thick and lustrous like mutton fat jade, and though Hsiang in his Album usually describes the white of his examples as "white like driven snow," it is worthy of note that in good imitations of the ware particular care seems to have been given to impart a distinct greenish tint to the glaze.

The honours of the period appear to have been shared by the "blue and white" and red painted wares. Out of twenty examples illustrated in Hsiang's Album, no fewer than twelve are decorated chiefly in red, either covering the whole or a large part of the surface or painted in designs, among which three fishes occur with monotonous frequency. The red in every case is called *chi hung*, and it is usually qualified by the illuminating comparison with "ape's blood," and in one case it is even redder than that!

The expression *chi hung* has evidently been handed down by oral traditions, for there is no sort of agreement among Chinese writers on the form of the first character. The *T'ao lu* uses the character 祭, which means "sacrificial," and Bushell[28] explains this "as the colour of the sacrificial cups which were employed by the Emperor in the worship of the Sun." Hsiang uses the character 積 which means "massed, accumulated." And others use the character 霽 which means "sky clearing," and is also applied to blue in the sense of the "blue of the sky after rain." In the oft quoted list of the Yung Chêng porcelains we find the item, "Imitations of Hsüan *chi hung* wares, including two kinds, *hsien hung* (fresh red) and *pao shih hung* (ruby red)." There can be little doubt that both these were shades of underglaze red derived from copper oxide, a colour with which we are quite familiar from the eighteenth century and later examples.

For in another context we find the *hsien hung* contrasted with *fan hung*, which is the usual term for overglaze iron red, and the description already given of the application of *pao shih hung* leaves no doubt whatever that it was an underglaze colour. The two terms are probably fanciful names for two variations of the same colour, or perhaps for two different applications of it, for we know that it was used as a pigment for brushwork as well as in the form of a ground colour incorporated in the glaze. The secret of the colour seems to have been well kept, and the general impression prevailing outside the factories was that its tint and brilliancy were due to powdered rubies, the red precious stone from the West which gave the name to the *pao shih hung*.[29] It is known that in some cases such stones as cornelian (*ma nao*) have been incorporated in the porcelain glazes in China to increase the limpidity of the glaze. This is reputed to have happened in the case of the Ju yao, but neither cornelian nor ruby could serve in any way as a colouring agent, as their colour would be dissipated in the heat of the furnace. The real colouring agent of the *chi hung* is protoxide of copper. If there were nothing else to prove this, it would be clear from the fact hinted in the *Po wu yao lan* that the failures came out a brownish or blackish tint. This colour has always proved a difficult one to manage, and in the early part of the last dynasty, when it was freely used after the manner of the Hsüan Tê potters, the results were most unequal, varying from a fine blood red to maroon and brown, and even to a blackish tint.

The peculiar merits of the Hsüan Tê red were probably due in some measure to the clay of which the ware was composed, and which contained some natural ingredient favourable to the development of the red. At any rate, we are told[30] that in the Chia Ching period (1522–1566) "the earth used for the *hsien hung* ran short."

Among the favourite designs[31] expressed in the Hsüan Tê red were three fishes, three fruits,[32] three funguses, and the character *fu* (happiness) repeated five times.[33] All these are mentioned among the Yung Chêng imitations. A good idea of the fish design is given by a cylindrical vase in the Franks Collection, which is plain except for two fishes in underglaze red of good colour, and rising in slight relief in the glaze. The glaze itself is of that faint celadon green which was apparently regarded as a necessary feature of the Hsüan Tê copies, and which incidentally seems to be favourable to the development of the copper red. The *sang de bœuf* red of the last dynasty is avowedly a revival of the Hsüan Tê red in its use as a glaze colour. Indeed, certain varieties of the *sang de bœuf* class are still distinguished as *chi hung*. The large bowls, "red as the sun and white at the mouth rim," as mentioned in the *Po wu yao lan*, have a counterpart in the large bowl of the last dynasty with *sang de bœuf* glaze, which, flowing downwards, usually left a colourless white band at the mouth.

The Hsüan Tê period extended only to ten years, and specimens of Hsüan red are excessively rare to-day, even in China. It is doubtful if a genuine specimen exists outside the Middle Kingdom, but with the help of the old Chinese descriptions and the clever imitations of a later date,[34] there is no difficulty in imagining the vivid splendours of the "precious stone red" of this brilliant period.

Among the "blue and white" wares of all periods, the Hsüan Tê porcelain is unanimously voted the first place by Chinese writers, and its excellence is ascribed principally to the superior quality of an imported mineral variously described as *su-ni-p'o*, *su-p'o-ni* and *su-ma-ni*. These outlandish names are, no doubt, attempts to render in Chinese the foreign name of the material, which was itself probably the name of the place or people whence it was exported. There is little doubt that this mysterious substance was the same species as the Mohammedan blue (*hui hui ch'ing*) of the following century. Indeed, this latter name is applied to it in Hsiang's Album. The Mohammedan blue was obtained from Arab traders, and its use for painting on pottery had been familiar in the Near East, in Persia and Syria for instance, at least as early as the twelfth century.[35] The *su-ni-p'o* blue was no doubt imported in the form of mineral cobalt, and though there was no lack of this mineral in the neighbourhood of Ching-tê Chên, the foreign material was of superior quality. It was, however, not only expensive but unsuited for use in a pure state. If applied by itself, it had a tendency to run in the firing, and it was necessary to blend it with proportions of the native mineral varying from one in ten for the finest quality to four in six for the medium quality. The native mineral used by itself tended to be heavy and dull in tone, owing to its inability to stand the intense heat of the kiln, and was only employed alone on the coarser wares. The supply of Mohammedan blue was uncertain and spasmodic. It ceased to arrive at the end of the Hsüan Tê period, and it was not renewed till the next century (see p. 29). Its nature, too, seems to have varied, for we are expressly told that the Hsüan Tê blue was pale in tone while the Mohammedan blue of the sixteenth century was dark. Possibly, however, this was not so much due to the nature of the material as to the method of its application, for Chinese writers are by no means unanimous about the paleness of the Hsüan Tê blue. The *Ch'ing pi ts'ang*, for instance, states that "they used *su-p'o-ni* blue and painted designs of dragons, phœnixes, flowers, birds, insects, fish and similar forms, deep and thickly heaped and piled and very lovely."

Authentic specimens of Hsüan Tê blue and white are virtually unknown, but the mark of the period is one of the commonest on Chinese porcelain of relatively modern date. In most cases this spurious dating means nothing more than that the period named was one of high repute; but there is a type of blue and white, usually bearing the period mark of Hsüan Tê, which is so mannered and characteristic that one feels the certainty that this really represents one kind at least of the Hsüan porcelain. It is usually decorated in close floral scrolls, and the blue is light dappled with darker shades, which are often literally "heaped and piled" (*tui t'o*) over the paler substratum.

I have seen examples of this style belonging to various periods, mostly eighteenth century, but some certainly late Ming[36] (see Plate 67, Fig. 4). Seven examples of Hsüan blue and white porcelain are figured in Hsiang's Album,[37] comprising an ink pallet, a vase shaped like a section of bamboo, a goose-shaped wine jar, a vase with an elephant on the cover, a tea cup, a sacrificial vessel, and a lamp with four nozzles. In five of these the blue is confined to slight pencilled borders, merely serving to set off the white ground, which is compared to driven snow. The glaze is rich and thick, and of uneven surface, rising in slight tubercles likened to "grains of millet." This is the "orange skin" glaze. The blue in each case is *hui hu*[38] *ta ch'ing* (deep Mohammedan blue). Of the two remaining instances, one is painted with a dragon in clouds, and the other with "dragon pines," and in the latter case the glaze is described as "lustrous like mutton fat jade," and the blue as "of intensity and brilliance to dazzle the eye."

The impression conveyed by all these examples is that they represent a type quite different from that described as "heaped and piled," a type in which delicate pencilling was the desideratum, the designs being slight and giving full play to the white porcelain ground. It is, in fact, far closer in style to the delicately painted Japanese Hirado porcelain than to the familiar Chinese blue and white of the K'ang Hsi period.

Plate 60 illustrates a little flask-shaped vase in the Franks Collection, which purports to be a specimen of Hsüan Tê blue and white porcelain. It has a thick, "mutton fat" glaze of faint greenish tinge, and is decorated with a freely drawn peach bough in underglaze blue which has not developed uniformly in the firing. The colour in places is deep, soft and brilliant, but elsewhere it has assumed too dark a hue.[39] Its certificate is engraved in Chinese fashion on the box into which it has been carefully fitted—*hsüan tz'ŭ pao yüeh p'ing*, "precious moon vase of Hsüan porcelain"—attested by the signature Tzŭ-ching, the studio name of none other than Hsiang Yüan-p'ien, whose Album has been so often quoted. Without attaching too much weight to this inscription, which is a matter easily arranged by the Chinese, there is nothing in the appearance of this quite unpretentious little vase which is inconsistent with an early Ming origin.

On the same plate is a brush rest in form of a log raft, on which is a seated figure, probably the celebrated Chang-Ch'ien, floating down the Yellow

River. The design recalls a rare silver cup of the Yüan dynasty, which was illustrated in the *Burlington Magazine* (December, 1912). Here the material is porcelain biscuit with details glazed and touched with blue, and the *nien hao* of Hsüan Tê is visible on the upper part of the log beside two lines of poetry. Whether this brush rest really belongs to the period indicated or not, it is a rare and interesting specimen. Two other possible examples of Hsüan Tê blue and white are described on p. 32.

PLATE 62

Barrel shaped Garden Seat: porcelain with coloured glazes on the biscuit, the designs outlined in slender fillets of clay. A lotus scroll between an upper band of clouds and a lower band of horses in flying gallop and sea waves. Lion mask handles. About 1500 A.D.

Height 14¼ inches.

British Museum.

As to the other types of Hsüan ware named in the *Po wu yao lan*, with one exception I can find no exact counterpart of them in existing specimens, though parts of the descriptions are illustrated by examples of apparently later date. Thus the form of the white tea cups, "with rounded body, convex base, and thread-like foot," is seen in such bowls as Fig. 1 of Plate 74, which is proved by its mount to be not later than the sixteenth century. Other examples of these bowls will be discussed later. They are characterised by a convexity in the centre which cannot be shown in reproductions.

The secret decoration (*an hua*) consists of designs faintly traced usually with a sharp-pointed instrument in the body and under the glaze. There is an excellent example of this in a high-footed cup in the Franks Collection which has the Hsüan Tê mark, the usual faintly greenish glaze, beneath which is a delicately etched lotus scroll so fine that it might easily be overlooked and is quite impossible to reproduce by photographic methods. It is, no doubt, an early eighteenth-century copy of Hsüan ware.

The one exception mentioned above is the type represented by the "barrel-shaped seats." The description of these leaves no room for doubt that they belonged to a fairly familiar class of Ming ware, whose strength and solidity has preserved it in considerable quantity where the more delicate porcelains have disappeared. Plate 62 gives a good idea of the Ming barrel-shaped garden seat, "with solid ground filled in with colours in engraved floral designs." The other kind, "with openwork ground, the designs filled in with colours (*wu ts'ai*), gorgeous as cloud brocades," must have been in the style of Plate 61. These styles of decoration are more familiar to us on potiche-shaped wine jars and high-shouldered vases than on garden seats, but the type is one and the same. Quite a series of these vessels was exhibited at the Burlington Fine Arts Club in 1910, and they are fully described in the catalogue. Some had an outer casing in openwork; others had the designs outlined in raised threads of clay, which contained the colours like the ribbons of cloisonné enamel[40]; in others, again, the patterns were incised with a point. The common feature of all of them was that the details of the pattern were defined by some emphatic method of outlining which served at the same time to limit the flow of the colours. The colours themselves consist of glazes containing a considerable proportion of lead, and tinted in the usual fashion with metallic oxides. They include a deep violet blue (sometimes varying to black or brown), leaf green, turquoise, yellow,[41] and a colourless glaze or a white slip which served as white colour, though at times the white was represented merely by leaving the unglazed body or biscuit to appear. These coloured glazes differ from the on-glaze painted enamels in that they are applied direct to the body of the ware, and are fired at a relatively high temperature in the cooler parts of the great kiln, a circumstance expressed by the French in the concise phrase, *couleurs de demi-grand feu*.[42]

The central ornament consisted chiefly of figures of sages or deities in rocky landscape, or seated under pine trees amid clouds, dragons in clouds, or beautiful lotus designs; and these were contained by various borders, such as floral scrolls, gadroons, *ju-i* head patterns, fungus scrolls, and symbols hanging in jewelled pendants. As a rule, the larger areas of these vases are invested with a ground colour and the design filled in with contrasting tints. Sometimes the scheme of decoration includes several bands of ornament, and in this case—as on Plate 62—more than one ground colour is used. The

Po wu yao lan speaks of green (*ch'ing*) and dark blue (*lan*) grounds, and existing specimens indicate that the dark violet blue was the commonest ground colour. Next to this, turquoise blue is the most frequently seen; but besides these there is a dark variety of the violet which is almost black, and another which is dark brown, both of which colours are based on cobaltiferous oxide of manganese. It has already been observed that this type of decoration was frequently used on a pottery body as well as on porcelain.

The question of the antiquity of the above method of polychrome decoration is complicated by the contradictory accounts which Dr. Bushell has given of a very celebrated example, the statuette of the goddess Kuan-yin in the temple named Pao kuo ssǔ at Peking. The following reference to this image occurs in the *T'ung ya*, published in the reign of Ch'ung Chêng (1625–1643): "The Chün Chou transmutation wares (*yao pien*) are not uncommon to-day. The Kuan-yin in the Pao kuo ssǔ is a *yao pien*." Dr. Bushell, who visited the temple several times, gives a minute description of the image, which contains the following passage[43]: "The figure is loosely wrapped in flowing drapery of purest and bluest turquoise tint, with the wide sleeves of the robe bordered with black and turned back in front to show the yellow lining; the upper part of the cloak is extended up behind over the head in the form of a plaited hood, which is also lined with canary yellow." To the ordinary reader, such a description would be conclusive. A fine example of Ming porcelain, he would say, decorated with the typical coloured glazes on the biscuit. Bushell's comment, however, is that the "colours are of the same type as those of the finest flower pots and saucers of the Chün Chou porcelain of the Sung dynasty." It should be said that the temple bonzes insist that they can trace the origin of the image back to the thirteenth century. If these are indeed the typical Chün Chou glazes, then all our previous information on that factory, including Bushell's own contributions, is worthless. In another work,[44] however, the same writer states that it (the image in question) is "really enamelled in 'five colours'—turquoise, yellow, crimson, red brown and black." This is precisely what we should have expected, and it can only be imagined that Bushell in the other passage was influenced by the statement in the *T'ung ya* that it was a furnace transmutation piece, a statement probably based on the superstition that it was a miraculous likeness of the goddess, who herself descended into the kiln and moulded its features. As to the other temple tradition, that it was made in the thirteenth century, it is not necessary to take that any more seriously than the myth concerning its miraculous origin, which derives from the same source.

It is hardly necessary to state that all the existing specimens of this class (and they are fairly numerous) do not belong to the Hsüan Tê period. Indeed, it is unlikely that more than a very small percentage of them were made in this short reign. Whether the style survived the Ming dynasty is an open question; but it is safe to assume that it was largely used in the sixteenth century.

The discussion of this group of polychrome porcelain leads naturally to the vexed question of the introduction of enamel painting over the glaze. By the latter I mean the painting of designs on the finished white glaze in vitrifiable enamels, which were subsequently fixed in the gentle heat of the muffle kiln (*lu*)—*couleurs de petit feu*, as the French have named them. No help can be got from the phraseology of the Chinese, for they use *wu ts'ai* or *wu sê* (lit. five colours) indifferently for all kinds of polychrome decoration, regardless of the number of colours involved or the mode of application. There is, however, no room for doubt that the delicate enamel painting, for which the reign of Ch'êng Hua (1465–1487) was celebrated, was executed with the brush over the fired glaze. It is inconceivable that the small, eggshell wine cups with peony flowers and a hen and chicken "instinct with life and movement" could have been limned by any other method. If this is the case, then what could the Chinese writers mean when they contrasted the *wu ts'ai* ornament of the Hsüan Tê and Ch'êng Hua periods, but that the same process of painting was in use in both reigns? The Ch'êng Hua colours were more artistic because they were thin and delicately graded, while the Hsüan Tê *wu ts'ai* were too thickly applied.[45] For this reason, if for no other, we may rightly infer that painting in on-glaze enamels was practised in the Hsüan Tê period, if, indeed, it had not been long in use.[46]

There is another and an intermediate method of polychrome decoration in which the low-fired enamels (*de petit feu*) are applied direct to the biscuit, as in the case of the *demi-grand feu* colours, but with the difference that they are fixed in the muffle kiln. This method was much employed on the late Ming and early Ch'ing porcelains, and it will be discussed later; but it is mentioned here because there are several apparent examples of it in Hsiang's Album, one[47] of which is dated Hsüan Tê. The example in question is a model of the celebrated Nanking pagoda, and it is described as *wu ts'ai*, the structure being white, the roofs green, the rails red, and the doors yellow, while the date is painted in blue. I have hesitated to assume that this is intended to represent an on-glaze painted piece, though there is much in the description to indicate such a conclusion; but it is certainly either this or a member of the class under discussion, viz. decorated in enamels of the muffle kiln applied to the biscuit.[48] In either case it proves the knowledge of vitrifiable enamels at this period to all who accept the evidence of Hsiang's Album.

Examples of Hsüan Tê polychrome porcelain enumerated in the *T'ao shuo* included wine pots in the form of peaches, pomegranates, double gourds, a pair of mandarin ducks and geese; washing dishes (for brushes) of "gong-shaped outline," with moulded fish and water-weeds, with sunflowers and with lizards; and lamp brackets, "rain-lamps," vessels for holding bird's food, and cricket[49] pots (see vol. i, p. 188).

Specimens of on-glaze painted porcelain with the Hsüan Tê mark are common enough, but I have not yet seen one which could be accepted without reserve. Perhaps the nearest to the period is a specimen in the Franks Collection, a box made of the lower part of a square vase which had been broken and cut down. It was fitted with a finely designed bronze cover in Japan, and it is strongly painted in underglaze blue and the usual green, yellow, red and purple on-glaze enamels. The mark is in a fine dark blue, and the porcelain has all the character of a Ming specimen.

There is, in the same collection, a dish of a different type, but with the Hsüan Tê mark in Mohammedan blue and other evidences of Ming origin. The glaze is of a faintly greenish white and of considerable thickness and lustre, and the design consists of lotus scrolls in gold. Painting in gold in the Hsüan Tê period is mentioned in the *T'ao shuo*[50] in connection with the pots for holding the fighting crickets alluded to above.

CHAPTER III

CH'ÊNG HUA 成花(1465–1487) AND OTHER REIGNS

The Ch'êng Hua porcelain shares with that of the Hsüan Tê period the honours of the Ming dynasty, and Chinese writers are divided on the relative merits of the two. Unfortunately, no material remains on which we might base a verdict of our own, but we may safely accept the summing up which the *Po wu yao lan*, the premier authority on early Ming wares, gives as follows[51]: "In my opinion, the blue and white porcelain of the Ch'êng Hua period does not equal that of the Hsüan Tê, while the polychrome of the Hsüan period does not equal that of the 'model[52] emperor's' reign. The reason is that the blue of the Hsüan ware was *su-ni-p'o*[53] blue, whereas afterward it was all exhausted, and in the Ch'êng Hua period only the ordinary blue was used. On the other hand, the polychrome (*wu ts'ai*) decoration on the Hsüan ware was deep and thick, heaped and piled, and consequently not very beautiful; while on the polychrome wares of the Ch'êng Hua period the colours used were thin and subdued,[54] and gave the impression of a picture."[55] Elsewhere we read that the Hsüan Tê porcelain was thick, the Ch'êng Hua thin, and that the blue of the Hsüan blue and white was pale, that of the Ch'êng Hua dark; but on this latter point there are many differences of opinion, and among the wares made at the Imperial factory in the Yung Chêng period we are told that there were "copies of Ch'êng Hua porcelain with designs pencilled in pale blue (*tan ch'ing*)."[56]

The only types of Ch'êng Hua porcelain considered worthy of mention by Chinese writers are the polychrome, the blue and white, and the red monochrome, though doubtless the other methods of previous reigns were still used. Stress is laid on the excellence of the designs which were supplied by artists in the palace,[57] and on the fine quality of the colours used, and an interesting list of patterns is given in the *T'ao shuo*,[58] which includes the following:

1. Stem-cups (*pa pei*), with high foot, flattened bowl, and spreading mouth; decorated in colours with a grape-vine pattern.

"Among the highest class of Ch'êng Hua porcelain these are unsurpassed, and in workmanship they far excel the Hsüan Tê cups." Such is the verdict of the *Po wu yao lan*, but they are only known to us by later imitations.

A poor illustration of one of these is given in Hsiang's Album,[59] and we are told in the accompanying text that the glaze is *fên pai*, "white like rice powder," while the decoration, a band of oblique vine clusters and tendrils, is merely described as *wu ts'ai* (polychrome), but it is obviously too slight to be executed by any other method than painting with enamels on the glaze. The price paid for this cup is stated as one hundred taels (or ounces) of silver.

2. Chicken cups (*chi kang*), shaped like the flat-bottomed, steep-sided, and wide-mouthed fish bowls (*kang*), and painted in colours with a hen and chickens beneath a flowering plant.

A valuable commentary on Ch'êng Hua porcelains is given by a late seventeenth-century writer in notes appended to various odes (e.g. on a "chicken cup" and on a Chün Chou vase). The writer is Kao Tan-jên, who also called himself Kao Chiang-ts'un, the name appended to a long dissertation on a Yüan dynasty silver wine cup, which now belongs to Sir Robert Biddulph and was figured in the *Burlington Magazine*.[60] "Ch'êng Hua wine cups," he tells us, "include a great variety of sorts. All are of clever workmanship and decoration, and are delicately coloured in dark and light shades. The porcelain is lustrous and clear, but strong. The chicken cups are painted with a *mu tan* peony, and below it a hen and chicken, which seem to live and move." Another writer[61] of the same period states that he frequented the fair at the *Tz'ŭ-iên* temple in the capital, where porcelain bowls were exhibited, and rich men came to buy. For Wan Li porcelain the usual price was a few taels of silver; for Hsüan Tê and Ch'êng Hua marked specimens two to five times that amount; but "chicken cups" could not be bought for less than a hundred taels, and yet those who had the means did not hesitate to buy, and porcelain realised higher prices than jade.

An illustration in Hsiang's Album[62] gives a poor idea of one of these porcelain gems, which is described as having the sides thin as a cicada's wing, and so translucent that the fingernail could be seen through them. The design, a hen and chicken beside a cock's-comb plant growing near a rock, is said to have been in the style of a celebrated Sung artist. The painting is in "applied colours (*fu sê*), thick and thin," and apparently yellow, green, aubergine and brown. Like that of the grape-vine cup, it is evidently in enamels on the glaze.

3. Ruby red bowls (*pao shao wan*)[63] and cinnabar red dishes (*chu sha p'an*). These were, no doubt, the same as the "precious stone red (*pao shih hung*) and cinnabar bowls red as the sun," described in the chapter on Hsüan Tê porcelain. Kao Chiang-ts'un remarks on these that "among the Ch'êng wares are chicken cups, ruby red bowls, and cinnabar dishes, very cleverly made, and fine, and more costly than Sung porcelain."

4. Wine cups with figure subjects and lotuses.

5. "Blue and white" (*ch'ing hua*) wine cups, thin as paper.

6. Small cups with plants and insects (*ts'ao ch'ung*).[64]

7. Shallow cups with the five sacrificial altar vessels (*wu kung yang*).

8. Small plates for chopsticks, painted in colours.

9. Incense boxes.

10. All manner of small jars.

All these varieties are mentioned in the *Po wu yao lan*, which gives the place of honour to the grape-vine stem-cups. The only kind specifically described as blue and white is No. 5, and the inference is that the other types were usually polychrome.

Plate 63.—Baluster Vase

With designs in raised outline, filled in with coloured glazes on the biscuit; dark violet blue background. About 1500. Height 14¾ inches.

Grandidier Collection (Louvre).

Fig. 1

Fig. 2

Fig. 3

Plate 64.—Fifteenth-century Polychrome Porcelain.

Fig. 1.—Vase with grey crackle and peony scrolls in blue and enamels. Ch'èng Hua mark. Height 16¼ inches. *British Museum.*

Fig. 2.—Vase with turquoise ground and bands of floral pattern and winged dragons incised in outline and coloured green, yellow and aubergine. Height 22 inches. *S. E. Kennedy Collection.*

Fig. 3.—Box with bands of *ju-i* clouds and pierced floral scrolls; turquoise and yellow glazes in dark blue ground. Diameter 10 inches. *Grandidier Collection.*

Plate 65.—Ming *san ts'ai* Porcelain.

Fig. 1.—Vase with winged dragons, *san ts'ai* glazes on the biscuit, dark blue ground. Dedicatory inscription on the neck, including the words "Ming dynasty." Cloisonné handles. Height 22¼ inches. *S. E. Kennedy Collection.*

Fig. 2.—Figure of Kuan-yin, turquoise, green and aubergine glazes, dark blue rockwork. Fifteenth century. Height 28 inches. *Grandidier Collection.*

Fig. 3.—Vase with lotus scrolls, transparent glazes in three colours. Late Ming. Height 20 inches. *Grandidier Collection.*

The following designs are enumerated and explained by Kao Chiang-ts'un in the valuable commentary which has already been mentioned:—

11. Wine cups with the design known as "the high-flaming candle lighting up red beauty," explained as a beautiful damsel holding a candle to light up *hai-t'ang* (cherry apple) blossoms.

12. Brocade heap pattern[65]; explained as "sprays of flowers and fruit massed (*tui*) on all sides."[66]

13. Cups with swings, with dragon boats, with famous scholars and with children.

The swings, we are told, represent men and women[67] playing with swings (*ch'iu ch'ien*): the dragon boats represent the dragon boat races[68]; the famous scholar (*kao shih*) cups have on one side Chou Mao-shu, lover of the lotus, and on the other T'ao Yüan-ming sitting before a chrysanthemum plant; the children (*wa wa*) consist of five small children playing together.[69]

14. Cups with grape-vines on a trellis, fragrant plants, fish and weeds, gourds, aubergine fruit, the Eight Buddhist Emblems (*pa chi hsiang*), *yu po lo* flowers, and Indian lotus (*hsi fan lien*) designs.

None of these need explanation except the Buddhist Emblems, which are described on p. 298, and the *yu po lo*, which is generally explained as a transcription of the Sanskrit *utpala*, "the dark blue lotus."

Though the reader will probably not have the opportunity of identifying these designs on Ch'êng Hua porcelain, they will help him in the description of later wares on which these same motives not infrequently occur. The nine illustrations[70] of Ch'êng Hua porcelain in Hsiang's Album, for the most part feebly drawn and badly coloured, form an absurd commentary on the glowing descriptions in the text. Their chief interest lies in their bearing on the question of polychrome painting. In some cases the designs have all the appearance of on-glaze enamels; in others they suggest transparent glazes or enamels on the biscuit. The colours used are green, yellow and aubergine brown, the *san ts'ai* or "three colours," notwithstanding which the decoration is classed under the general term *wu ts'ai* (lit. five colours), or polychrome. The phrases used to describe the colouring include *wu ts'ai, fu sê, t'ien yu*, of which *fu sê*[71] means "applied colours," which might equally suggest on-glaze enamels or on-biscuit colours, and *t'ien yu*[72] decidedly suggests on-biscuit colouring. On the other hand, in one case[73] we are expressly told that the "colour of the glaze is lustrous white and the painting *upon it*[74] consists of geese, etc.," an unequivocal description of on-glaze painting.

Though the Ch'êng Hua mark is one of the commonest on Chinese porcelain, genuine examples of Ch'êng Hua porcelain are virtually unknown in Western collections. The Imperial wares of the period were rare and highly valued in China in the sixteenth century, and we can hardly hope to obtain them in Europe to-day; but there must be many survivors from the wares produced by the private kilns at the time, and possibly some few examples are awaiting identification in our collections. Unfortunately, the promiscuous use of the mark on later wares, the confused accounts of the blue in the "blue and white," and the conflicting theories on the polychrome decoration, have all helped to render identifications difficult to make and easy to dispute. The covered cake box in the Bushell collection, figured by Cosmo Monkhouse[75] as a Ch'êng Hua specimen, is closely paralleled in make and style of decoration by a beaker-shaped brush pot in the Franks Collection.[76] Both are delicately pencilled in pale blue; both have a peculiar brown staining in parts of the glaze and a slight warp in the foot rim. In the British Museum piece, however, the foot rim is grooved at the sides to fit a wooden stand, a feature which was not usual before the K'ang Hsi period, and something in the style of the drawing is rather suggestive of Japanese work. There is, however, another specimen in the Franks Collection[77] which is certainly Chinese of the Ming dynasty, and possibly of the Ch'êng Hua period, of which it bears the mark. It is a vase of baluster form, thick and strongly built, with great weight of clay at the foot, and unfortunately, like so many of the early polychrome vases which have come from China in recent years, it is cut down at the neck. It has a greyish crackled glaze, painted with a floral scroll design, outlined in brown black pigment and washed in with leaf green, yellow, manganese purple and bluish green enamels, which are supplemented by a little underglaze blue, and the mark is in four characters in blue in a sunk panel under the base.

Though too clumsy to belong to any of the groups of Imperial wares described in the *Po wu yao lan*, this vase is certainly an old piece, and possibly the production of one of the private factories of the Ch'êng Hua period. In the Eumorfopoulos and Benson Collections[78] there are a few examples of these massive-footed vases, most of them unfortunately incomplete above, decorated in polychrome glazes with engraved or relief-edged designs, but not, as a rule, in on-glaze enamels. These are clearly among our earliest examples of polychrome porcelain, and we should expect to find here, if anywhere, specimens of the coloured porcelain of the fifteenth century. See Plate 64.

Though the fifteenth century was distinguished by two brilliant periods, there are considerable gaps in the ceramic annals of the time. The reign of the Emperor Chêng T'ung,[79] who succeeded to the throne in 1436, was troubled by wars, and in his first year the directorate of the Imperial factory was abolished; and, as soldiers had to be levied, relief was given by stopping the manufacture of porcelain for the palace. In 1449 this emperor was actually taken captive by the Mongols, and his brother, who took his place from 1450 to 1456 under the title of Ching T'ai,[80] reduced the customary supplies of palace wares in 1454 by one third. The reign of Ching T'ai is celebrated for cloisonné enamel on metal.

In 1457, when Chêng T'ung was released and returned to the throne under the title of T'ien Shun[81] (1457–1464), the Imperial factory was re-established, and the care of it again entrusted to a palace eunuch. There are no records, however, of the wares made in these periods, though we may assume that the private factories continued in operation even when work at the Imperial pottery was suspended. The directorship was again abolished in 1486, and porcelain is not mentioned in the official records until the end of the reign of Hung Chih[82] (1488–1505).

In Hsiang's Album[83] we are told that the pale yellow of the Hung Chih period was highly prized, and that the polychrome wares vied with those of the reign of Ch'êng Hua. Four examples are given: an incense burner, a cup moulded in sunflower design, and a spirit jar (all yellow), besides a gourd-shaped wine pot with yellow ground and accessories in green and brown, apparently coloured glazes or enamels applied to the biscuit. The yellow glazes are described as pale yellow (*chiao*[84] *huang*), and likened to the colour of steamed chestnuts (*chêng li*[85]) or the sunflower (*k'uei hua*[86]).

The yellow colour is of old standing in Chinese ceramics. We have found it on T'ang pottery, in the *mi sê* of the Sung period, in the blackish yellow of the Yüan ware made at Hu-t'ien, and in the early Ming porcelains. Peroxide of iron or antimony are the usual metallic bases of the colour, and it was used either in high-fired glazes or in enamels of the muffle stove. The yellow for which the Hung Chih period was noted was a yellow glaze, applied direct to the biscuit, or added as an overglaze to the ordinary white porcelain. When applied to the biscuit it assumes a fuller and browner tint than when backed by a white glaze. These yellow glazes often have a slightly mottled or stippled look, the colour appearing as minute particles of yellow held in suspension in the glaze.

Marked examples, purporting to be Hung Chih yellow, are occasionally seen, but the most convincing specimen is a saucer dish in the Victoria and Albert Museum, of good quality porcelain, with a soft rich yellow glaze and the Hung Chih mark under the base in blue. Part of its existence was spent in Persia, where it was inscribed in Arabic with the date 1021 A.H., which corresponds to 1611 A.D.

A beautiful seated figure of the goddess Kuan-yin in the Pierpont Morgan Collection, not unlike Plate 65, Fig. 2, but smaller, is decorated with yellow, green and aubergine glazes on the biscuit, and bears a date in the Hung Chih period which corresponds to 1502.

A dish of fine white porcelain with the Hung Chih mark is in the British Museum, and examples of the blue and white of the period may be seen in the celebrated Trenchard bowls. These last are the earliest known arrivals in the way of Chinese porcelain in this country, and they were given by Philip of Austria, King of Castile, to Sir Thomas Trenchard in 1506. One of them is illustrated in Gulland's *Chinese Porcelain*,[87] with a description written by Mr. Winthrop after a personal inspection. The decoration consists of floral scrolls outside and a fish medallion surrounded by four fishes inside. The account of the colour, however, is not very flattering: "One of the bowls bore this decoration very distinctly traced in blackish cobalt, while the other bowl had a very washed-out and faded appearance." The ware itself is described as "rather greyish." Probably these bowls were made for the export trade, and need not necessarily be regarded as typical of the Hung Chih blue and white.

Chêng Tê 正德 (1506–1521)

The reign of Chêng Tê, though not mentioned in the *Po wu yao lan* and but briefly noticed in the *T'ao shuo*, must have been an important period in the history of Chinese porcelain. The *yü ch'i ch'ang* (Imperial ware factory) was rebuilt[88] and the direct supervision of a palace eunuch renewed. The porcelain, we are told in the *T'ao lu*, was chiefly blue painted and polychrome, the finest being in the underglaze red known as *chi hung*. An important factor in the blue decoration was the arrival of fresh supplies of the Mohammedan blue.[89] The story is that the governor of Yunnan obtained a supply of this *hui ch'ing* from a foreign country, and that it was used at first melted down with stone for making imitation jewels. It was worth twice its weight in gold. When, however, it was found that it would endure the heat of the kiln, orders were given for its use in porcelain decoration, and its colour was found to be "antique and splendid." Hence the great esteem in which the blue and white of the period was held.[90] The merit of this new Mohammedan blue was its deep colour, and the choicest kind was known as "Buddha's head blue" (*Fo t'ou ch'ing*). Its use at this period was not confined to the Imperial factory, for we read that the workmen stole it and sold it to the private manufacturers. In the following reign a method of weighing the material was instituted, which put an end to this pilfering.

Some account has already been given[91] of this material and its use in combination with the commoner native mineral blue. It was, no doubt, the blue used on Persian, Syrian and Egyptian pottery of the period exported by the Arab traders. One of the oldest routes[92] followed by Western traders with China was by river (probably the Irrawady) from the coast of Pegu, reaching Yung-ch'ang, in Yunnan, and so into China proper. This will explain the opportunities enjoyed by the viceroy of Yunnan. There were, of course, other lines of communication between China and Western Asia by sea and land, and a considerable interchange of ideas had passed between China and Persia for several centuries, so that reflex influences are traceable in the pottery of both countries. Painting in still black under a turquoise blue glaze is one of the oldest Persian methods of ceramic decoration, and we have seen that it was closely paralleled on the Tz'ŭ Chou wares (vol. i, p. 103).

It is related that a thousand Chinese artificers were transplanted to Persia by Hulagu Khan (1253–1264), and it is probable that they included potters. At any rate, the Chinese dragon and phœnix appear on the Persian lustred tiles of the fourteenth century. At a later date Shah Abbas (1585–1627) settled some Chinese potters in Ispahan. Meanwhile, quantities of Chinese porcelain had been traded in the Near East, where it was closely copied by the Persian, Syrian and Egyptian potters in the sixteenth century. The Persian pottery and soft porcelain of this time so closely imitates the Chinese blue and white that in some cases a very minute inspection is required to detect the difference, and nothing is commoner than to find Persian ware of this type straying into collections of Chinese porcelain.[93] Conversely, the Persian taste is strongly reflected in some of the Chinese decorations, not only where it is directly studied on the wares destined for export to Persia, but in the floral scrolls on the Imperial wares of the Ming period. The expressions *hui hui hua* (Mohammedan ornament or flowers) and *hui hui wên* (Mohammedan designs) occur in the descriptions of the porcelain forwarded to the palace, and there can be little doubt that they refer to floral arabesque designs in a broad sense, though it would, of course, be possible to narrow the meaning to the medallions of Arabic writing not infrequently seen on Chinese porcelain, which was apparently made for the use of some of the numerous Mohammedans in China.

An interesting series of this last-mentioned type is exhibited in the British Museum along with a number of bronzes similarly ornamented. Many of these are of early date, and five of the porcelains bear the Chêng Tê mark and unquestionably belong to that period. These comprise a pair of vases with spherical tops which are hollow and pierced with five holes, in form resembling the peculiar Chinese hat stands; the lower part of a cut-down vase, square in form; an ink slab with cover, and a brush rest in the form of a conventional range of hills. The body in each case is a beautiful white material, though thickly constructed, and the glaze, which is thick and of a faint greenish tinge, has in three of these five pieces been affected by some accident of the firing, which has left its surface dull and shrivelled in places like wrinkled skin.[94] The designs are similar throughout—medallions with Arabic writing surrounded by formal lotus scrolls or cloud-scroll designs, strongly outlined and filled in with thin uneven washes of a beautiful soft Mohammedan blue. The glaze being thick and bubbly gives the brush strokes a hazy outline, and the blue shows that tendency to run in the firing which we are told was a peculiarity of the Mohammedan blue if not sufficiently diluted with the native mineral cobalt. The inscriptions are mainly pious Moslem texts, but on the cover of the ink slab is the appropriate legend, "Strive for excellence in penmanship, for it is one of the keys of livelihood," and on the brush rest is the Persian word *Khāma-dān* (pen rest). In the same case are three cylindrical vases, apparently brush pots, decorated in the same style but unmarked. One has dark Mohammedan blue and probably belongs to the next reign. The other two, I venture to think, are earlier. They are both of the same type of ware, a fine white material, which takes a brownish red tinge in the exposed parts, and the glaze, which is thick and of a soft greenish tint, has a tendency to scale off at the edges. The bases are unglazed and show the marks of a circular support. The larger piece is remarkably thick in the wall, and has a light but vivid blue of the Mohammedan sort; the smaller piece is not quite so stoutly proportioned, but the blue is peculiarly soft, deep, and beautiful, though it has run badly into the glaze, and where it has run it has changed to a dark indigo.[95] One would say that this is the Mohammedan blue, almost pure; and if, as I have suggested, these two specimens are earlier types, they can only belong to the Hsüan Tê period.

Another blue and white example with Chêng Tê mark in the British Museum is of thinner make and finer grain; but, as it is a saucer-dish, this refinement was only to be expected. It is painted in a fine bold style, worthy of the best Ming traditions, with dragons in lotus scrolls, but the blue is duller and greyer in tone than on the pieces just described.

Two specimens of Chêng Tê ware are figured in Hsiang's Album,[96] one a tripod libation cup of bronze form and the other a lamp supported by a tortoise, and the glaze of both is "deep yellow, like steamed chestnuts."

Fig. 1

Fig. 2

Plate 66.—Porcelain with Chêng Tê mark.

Fig. 1.—Slop Bowl with full-face dragons holding *shou* characters, in underglaze blue in a yellow enamel ground. Height 3½ inches. *British Museum.*

Fig. 2.—Vase with engraved cloud designs in transparent coloured glazes on the biscuit, green ground. Height 8⅛ inches. *Charteris Collection.*

Plate 67.—Blue and White Porcelain. Sixteenth Century.

Fig. 1.—Bowl with Hsüan Tê mark. Diameter 4 inches. *Dresden Collection.*

Fig. 2.—Covered Bowl with fish design. *Dresden Collection.*

Fig. 3.—Bottle, peasant on an ox. Height 8½ inches. *Eumorfopoulos Collection.*

Fig. 4.—Bottle with lotus scrolls in mottled blue. Height 9 inches. *Alexander Collection.*

The Chêng Tê mark is far from common, but it occurs persistently on certain types of polychrome porcelain. One is a saucer-dish with carved dragon designs under a white glaze, the depressions of the carving and a few surrounding details being washed over with light green enamel. The design consists of a circular medallion in the centre enclosing a dragon among clouds, and two dragons on the outside, the space between them faintly etched with sea waves. The ware is usually thin and refined. These dishes are not uncommon, and it is difficult to imagine that they can all belong to such an early period. On the other hand, one also meets with copies of the same design with the Ch'ien Lung mark (1736–1795), which display unmistakable difference in quality. Another type has the same green dragon design with engraved outlines set in a yellow ground, and in most cases its antiquity is open to the same doubts. It is certain, however, that these pieces represent a style which was in vogue in the Chêng Tê period. A small vase of this kind was the only piece with the Chêng Tê mark in the exhibition at the Burlington Fine Arts Club in 1910,[97] and it had the appearance of a Ming specimen. A good example of this Chêng Tê polychrome belonging to the Hon. Evan Charteris is illustrated in Fig. 2 of Plate 66. It has the designs etched in outline, filled in with transparent green, yellow and aubergine glazes, the three colours or *san ts'ai* of the Chinese; and the Chêng Tê mark is seen on the neck.[98] And a square bowl in the British Museum, similar in body and glaze to the blue and white specimens with Arabic inscriptions, is painted in fine blue on the exterior with dragons holding *Shou* (longevity) characters in their claws, the background filled in with a rich transparent yellow enamel. This piece (Plate 66, Fig. 1) has the mark of Chêng Tê in four characters painted in Mohammedan blue, and is clearly a genuine specimen.

CHAPTER IV

CHIA CHING 嘉靖(1522–1566) AND LUNG CH'ING 隆慶(1567–1572)

The Imperial potteries at Ching-tê Chên were busy in the long reign of Chia Ching, grandson of Ch'êng Hua, under the supervision of one of the prefects of the circuit who took charge in place of the palace eunuch of previous reigns. Chinese accounts of the porcelain of this important period, summarised in the *T'ao shuo*, include passages from the late Ming and therefore almost contemporary works, the *Shih wu kan chu* and the *Po wu yao lan*. In the former we are told that the Mohammedan blue was largely used, but that the material for the "fresh red" (*hsien hung*)[99] was exhausted, and that the method of producing the red colour was no longer the same as of old, the potters being capable only of making the overglaze iron red called *fan hung*. The *Po wu yao lan* gives a more intimate description of the ware, and the passage[100]—the last in that work on the subject of porcelain—may be rendered as follows:—

"Chia Ching porcelain includes blue-decorated and polychrome wares of every description; but unfortunately the clay brought to the place from the neighbouring sources in Jao Chou gradually deteriorated, and when we compare these two classes of porcelain with the similar productions of the earlier periods of the dynasty the (Chia Ching) wares do not equal the latter. There are small white bowls (*ou*) inscribed inside with the character *ch'a* 酒 (tea), the character *chiu* 茶 (wine), or the characters *tsao t'ang* 棗湯 (decoction of dates), or *chiang t'ang*[101] 薑湯(decoction of ginger); these are the sacrificial altar vessels regularly used by the Emperor Shih Tsung (i.e. Chia Ching), and they are called white altar cups, though in form and material they are far from equalling the Hsüan Tê vessels. The Chia Ching shallow wine cups with rimmed mouth,[102] convex centre,[103] and foot with base rim,[104] decorated outside in three colours with fish design, and the small vermilion boxes, no bigger than a "cash," are the gems of the period. As for the small boxes beautifully painted with blue ornament, I fear that the Imperial factories of after times will not be able to produce the like. Those who have them prize them as gems."

A few supplementary comments in the *T'ao shuo* further inform us that the Mohammedan blue of the Chia Ching period was preferred very dark (in contrast with the pale blue of the Hsüan Tê porcelain), that it was very lovely, and that supplies of this blue arrived providentially at the time when the "fresh red" failed[105]; and also that the supplies of earth from Ma-ts'ang were daily diminishing till they were nearly exhausted, and consequently the material of the ware was far from equalling that of the Hsüan Tê period. The *T'ao lu* adds practically nothing to the above statements.

Fortunately, there are still to be found a fair number of authentic specimens of Chia Ching porcelain, but before considering these in the light of the Chinese descriptions, it will be helpful as well as extremely interesting to glance at the lists of actual porcelain vessels supplied to the palace at this time. From the eighth year of this reign, the annual accounts of the palace porcelains have been preserved in the Annals of Fou-liang, from which they were copied in the provincial topographies. Two of these lists (for the years 1546 and 1554) are quoted by Bushell,[106] and a general summary of them is given in the *T'ao shuo*.[107] To quote them in full here would take too much space, but the following notes may be useful to the reader, who, with his knowledge of the later porcelains, should have no difficulty in reconstructing for himself the general appearance of the court wares of the time.

The actual objects[108] supplied consisted chiefly of fish bowls (*kang*), covered and uncovered jars (*kuan*), of which some were octagonal, bowls (*wan*), dinner bowls (*shan wan*) of larger size, saucer dishes (*tieh*) and round dishes (*p'an*), tea cups (*ch'a chung*), tea cups (*ou*), wine cups (*chiu chan*), and libation cups (*chüeh*) with hill-shaped saucers (*shan p'an*) to support their three feet, various vases (*p'ing*), slender ovoid jars for wine (*t'an*), ewers or wine pots (*hu p'ing*), and wine seas (*chiu hai*) or large bowls. A large number of complete dinner-table sets (*cho ch'i*) occur in one of the lists, and we learn from the *T'ao shuo* that uniform sets with the same pattern and colours throughout were an innovation of the Ming dynasty. A set[109] comprised 27 pieces, including 5 fruit dishes (*kuo tieh*), 5 food dishes (*ts'ai tieh*), 5 bowls (*wan*), 5 vegetable dishes (*yün tieh*), 3 tea cups (*ch'a chung*), 1 wine cup (*chiu chan*), 1 wine saucer (*chiu tieh*), 1 slop receptacle (*cha tou*), and 1 vinegar cruse (*ts'u chiu*). The slop receptacle appears to have been a square bowl used for the remnants of food (see Plate 66, Fig. 1).

The sacrificial vessels of the period included tazza-shaped bowls and dishes (*pien tou p'an*), large wine jars (*t'ai tsun*), with swelling body and monster masks for handles, "rhinoceros" jars (*hsi tsun*) in the form of a rhinoceros carrying a vase on its back, besides various dishes, plates, cups, and bowls of undefined form.

The decorations are grouped in six headings:—

(1) Blue and white (*ch'ing hua pai ti*, blue ornament on a white ground), which is by far the largest.

(2) Blue ware, which included blue bowls (*ch'ing wan*), sky-blue bowls (*t'ien ch'ing wan*), and turquoise bowls (*ts'ui ch'ing wan*). In some cases the ware is

- 39 -

described as plain blue monochrome, and in one item it is "best blue monochrome" (*t'ou ch'ing su*), while in others there are designs engraved under the glaze (*an hua*). In others, again, ornament such as dragons and sea waves is mentioned without specifying how it was executed. Such ornament may have been etched with a point in the blue surface,[110] or pencilled in darker blue on a blue background or reserved in white in a blue ground. Another kind is more fully described as "round dishes of pure blue (*shun ch'ing*) with dragons and sea waves inside, and on the exterior a background of dense cloud scrolls[111] with a gilt[112] decoration of three lions and dragons." Bushell[113] speaks of the "beautiful mottled blue ground for which this reign is also remarkable," and which, he says, was produced by the usual blend of Mohammedan and native blue suspended in water.

(3) Wares which were white inside and blue outside.

(4) White ware, plain[114] or with engraved designs under the glaze (*an hua*, lit. secret ornament).

(5) Ware with brown glaze in two varieties, *tzŭ chin* (golden brown), and *chin huang* (golden yellow), with dragon designs engraved under the glaze. These are the well-known lustrous brown glazes, the former of dark coffee brown shade, and the latter a light golden brown.

(6) Ware with mixed colours (*tsa sê*), which included bowls and dishes decorated in iron red[115] (*fan hung*) instead of the "fresh red" (*hsien hung*); others with emerald green colour (*ts'ui lü sê*); bowls with phœnixes and flowers of Paradise in yellow in a blue ground; cups with blue cloud and dragon designs in a yellow ground; boxes with dragon and phœnix designs engraved under a yellow glaze; dishes with design of a pair of dragons and clouds in yellow within a golden brown (*tzŭ chin*) ground; and globular bowls with embossed[116] ornament in a single-coloured ground.

To these types Bushell adds from other similar lists crackled ware (*sui ch'i*), tea cups of "greenish white porcelain" (*ch'ing pai tz'ŭ*), which seems to be a pale celadon, and large fish bowls with pea green (*tou ch'ing*) glaze.

The source of the designs of the porcelain is clearly indicated in the following passage in the *T'ao shuo*[117]: "Porcelain enamelled in colours was painted in imitation of the fashion of brocaded silks, and we have consequently the names of blue ground, yellow ground, and brown gold (*tzŭ chin*) ground. The designs used to decorate it were also similar, and included dragons in motion (*tsou lung*), clouds and phœnixes, *ch'i-lin*, lions, mandarin ducks, myriads of gold pieces, dragon medallions (*p'an lung*, lit. coiled dragons), pairs of phœnixes, peacocks, sacred storks, the fungus of longevity, the large lion in his lair, wild geese in clouds with their double nests, large crested waves, phœnixes in the clouds, the son-producing lily, the hundred flowers, phœnixes flying through flowers, the band of Eight Taoist Immortals, dragons pursuing pearls, lions playing with embroidered balls, water weeds, and sporting fishes. These are the names of ancient brocades, all of which the potters have reproduced more or less accurately in the designs and colouring of their porcelain."

The following analysis of the designs named in the Chia Ching lists will show that the blue and white painters of the period took their inspiration from the same source:—

Floral Motives.

Celestial flowers (*t'ien hua*), supporting the characters *shou shan fu hai* 壽山福海, "longevity of the hills and happiness (inexhaustible as) the sea."

Flowers of the four seasons (the tree peony for spring, lotus for summer, chrysanthemum for autumn, and prunus for winter).

Flowering and other plants (*hua ts'ao*).

The myriad-flowering wistaria (*wan hua t'êng*).

The water chestnut (*ling*).

The pine, bamboo, and plum.

Floral medallions (*t'uan hua*).

Indian lotus (*hsi fan lien*).

Knots of lotus (*chieh tzŭ lien*[118]).

Interlacing sprays of lotus supporting the Eight Precious Symbols or the Eight Buddhist Emblems.[119]

Branches of *ling chih*[120] fungus supporting the Eight Precious Symbols.

Ling chih fungus and season flowers.

Lotus flowers, fishes, and water weeds.

Floral arabesques (*hui hui hua*).

Flowers of Paradise (*pao hsiang hua*) 寶相花.

The celestial flowers and the flowers of Paradise are no doubt similar designs of idealised flowers in scrolls or groups.[121] The *pao hsiang hua*, which is given in Giles's Dictionary as "the rose," is rendered by Bushell "flowers of Paradise" or "fairy flowers." Judging by the designs with this name in Chinese works, and also from the fact that the rose is a very rare motive on Chinese wares before the Ch'ing dynasty, whereas the *pao hsiang hua* is one of the commonest in the Ming lists, Bushell's rendering is probably correct in the present context.

Animal Motives, mythical or otherwise.

Dragons, represented as pursuing jewels (*kan chu*); grasping jewels (*k'ung chu*); in clouds; emerging from water; in bamboo foliage and fungus plants; among water chestnut flowers; among scrolls of Indian lotus; emerging from sea waves and holding up the Eight Trigrams (*pa kua*); holding up the characters *fu* 福 (happiness) or *shou* 壽 (longevity), as on Fig. 1 of Plate 66.

Dragons of antique form. These are the lizard-like creatures (*ch'ih*) with bifid tail which occur so often in old bronzes and jades.

Dragon medallions (*t'uan lung*).

Nine dragons and flowers.

Dragons and phœnixes moving through flowers.

Dragon, and phœnixes with other birds.

Phœnixes flying through flowers.

A pair of phœnixes.

Lions[122] rolling balls of brocade.

Flying lions.

Hoary[123] lions and dragons.

Storks in clouds.

Peacocks (*k'ung ch'iao*) and *mu-tan* peonies.

Birds flying in clouds.

Fish and water weeds.

Four fishes.[124]

Human Motives.

Children (*wa wa*) playing.

Three divine beings (*hsien*) compounding the elixir of Immortality.

Two or four Immortals.

The Eight Immortals (*pa hsien*) crossing the sea; or paying court to the god of Longevity (*p'êng shou*), or congratulating him (*ch'ing shou*).

A group of divine beings (*hsien*) paying court to the god of Longevity.

Two designs of doubtful meaning may be added here:

(1) "Jars decorated with *chiang hsia pa chün*,"[125] a phrase which means "the eight elegant (scholars) of Chiang-hsia (i.e. below the river)," but has been translated by Bushell, using a variant reading,[126] as "the eight horses of Mu Wang." The latter rendering ignores the presence of *chiang hsia*, and the former, though a correct reading of the original, is not explained in any work of reference to which I have had access.

(2) "Bowls with *man ti ch'iao*," lit. "graceful (designs) filling the ground." The meaning of *ch'iao* is the difficulty, and Bushell in one translation[127] has rendered it "graceful sprays of flowers," which sorts well with rest of the phrase, but in another[128] he has assumed that it means "graceful beauties" in reference to the well-known design of tall, slender girls, which the Dutch collectors named *lange lijsen* (see Plate 92, Fig. 2). The latter rendering, however, goes badly with *man ti*, "filling the ground," which is certainly more applicable to some close design, such as floral scroll work. This is, however, a good example of the difficulty of translating the Chinese texts, where so much is left to the imagination, and consequently there is so much room for differences of opinion.

Plate 68.—Blue and White Porcelain. Sixteenth Century.

Fig. 1.—Perfume Vase, lions and balls of brocade. Height 8¾ inches. *V. &*
A. Museum.

Fig. 2. Double Gourd Vase, square in the lower part. Eight Immortals paying
court to the God of Longevity, panels of children (*wa wa*). Height 21 inches.
Eumorfopoulos Collection.

Fig. 3.—Bottle with medallions of *ch'i-lin* and incised fret pattern between. Late Ming. Height 9 inches. *Halsey Collection.*

Fig. 1

Fig. 2

Plate 69.—Sixteenth Century Porcelain.

Fig. 1.—Bowl of blue and white porcelain with silver gilt mount of Elizabethan period. Height 3¾ inches. *British Museum.*

Fig. 2.—Covered Jar, painted in dark underglaze blue with red, green and yellow enamels; fishes and water plants. Chia Ching mark. Height 17 inches. *S. E. Kennedy Collection.*

Fig. 1

Fig. 2

Plate 70.—Porcelain with Chia Ching mark.

Fig. 1.—Box with incised Imperial dragons and lotus scrolls; turquoise and dark violet glazes on the biscuit. Diameter 9½ inches. *V. & A. Museum.*

Fig. 2.—Vase with Imperial dragons in clouds, painted in yellow in an iron red ground. Height 8½ inches. *Cologne Museum.*

Fig. 1   Fig. 2

Fig. 3

Plate 71.—Sixteenth Century Porcelain.

Figs. 1 and 2.—Two Ewers in the Dresden Collection, with transparent green, aubergine and turquoise glazes on the biscuit, traces of gilding. In form of a phœnix (height 11 inches), and of a crayfish (height 8¼ inches).

Fig. 3.—Bowl with flight of storks in a lotus scroll, enamels on the biscuit, green, aubergine and white in a yellow ground. Chia Ching mark. Diameter 7 inches. *Alexander Collection.*

Emblematic Motives.

Heaven and Earth, and the six cardinal points (*ch'ien k'un liu ho*[129]), or "emblems of the six cardinal points of the Universe."

Ch'ien and *k'un* are the male and female principles which are represented by Heaven and Earth, and together make up the Universe. The identification of these emblems is obscure. They might simply be the Eight Trigrams (*pa kua*), which are explained next, for two of these are known as *ch'ien* and *k'un*, and together with the remaining six they are arranged so as to make up eight points of the compass. But in that case, why not simply say *pa kua* as elsewhere?

On the other hand, we know that certain emblems were used in the Chou dynasty[130] in the worship of the six points of the Universe, viz. a round tablet with pierced centre (*pi*) of bluish jade for Heaven; a yellow jade tube with square exterior (*ts'ung*) for Earth; a green tablet (*kuei*), oblong with pointed top, for the East; a red tablet (*chang*), oblong and knife-shaped, for the South; a white tablet, in the shape of a tiger (*hu*), for the West; and a black jade piece of flat semicircular form (*huang*) for the North. All these objects are illustrated in Laufer's *Jade*, but as they have not, to my knowledge, appeared together in porcelain decoration, the question must for the present be left open.

The *pa-kua* 八卦 or Eight Trigrams, supported by dragons or by waves and flames.

These are eight combinations of triple lines. In the first the lines are unbroken, and in the last they are all divided at the centre, the intermediate figures consisting of different permutations of broken and unbroken lines (see p. 290). These eight diagrams, by which certain Chinese philosophers explained all the phenomena of Nature, are supposed to have been constructed by the legendary Emperor Fu Hsi (B.C. 2852) from a plan revealed to him on the back of the "dragon horse" (*lung ma*) which rose from the Yellow River.[131] Among other things, they are used to designate the points of the compass, one arrangement making the first figure represent the South (also designated *ch'ien* 乾 or Heaven), and the last figure the North (also designated *k'un* 坤 or Earth), the remaining figures representing South-West, West, North-West, North-East, East, and South-East.

The *pa pao* 八寶, or Eight Precious Symbols, supported by fungus sprays.

These are usually represented by (1) a sphere or jewel, which seems to have originally been the sun disc; (2) a circle enclosing a square, which suggests the copper coin called a "cash"; (3) an open lozenge, symbol of victory or success; (4) a musical stone (*ch'ing*); (5) a pair of books; (6) a pair of rhinoceros horns (cups); (7) a lozenge-shaped picture (*hua*); (8) a leaf of the artemisia, a plant of good omen, which dispels sickness. (See p. 299.)

The *pa chi hsiang* 八吉祥, or Eight Buddhist Symbols, supported on lotus scrolls.

These symbols, which appeared among the auspicious signs on the foot of Buddha, comprise (1) the wheel (*chakra*), which is sometimes replaced by the hanging bell; (2) the shell trumpet of Victory; (3) the umbrella of state; (4) the canopy; (5) the lotus flower; (6) the vase; (7) the pair of fish, emblems of fertility; (8) the angular knot (representing the entrails), symbol of longevity. (See p. 298.)

The hundred forms of the character *shou* (longevity)—*pai shou tz'ŭ*.

Ju-i sceptres and phœnix medallions.

The *ju-i* 如意("as you wish") sceptre brings fulfilment of wishes, and is a symbol of longevity (see vol. i., p. 227). The head of the *ju-i*, which has a strong resemblance to the conventional form of the *ling chih* fungus, is often used in borders and formal patterns variously described as "*ju-i* head patterns," "cloud-scroll patterns," or "*ju-i* cloud patterns."

Close ground patterns of propitious clouds (*yung hsiang yün ti*).

Cloud designs are propitious because they symbolise the fertilising rain, and they are commonly represented by conventional scrolls as well as by the more obvious cloud patterns.

Crested sea waves (*chiang ya hai shui*).

Chiang ya 薑芽 (lit. ginger shoots) is rendered by Bushell "crested waves," the metaphor being apparently suggested by the curling tops of the young plant.

Cups decorated[132] with the characters *fu shou k'ang ning* 福壽康寧(happiness, long life, peace, and tranquillity).

A blue and white vase with these characters in medallions framed by cloud scrolls on the shoulders is shown on Plate 68.

Miscellaneous Motives.

The waterfalls of Pa Shan 巴山 in the province of Szechuan.

Gold weighing-scales (*ch'ēng chin* 秤金).

A design named *san yang k'ai t'ai* 三陽開泰, a phrase alluding to the "revivifying power of spring," and said by Bushell to be symbolised by three rams. Cf. Fig. 2 of Plate 122.

The mark of the Chia Ching period, though not so freely used as those of Hsüan Tê and Ch'êng Hua, has been a favourite with Japanese copyists, whose imitations have often proved dangerously clever. Still, there are enough genuine specimens in public and private collections in England to provide a fair representation of the ware. In studying these the blue and white will be found to vary widely, both in body material and in the colour of the blue, according to the quality of the objects.

Plate 77 illustrates a remarkably good example of the dark but vivid Mohammedan blue on a pure white ware of fine close grain with clear glaze. The design, which consists of scenes from the life of a sage, perhaps Confucius himself, is painted in typical Ming style, and bordered by *ju-i* cloud scrolls and formal brocade patterns. The Chia Ching blue is often darker[133] and heavier than here, resembling thick patches of violet ink, to use Mr. Perzynski's phrase. This powerful blue is well shown in the large vase given by Mr. A. Burman to the Victoria and Albert Museum (Plate 72), and by a fine ewer in Case 22 in the same gallery. The latter has an accidentally crackled glaze on the body with brownish tint, due, no doubt, to staining.

On the other hand, a large double-gourd vase in the British Museum, heavily made (probably for export), is painted with the eighteen Arhats, or Buddhist apostles, in a dull greyish blue, which would certainly have been assigned to the Wan Li period were it not for the Chia Ching mark. This is, no doubt, the native cobalt without any admixture of Mohammedan blue.

The body material in these specimens varies scarcely less than the blue. In the colour stand on Plate 77 the ware is a pure clean white, both in body and glaze. On other specimens—particularly the large, heavily built jars and vases made for export to India and Persia—the ware is of coarser grain, and the glaze of grey or greenish tone. The tendency of the Ming biscuit to assume a reddish tinge where exposed to the fire is exaggerated on some of these large jars, so that the exposed parts at the base and foot rim are sometimes a dark reddish brown. Doubtless the clay from different mines varied considerably, and the less pure materials would be used on these relatively coarse productions. On the other hand, the better class of dish and bowl made for service at the table is usually of clean white ware, potted thin and neatly finished, and differing but little in refinement from the choice porcelains of the eighteenth century. Such are the dragon dish described on p. 32 and the polychrome saucers which will be mentioned presently.

The export trade with Western Asia and Egypt, both by sea and land, must have been of considerable dimensions in the middle of the sixteenth century.

Broken pieces of Chinese blue and white are found on all the excavated sites in the Near East, and the influence of the Chinese porcelain is clearly seen in the blue, or blue and brown, painted faience made in Persia, Syria, and Egypt in the sixteenth century. The reflex influence of Persia on the Chinese wares has already been noted, and it is clear that Persian taste was studied by the makers of the dishes, bottles, pipes, and other objects with birds and animals in foliage and floral scrolls of decidedly Persian flavour, which are still frequently found in the Near East. It was this type of Chinese porcelain which inspired Italian maiolica potters in their decoration *alla porcellana*, as well as the decorators of the Medici or Florentine porcelain, the first European porcelain of any note. Françesco Maria, the patron of the Medici porcelain, died in 1587, and as little, if any, of the ware was made after his death, the rare surviving examples may be safely taken as reflecting, where any Chinese influence is apparent, the influence of the mid-sixteenth century porcelains.

PLATE 72

Vase with Imperial five-clawed dragons in cloud scrolls over sea waves: band of lotus scrolls on the shoulder. Painted in dark Mohammedan blue. Mark on the neck, of the Chia Ching period (1522–1566) in six characters.

Height 21 inches.

Victoria and Albert Museum.

An interesting series of Ming blue and white export wares collected in India was lent to the Burlington Fine Arts Club in 1910 by Mrs. Halsey. It included a few Chia Ching specimens, and among them a melon-shaped jar with lotus scrolls in the dark blue of the period. This melon form has been popular with the Chinese potters from T'ang times, and it occurs fairly often in the Ming export porcelains. A companion piece, for instance, at the same exhibition was decorated with handsome pine, bamboo, and plum designs. Others, again, are appropriately ornamented with a melon vine pattern, a gourd vine, or a grape vine with a squirrel-like animal on the branches. The drawing of these pieces is usually rough but vigorous, the form is good, and the blue as a rule soft and pleasing; and though entirely wanting in the superfine finish of the choice K'ang Hsi blue and white, they have a decorative value which has been sadly underrated.

The polychrome porcelains of the Chia Ching period are rarer than the blue and white, but still a fair number of types are represented in English collections. Of the colours applied direct to the biscuit the early glazes of the *demi-grand feu*—turquoise, aubergine violet, green and yellow—were doubtless applied as in the previous century to the large wine jars, vases and figures in the round. An unusual specimen of this class is the marked Chia Ching cake box in the Victoria and Albert Museum, illustrated on Plate 70. The design—Imperial dragons among floral scrolls—is traced with a point in the paste and covered with a delicate turquoise glaze, the background being filled with violet aubergine. Similarly engraved designs coloured by washes of transparent glazes in the three colours—green, yellow and aubergine brown—are found with the Chia Ching mark as with that of Chêng Tê, and Plate 73 illustrates two singularly beautiful bowls with designs outlined in brown and washed in with transparent glazes. The one has flowering branches of prunus, peach and pomegranate in white, green and aubergine in a yellow ground, and the other phœnixes and floral scrolls in yellow, green and white in a ground of pale aubergine. Both have the Chia Ching mark. Fig. 2 of Plate 71 is another member of the same group, with a beautiful design of cranes and lotus scrolls in a yellow ground. There are, besides, examples of these yellow and aubergine glazes in monochrome. A good specimen of the latter with Chia Ching mark in the British Museum has fine transparent aubergine glaze with iridescent surface, the colour pleasantly graded, which contrasts with the uniform smooth glaze and trim finish of a Ch'ien Lung example near to it.

Two interesting ewers in the Dresden collection (Figs. 1 and 2 of Plate 71) probably belong to this period, or at any rate to the sixteenth century. They are fantastically shaped to represent a phœnix and a lobster, and are decorated with green, yellow, aubergine and a little turquoise applied direct to the biscuit. Parts of the surface have been lightly coated with gilding, which has almost entirely disappeared. These pieces are mentioned in an inventory of 1640, and a lobster ewer precisely similar was included in the collection made by Philipp Hainhofer in the early years of the seventeenth century.[134]

Among the examples of on-glaze enamels of this period are those in which the coral red derived from iron oxide (*fan hung*) is the most conspicuous colour. This red is often highly iridescent, displaying soft ruby reflections like Persian lustre; at other times it is richly fluxed, and has a peculiarly vitreous and almost sticky appearance. The former effect is well seen in a small saucer in the British Museum, which has a wide border of deep lustrous red surrounding a medallion with lions and a brocade ball in green. The latter is seen on a square, covered vase in the same case, decorated on each side with full-faced dragons in red and the usual cloud accessories in inconspicuous touches of green and yellow. The yellow enamel of the period is often of an impure, brownish tint and rather thickly applied, but these peculiarities of both yellow and red continued in the Wan Li period.

Fig. 1

Fig. 2

PLATE 73

Two Bowls with the Chia Ching mark (1522–1566), with designs outlined in brown and washed in with colours in monochrome grounds.

Fig. 1 with peach sprays in a yellow ground. Diameter 8 inches. *Alexander Collection.*

Fig. 2 with phœnixes (*fêng-huang*) flying among scrolls of *mu-tan* peony. Diameter 7 inches. *Cumberbatch Collection.*

The combination of enamel colours with underglaze blue, which was so largely used in the Wan Li period as to be generally known by the name *Wan li wu ts'ai* (Wan Li polychrome), is not unknown on Chia Ching wares. The wide-mouthed jar, for instance, from the collection of Mr. S. E. Kennedy[135] (Plate 69, Fig. 2) is decorated with a design of fish among water plants in deep Chia Ching blue combined with green, yellow and iron red enamels; and a small bottle-shaped vase in the British Museum has the same blue combined with on-glaze red, green, yellow and aubergine, the design being fish, waves, and water plants. The greens of this and the Wan Li period include various shades—bright leaf green, pale emerald, and a bluish green[136] which seems to be peculiar to the late Ming period.

A box in the collection of Dr. C. Seligmann has a dragon design reserved in a blue ground and washed over with yellow enamel, on which in turn are details traced in iron red; and another peculiar type of Chia Ching polychrome in the Pierpont Morgan Collection (Cat. No. 882) is a tea cup with blue Imperial dragons inside, "on the outside deep yellow glaze with decoration in brownish red of intensely luminous tone, derived from iron, lightly brushed on the yellow ground: the decoration consists of a procession of boys carrying vases of flowers round the sides of the cup with addition of a scroll of foliage encircling the rim." Both these specimens have the Chia Ching mark.

Allusion has already been made (p. 6) to a type of bowl which belongs to the Ming period, though opinions differ as to the exact part of that dynasty to which it should be assigned. The bowls vary slightly in form, but the most usual kind is that shown on Plate 74 with well rounded sides. A common feature, which does not appear in the photograph, is a convex centre. Others, again, are shallow with concave base, but no foot rim. The decoration of those in the British Museum includes (1) a coral red exterior with gilt designs as described on p. 6, combined with slight underglaze blue interior ornament, (2) a beautiful pale emerald green exterior similarly gilt, with or without blue ornament inside, and (3) a single specimen with white slip traceries in faint relief under the glaze inside, the outside enamelled with turquoise blue medallions and set with cabochon jewels in Persia or India. There are similar bowls in the Dresden collection, with pale sky blue glaze on the exterior. As already noted, one or two of the red bowls have the Yung Lo mark, but, as a rule, they are marked with phrases of commendation or good wish,[137] such as *tan kuei* (red cassia, emblem of literary success), *wan fu yu t'ung* (may infinite happiness embrace all your affairs!) Two of them are known to have sixteenth-century European mounts, viz. the red bowl mentioned on p. 6, and a green specimen in the British Museum.[138] Without denying the possibility of some of the red examples dating back to the Yung Lo period, the conclusion is almost irresistible that we have here in one case the *fan hung* decoration which replaced the *hsien hung* in the Chia Ching period, and in another the *ts'ui lü* (emerald green), named among the colours of the Imperial Chia Ching porcelains.

The Chia Ching monochromes already mentioned include white, blue, sky blue, lustrous brown, turquoise, green, yellow, and aubergine, with or without designs engraved in the paste (*an hua*). None of these call for any further comment, unless it be the distinction between blue and sky blue of the Imperial wares. The former, no doubt, resulted from the Mohammedan blue (blended with native cobalt) mixed with the glaze, and must have been a fine blue of slightly violet tone: the latter was apparently the lavender-tinted blue which goes by the name of sky blue on the more modern porcelains.

We read in more than one passage in the Chinese works that the imitation of the classical porcelains of Hsüan Tê and Ch'êng Hua was practised in the Chia Ching period, and the name of a private potter who excelled in this kind of work has been preserved. A note on this artist, given in the *T'ao lu*[139] under the heading *Ts'ui kung*[140] *yao*, or Wares of Mr. Ts'ui, may be rendered as follows:—

"In the Chia Ching and Lung Ch'ing periods there lived a man who was clever at making porcelain (*t'ao*). He was famed for imitations of the wares in the traditional style and make of the Hsüan Tê and Ch'êng Hua periods, and in his time he enjoyed the highest reputation. The name given to his wares was Mr. Ts'ui's porcelain (*ts'ui kung yao tz'ǔ*), and they were eagerly sought in all parts of the empire. As for the shape of his cups (*ch'ien*), when compared with the Hsüan and Ch'êng specimens[141] they differed in size but displayed the same skill and perfection of design. In the blue and polychrome wares his colours were all like the originals. His were, in fact, the cream of the porcelains made in the private factories (*min t'ao*)."

PLATE 74

Two Bowls in the British Museum with gilt designs on a monochrome ground. Probably Chia Ching period (1522–1566)

Fig. 1 with lotus scroll with etched details on a ground of iron red (*fan hung*) outside. Inside is figure of a man holding a branch of cassia, a symbol of literary success, painted in underglaze blue. Mark in blue, *tan kuei* (red cassia.) Diameter 4½ inches.

Fig. 2 with similar design on ground of emerald green enamel. Mark in blue in the form of a coin or *cash* with the characters *ch'ang ming fu kuei* (long life, riches and honours!). Diameter 4¾ inches.

It is interesting to note that the imitation of the early Ming porcelains began as soon as this, and we may infer from the usual Chinese procedure that the marks of the Hsüan Tê and Ch'êng Hua periods were duly affixed to these clever copies.

Lung Ch'ing 隆慶 (1567–1572)

We read in the *T'ao shuo*[142] that the Imperial factory was re-established in the sixth year of this reign (1572), and placed under the care of the assistant prefects of the district. This would seem to imply that for the greater part of this brief period the Imperial works had been in abeyance. Be this as it may, there was no falling off in the quantity of porcelain commanded for the Court, and the extravagant and burdensome demands evoked a protest from Hsü Ch'ih, the president of the Censorate,[143] in 1571. It was urged among other things that the secret of the copper red colour (*hsien hung*) had been lost, and that the potters should be allowed to use the iron red (*fan hung*) in its place: that the size and form of the large fish bowls which were ordered made their manufacture almost impossible: that the designs for the polychrome (*wu ts'ai*) painting were too elaborate, and that square boxes made in three tiers were a novelty difficult to construct. Fire and flood had devastated Ching-tê Chên, and many of the workmen had fled, and he (the president) begged that a large reduction should be made in the palace orders.

We are not told whether this memorial to the emperor had the desired effect. In the case of the next emperor a similar protest resulted in a large reduction of the demands. But the document discloses several interesting facts, and among other things we learn that the designs for some of the ware and for the coloured decoration were still sent from the palace as in the days of Ch'êng Hua.

The official lists of porcelain actually supplied to the Court of Lung Ch'ing have been briefly summarised in the *T'ao shuo*[144]; but they do not include any new forms, and the motives of decoration were in the main similar to those recorded in the Chia Ching lists. The following, however, may be added to the summary in the previous chapter:—

The *yü tsan hua*, rendered in Giles's Dictionary as the "tuberose," by Bushell as the "iris."

Clumps of chrysanthemum flowers.

Interlacing scrolls of *mu-tan* peony.

Ch'ang ch'un (long spring) flowers, identified by Bushell with the "jasmine."

A "joyous meeting," symbolised according to Bushell by a pair of magpies.

The Tartar pheasant (*chai chih*).

The season flowers supporting the characters 乾坤清泰 *ch'ien k'un ch'ing t'ai*, "Heaven and earth fair and fruitful!"

Monsters (*shou*) in sea waves.

Flying fish.

Historical scenes (*ku shih*), as well as genre subjects (*jên wu*).

Children playing with branches of flowers.

This last design occurs both in the form of belts of foliage scrolls, among which are semi-nude boys, and of medallions with a boy holding a branch, on blue and white and polychrome wares of the late Ming period. But it is a design of considerable antiquity, and it is found engraved on the early Corean bowls which, no doubt, borrowed from Sung originals.

Though all these designs are given under the general heading of blue and white, we may infer that the polychrome which is occasionally mentioned was used in combination with the blue. Thus the mention of "phœnixes in red clouds flying through flowers," of "nine red dragons in blue waves," and of "a pair of dragons in red clouds," recalls actual specimens which I have seen of Lung Ch'ing and Wan Li boxes with designs of blue dragons moving through clouds touched in with iron red. Again, where the blue designs are supplemented with "curling waves and plum blossoms in polychrome (*wu ts'ai*)," one thinks of the well-known pattern of conventional waves on which blossom and symbols are floating, as on Plate 79. Other types of decoration mentioned are yellow grounds and white glaze, both with dragon designs engraved under the glaze (*an hua*), peacocks and *mu-tan* peonies in gilding, and moulded ornament. A specific example of the last are the lions which served as knobs on the covers of the ovoid wine jars (*t'an*).

The author of the *T'ao shuo* pays a handsome tribute to the skill of the late Ming potters. "We find," he says, "that the porcelain of the Ming dynasty daily increased in excellence till we come to the reigns of Lung Ch'ing and Wan Li, when there was nothing that could not be made." At the same time he finds fault with a particular kind of decoration which was encouraged by the degraded and licentious tastes of the Emperor Lung Ch'ing, and seems to have only too frequently marred the porcelain of the period.[145]

The rare examples of marked Lung Ch'ing porcelain in our collections do not call for special comment, and the unmarked specimens will hardly be distinguished from the productions of the succeeding Wan Li period. There are, however, two boxes in the British Museum which may be regarded as characteristic specimens of the Imperial blue and white porcelains. Both are strongly made with thick but fine-grained body material and a glaze of slightly greenish tone; and the designs are boldly sketched in strong outline and washed in with a dark indigo blue. One is a square box with four compartments decorated with five-clawed dragons in cloud scrolls, extended or coiled in medallions according as space demanded; and the other is oblong and rectangular, and painted on the sides (the cover is missing) with scenes of family life (*jên wu*). In both cases the base is unglazed except for a sunk medallion in which the six characters of the Lung Ch'ing mark are finely painted in blue.

CHAPTER V

WAN LI 萬曆 (1573–1619) AND OTHER REIGNS

The long reign of Wan Li, the last important period of the Ming dynasty, is certainly the best represented in European collections, a circumstance due to the ceramic activity of the time not less than to its nearness to our own age. In the first year of the reign orders were given that one of the sub-prefects of Jao-chou Fu should be permanently stationed at Ching-tê Chên to supervise the Imperial factory. It appears that he proved a stern taskmaster, and at the same time that the potters were severely burdened by excessive demands from the palace. The picture drawn by the censor in the previous reign of the afflicted condition of the potters, and the story told elsewhere[146] how they had made intercession daily in the temple of the god that the Imperial orders might be merciful, are fitting preface to the tale of the dragon bowls told as follows by T'ang Ying,[147] the director of the factory in the first half of the eighteenth century.

"By the west wall of the Ancestral-tablet Hall of the spirit who protects the potters is a dragon fish bowl (*lung kang*). It is three feet in diameter and two feet high, with a fierce frieze of dragons in blue and a wave pattern below. The sides and the mouth are perfect, but the bottom is wanting. It was made in the Wan Li period of the Ming. Previously these fish bowls had presented great difficulty in the making, and had not succeeded, and the superintendent had increased his severity. Thereupon the divine T'ung took pity on his fellow potters, and served them by alone laying down his life. He plunged into the fire, and the bowls came out perfect. This fish bowl was damaged after it had been finished and selected (for palace use), and for a long time it remained abandoned in a corner of the office. But when I saw it I sent a double-yoked cart and men to lift it, and it was brought to the side of the Ancestral-tablet Hall of the god, where it adorns a high platform, and sacrifice is offered. The vessel's perfect glaze is the god's fat and blood; the body material is the god's body and flesh; and the blue of the decoration, with the brilliant lustre of gems, is the essence of the god's pure spirit."

The deification of T'ung was a simple matter to the Chinese, who habitually worship before the tablets of their ancestors; but he seems to have become the genius of the place, and in this capacity to have superseded another canonised potter named Chao,[148] who had been worshipped at Ching-tê Chên since 1425.

To add to the difficulties experienced by the potters in satisfactorily fulfilling the Imperial demands, it had been reported in 1583 that the supplies of earth from Ma-ts'ang were practically worked out, and though good material was found at Wu-mên-t'o, which is also in the district of Fu-liang, the distance for transport was greater, and as the price was not correspondingly raised the supply from this source was difficult to maintain. Consequently we are not surprised to learn that in this same year another memorial was forwarded to the emperor by one of the supervising censors, Wang Ching-min, asking for alleviation of the palace orders, and protesting specifically against the demands for candlesticks, screens, brush handles, and chess apparatus as unnecessarily extravagant. It was urged at the same time that blue decoration should be substituted for polychrome, and that pierced work (*ling lung*) should not be required, the objection to both these processes being that they were difficult to execute and meretricious in effect.

It is stated in the *T'ao lu*[149] that the supply of Mohammedan blue had ceased completely in the reign of Wan Li, and that on the other hand the *chi hung* or underglaze copper red was made, though it was not equal in quality to the *hsien hung* or *pao shih hung*[150] of the earlier periods. Both these assertions are based on the somewhat uncertain authority of the *T'ang shih ssŭ k'ao*, and though the truth of the second is shown by existing specimens, the first is only partially true, for there are marked examples of Mohammedan blue in the British Museum and probably elsewhere. Either there were supplies of the Mohammedan material in hand at the beginning of the reign, or they continued to arrive for part at least of the period.

The lists of porcelain supplied to the Court of Wan Li may be consulted with advantage, and the extracts from those of the previous reigns may be supplemented by the following, which, though not necessarily new forms and designs, do not appear in the Chia Ching and Lung Ch'ing records:—

Forms.

Trays for wine cups (*pei p'an*).[151]

Beaker-shaped[152] vases (*hu p'ing* 壺缾).

Flat-backed wall vases in the form of a double gourd split vertically.

Chess boards (*ch'i p'an*).

Hanging oil lamps[2] (*ch'ing t'ai* 檠臺).

Pricket candlesticks (*chu t'ai*). See *Cat. B. F. A.*, 1910, E 6: a pricket candlestick with cloud and dragon designs in blue and the Wan Li mark.

Jars for candle snuff (*chien chu kuan*).

Screens (*p'ing*).

Brush handles (*pi kuan*).

Brush rests (*pi chia*).

Brush pots (*pi ch'ung*). Apparently the cylindrical jars usually known as *pi t'ung*.

Fan cases (*shan hsia*).

Water droppers for the ink pallet (*yen shui ti*).

Betel-nut boxes (*pin lang lu*).

Handkerchief boxes (*chin lu*).

Hat boxes (*kuan lu*).

Cool seats (*liang tun*), for garden use in summer.

Motives for Painted Decoration.

Floral, etc.:

Lily flowers (*hsüan hua*).

Hibiscus (*kuei*) flowers on a brocade ground.

Round medallions of season flowers.

Flower designs broken by medallions of landscape.

Marsh plants.

Sections of water melons (*hsi kua pan*).

Foreign pomegranates; sometimes tied with fillets.

The sacred peach.

Medallions of peach boughs with the seal character *shou* (longevity).

Apricot (*hsing*) foliage.

Pine pattern brocade.

Ginseng (*hsien*).

Hemp-leaved (*ma yeh*) Indian lotus.

Borders of bamboo foliage and branching prunus.

Grape-vine borders.

Animals, etc.:

Monsters: variously described as *hai shou* (sea monsters) and *i shou* (strange monsters).

Nine blue monsters in red waves.

Strange monsters attending the celestial dragon.

Sea horses.

Full-faced dragons (*chêng mien lung*). See Plate 66.

Medallions of archaic dragons (*ch'ih*) and tigers.

Ascending and descending dragons.

Couchant, or squatting (*tun*) dragons.

Flying dragons.

The hundred dragons.

The hundred storks.

The hundred deer. (As in the "Hundred Shou Characters" and other similar phrases, the "hundred" is merely an indefinite numerative signifying a large number.)

Elephants with vases of jewels (of Buddhistic significance).

Water birds in lotus plants.

Six cranes, "symbolising the cardinal points of the universe" (*liu ho ch'ien k'un*).

Phœnixes among the season flowers.

Bees hovering round plum blossom.

Human:

Men and women (*shih nü*).

Medallions with boys pulling down (branches of) cassia (*p'an kuei*).

The picture of the Hundred Boys.

Fu, Lu, Shou (Happiness, Rank, and Longevity). It is not stated whether the characters only are intended, or, as is more probable, the three Taoist deities who distribute these blessings.

Emblematic Motives and Inscriptions.

The eight Buddhist emblems, bound with fillets (*kuan t'ao*).

Ju-i sceptres bound with fillets.

Ju-i cloud borders (*ju i yün pien*).

Midsummer holiday symbols (*tuan yang chieh*). Explained by Bushell as sprigs of acorns and artemisia hung up on the fifth day of the fifth moon.

Emblems of Longevity (*shou tai*), e.g. gourd, peach, fungus, pine, bamboo, crane, deer.

The "monad symbol" (*hun yüan*), which is apparently another name for the *yin yang*, and the Eight Trigrams. See p. 290.

Lozenge symbols of victory (*fang shêng*).

"The four lights worshipping the star of Longevity" (*ssǔ yang p'êng shou*).

Spiral (*hui* 廻) patterns.

Sanskrit invocations (*chên yen tz'ǔ*). See Plate 93.

Ancient writings found at Lo-yang (*lo shu*). Lo-yang (the modern Honan Fu) was the capital of the Eastern Han (25–220 A.D.).

Inscriptions in antique seal characters (*chuan*).

Dragons holding up the characters 永保萬壽*yung pao wan shou* (ever insuring endless longevity); and 永保洪福齊天*yung pao hung fu ch'i t'ien* (ever insuring great happiness equalling Heaven).

Borders inscribed 福如東海*fu ju tung hai* (happiness like the eastern sea); and 風調雨順天下太平*fêng t'iao yü shun t'ien hsia t'ai p'ing* (favouring winds and seasonable rain: great peace throughout the empire).

"A symbolical head with hair dressed in four puffs"[153] bearing the characters 永保長春*yung pao ch'ang ch'un* (ever insuring long spring).

Taoist deities holding the characters 萬古長春四海來朝*wan ku ch'ang ch'un ssǔ hai lai ch'ao* (through myriads of ages long spring; tribute coming from the four seas); or the same sentiment with *yung pao* (ever insuring) in place of *wan ku*.

Dragons in clouds holding the characters 聖壽*shêng shou*, the emperor's birthday.

Miscellaneous.

Representations of ancient coins (*ku lao ch'ien*).

Landscapes (*shan shui*).

Necklaces (*ying lo* 瓔珞).

Jewel mountains in the sea waves (*pao shan hai shui*). This is, no doubt, the familiar border pattern of conventional waves with conical rocks standing up at regular intervals.

Round medallions (*ho tzŭ*, lit. boxes) in brocade grounds.

Most of these designs are given under the heading of "blue and white," though, as in the Lung Ch'ing list, the blue is in many cases supplemented by colour or by other forms of decoration such as patterns engraved in the body (*an hua*), and "designs on a blue ground," the nature of them not explained, but no doubt similar to those described on p. 61. The method of reserving the decoration in white in a blue ground (*ch'ing ti pai hua*) is specifically mentioned under the heading of "mixed decorations." The supplementary decoration consists of on-glaze enamels mixed with the underglaze blue; bowls with coloured exterior and blue and white inside or vice versa; yellow grounds with designs engraved under the glaze; gilded fishes among polychrome water weeds, and other gilded patterns; curling waves in polychrome and plum blossoms; red dragons in blue waves, the red either under or over the glaze; relief designs (*ting chuang*[154]) and pierced work (*ling lung*[155]).

The "mixed colours" included garden seats with lotus designs, etc., in polychrome (*wu ts'ai*) and with aubergine brown (*tzŭ*) lotus decoration in a monochrome yellow ground; tea cups with dragons in fairy flowers engraved under a yellow glaze; yellow ground with polychrome (*wu ts'ai*) decoration; banquet dishes, white inside, the outside decorated with dragons and clouds in red, green, yellow, and aubergine.

The custom of minutely subdividing the work in the porcelain factories so that even the decoration of a single piece was parcelled out among several painters existed in the Ming dynasty, though perhaps not carried so far as in the after periods. It is clear that under such a system the individuality of the artists was completely lost, and we never hear the name of any potter or painter who worked at the Imperial factory. In the private factories probably the division of labour was less rigorous, and it is certain that many of the specimens were decorated by a single brush. But even so, signatures of potters or painters are almost unknown; and only one or two private potters of conspicuous merit at the end of the Ming period are mentioned by name in the Chinese books. Mr. Ts'ui, for instance, has already been mentioned in the chapter on the Chia Ching period, and three others occur in the annals of the Wan Li period.

Fig. 1

Fig. 2

Fig. 3

Fig. 4

Plate 75.—Ming Porcelain.

Fig. 1.—Tripod Bowl with raised peony scrolls in enamel colours. Wan Li mark. Height 5¾ inches. *Eumorfopoulos Collection.*

Fig. 2.—Blue and white Bowl, Chia Ching period. Mark, *Wan ku ch'ang ch'un* ("A myriad antiquities and enduring spring!"). Height 3 inches. *Kunstgewerbe Museum, Berlin.*

Fig. 3.—Ewer with white slip *ch'i-lin* on a blue ground. Wan Li period. Height 9 inches. *Eumorfopoulos Collection.*

Fig. 4.—Gourd-shaped Vase with winged dragons and fairy flowers, raised outlines and coloured glazes on the biscuit. Sixteenth century. Height 8¾ inches. *Salting Collection.*

Of these, the most interesting personality was Hao Shih-chiu,[156] scholar, painter, poet, and potter, who signed his wares with the fanciful name *Hu yin tao jên*[157] (Taoist hidden in a tea pot), to show that he "put his soul" into the making of his pots. He lived, we are told,[158] in exaggerated simplicity, in hut, with a mat for a door and a broken jar for a window; but he was so celebrated as a man of talent and culture that his hut was frequented by the *literati*, who capped his verses and admired his wares. The latter were of great refinement and exquisitely beautiful, and his white "egg shell"[159] wine cups were so delicate as to weigh less than a gramme.[160] No less famous were his red wine cups, bright as vermilion, the colour floating in the glaze like red clouds. They were named *liu hsia chan*[161] (*lit.* floating red cloud cups), which has been poetically rendered by Bushell as "dawn-red wine cups" and "liquid dawn cups," and were evidently one of the reds of the *chi hung* class produced by copper oxide in the glaze, like the beautiful wine cups with clouded maroon red glaze of the early eighteenth century. All these wares were eagerly sought by connoisseurs throughout the Chinese empire. "There were also elegantly formed pots (hu), in colour pale green, like Kuan and Ko wares, but without the ice crackle, and golden brown[162] tea pots with reddish tinge, imitating the contemporary wares of the Ch'ên family at Yi-hsing, engraved underneath with the four characters, *Hu yin tao jên*."

The "red cloud" cups are eulogised by the poet Li Jih-hua in a verse addressed to their maker as fit to be "started from the orchid pavilion to float down the nine-bend river."[163]

Fig. 1

Fig. 2

Fig. 3

Fig. 4

Plate 76.—Blue and White Porcelain. Sixteenth Century.

Fig. 1.—Vase with monster handles, archaic dragons. Height 10⅞ inches. *Halsey Collection.*

Fig. 2.—Hexagonal Bottle, white in blue designs. Mark, a hare. Height 11½ inches. *Alexander Collection.*

Fig. 3.—Bottle with "garlic mouth," stork and lotus scrolls, white in blue. Height 11 inches. *Salting Collection.*

Fig. 4.—Vase (*mei p'ing*), Imperial dragon and scrolls. Wan Li mark on the shoulder. Height 15 inches. *Coltart Collection.*

The two other potters of this period whose names have survived are Ou of Yi-hsing fame (vol. i., p. 181) and Chou Tan-ch'üan, whose wonderful imitations of Sung Ting ware have been described in vol. i., p. 94. Many clever imitations of this latter porcelain were made at Ching-tê Chên in the Wan Li period, and a special material, *ch'ing-t'ien*[164] stone, was employed for the purpose; but the followers of Ch'ou Tan-ch'üan were not so successful as their master, and their wares are described as over-elaborate in decoration and quite inferior to Ch'ou's productions. There was one type, however, which is specially mentioned, the oblong rectangular boxes made to hold seal-vermilion. These are described in a sixteenth-century work[165] as either pure white or painted in blue, and usually six or seven inches long. They are accorded a paragraph in the *T'ao shuo*[166] under the heading of *fang ting* or "imitation Ting ware," and they were probably of that soft-looking, creamy white crackled ware to which Western collectors have given the misleading name of "soft paste."[167]

Another private manufacture specially mentioned in the *T'ao lu*[168] was located in a street called *Hsiao nan* 小南 where, we are told, "they made wares of small size only, like a squatting frog, and called for that reason frog wares (*ha ma*[169] *yao*). Though coarse, they were of correct form; the material was yellowish, but the body of the ware was thin; and though small, the vessels were strong. One kind of bowl was white in colour with a tinge of blue (*tai ch'ing*), and decorated in blue with a single orchid spray or bamboo leaves; and even those which had no painted design had one or two rings of blue at the mouth. These were called "white rice vessels" (*pai fan ch'i*). There were, besides, bowls with wide mouths and flattened rims (*p'ieh t'an*)[170] but shallow, and pure white, imitating the Sung bowls. All these wares had a great vogue, both at the time and at the beginning of the present (i.e. the Ch'ing) dynasty."

Out of the comparatively large number of Wan Li porcelains in European collections the majority are blue and white. This is only to be expected, having regard to the preponderance of this style of decoration in the Imperial lists, and also to the fact that it was found easiest of all processes to execute. In fact, the censor pleading on behalf of the potters in 1583 asks that this style may be substituted for the more exacting polychrome and pierced work. It has already been mentioned that the supplies of Mohammedan blue apparently came to an end early in the reign, but there are enough examples of this colour associated with the Wan Li mark to show that it was used for part at least of the period. One of these is a well-potted bowl of fine white porcelain, entirely covered with Sanskrit characters (*chên yen tẓ'ŭ*), in the British Museum; and another piece* is a dish moulded in the form of an open lotus flower with petals in relief, and in the centre a single Sanskrit character. Both are painted in a clear and vivid Mohammedan blue, and have the Wan Li mark under the base. A dark violet blue, closely akin to the typical Chia Ching colour but with a touch of indigo, occurs on two dishes,* decorated with a pair of fishes among aquatic plants and bearing the four characters of the Wan Li mark surrounding a cartouche, which contains the felicitous legend, "Virtue, culture, and enduring spring" (see vol. i., p. 225). An intense but more vivid violet blue, which betrays something of the Mohammedan blend, is seen on a ewer* of Persian form, decorated with a *ch'i-lin* reclining before a strangely Italian-looking fountain. The ware of this piece, though thick, is of fine grain, and the glaze has a faint greenish tinge, and its mark, a hare,[171] (see vol. i., p. 227) occurs on several other examples of varying quality, but all of late Ming character.

Another group of marked Wan Li ware, comprising bowls and dishes with trim neat finish and obviously destined for table use, has a soft-looking glaze, often much worn, but, even in the less used parts, with a peculiar smoothness of surface which is, no doubt, largely due to age. There are three examples of this group in the British Museum, all painted in the same soft, dark indigo-tinged blue. One is a bowl with baskets of season flowers round the exterior, insects, and a border of dragon and phœnix pattern; while inside is a blue medallion with a full-face dragon reserved in white. The other two are dishes with figure subjects and gourd vine borders, which are interesting because the painting shows signs of a transition state, part being in flat Ming washes, and part showing the marbled effect which was afterwards characteristic of the K'ang Hsi blue and white.

In striking contrast with this smooth, soft-surfaced ware is a vase* of square, beaker shape, and details which indicate a form derived from bronze. Though evidently an Imperial piece, it is of strong, heavy build, with a hard thick glaze of greenish tinge, so full of minute bubbles as to spread in places a veritable fog over the blue decoration beneath. The design, consisting of a dragon and phœnix among sprays of (?) lily, with rock and wave borders, is repeated in all the spaces, and below the lip in front is the Wan Li mark extended in a single line. A similar vase,* but with polychrome decoration, illustrated on Plate 81, will serve to show the form and design. Both are fine, decorative objects, in a strong, rugged style, which takes no account of small fire-flaws and slight imperfections in the glaze. The same strong, hard body and glaze is seen again on three flat, narrow-rimmed dishes,* which are conspicuous for unusual borders, two having a large checker and the third a chevron pattern, in addition to a thin blue line on either side of the edge. Sand adhering to the foot rim and faint radiating lines scored in the base are indications of rough finish, and they are clearly all the work of a private factory perhaps catering for the export trade.

A variety of boxes figured in the Imperial lists, destined for holding incense, vermilion, chess pieces, handkerchiefs, caps, sweetmeats, cakes, etc. A fair number of these have survived and found their way into Western collections. Round, square, oblong with rounded ends, and sometimes furnished with interior compartments, they are usually decorated with dragon designs in dark blue, occasionally tricked out with touches of iron red; but miscellaneous subjects also occur in their decoration, as in a fine example exhibited at the Burlington Fine Arts Club in 1910,[172] which has figure subjects on the cover and a landscape with waterfall, probably from a picture of the celebrated mountain scenery in Szechuan. Sometimes the covers of these boxes are perforated as though to allow some perfume to escape. Other interesting late Ming porcelains in the same exhibition were a pricket candlestick with cloud and dragon ornament and the Wan Li mark; a curious perfume vase (Plate 68, Fig. 1), which illustrates the design of lions sporting with balls of brocade, an unmarked piece which might even be as early as Chia Ching; and a wide-mouthed vase lent by the Ashmolean Museum, Oxford, with the familiar design of fantastic lions moving among peonies and formal scrolls on the body and panels of flowers separated by trellis diaper on the shoulder. The last is a type which is not uncommon, but this particular example is interesting because it belonged to one of the oldest collections in England, presented to the Oxford Museum by John Tradescant, and mostly collected before 1627.

The export trade with Western Asia was in full swing in the reign of Wan Li, and the Portuguese traders had already made their way to the Far East and brought back Chinese porcelain for European use. That it was, however, still a rare material in England seems to be indicated by the sumptuous silver-gilt mounts in which stray specimens were enshrined. Several of these mounted specimens still exist, and seven of them were seen at the Burlington Fine Arts Exhibition, 1910,[173] the date of the mounts being about 1580–1590. Taken, as they may fairly be, as typical specimens, they show on the whole a porcelain of indifferent quality, with all the defects and virtues of export ware—the summary finish of skilful potters who worked with good material but for an uncritical public, and rapid, bold draughtsmanship in an ordinary quality of blue usually of greyish or indigo tint. The most finished specimen was a bowl from the Pierpont Morgan Collection, with a design of phœnixes and lotus scrolls finely drawn in blue of good quality. Unlike the others, it had a reign mark (that of Wan Li), and probably it was made at the Imperial factory. A bottle mounted as a ewer from the same collection had a scale pattern on the neck, flowering plants and birds on the body, and a saucer dish was painted in the centre with a typical late Ming landscape, with mountains, pine trees, pagoda, a pleasure boat, and sundry figures. The blue of this last piece was of fair quality but rather dull, and it had a double ring under the base void of mark. Another bowl had on the exterior panel designs with deer in white reserved in a blue ground, in a style somewhat similar to that of the bottle illustrated on Plate 76, Fig. 3. There is a bowl in the British Museum, mounted with silver-gilt foot and winged caryatid handles of about 1580 (Plate 69, Fig. 1). The porcelain is of fine white material with thick lustrous glaze of slightly bluish tint and "pinholed" here and there; and the design painted in blue with a faint tinge of indigo consists of a vase with a lotus flower and a lotus leaf and three egrets, in a medallion inside and four times repeated on the exterior. This is clearly an early Wan Li specimen, if, indeed, it is not actually as old as Chia Ching.

The most remarkable collection of Chinese export porcelain is illustrated by Professor Sarre[174] from a photograph which he was able to make of the *Chini-hane* or porcelain house attached to the mosque of Ardebil, in Persia. Ranged on the floor are some five hundred specimens—jars, vases, ewers, and stacks of plates, bowls and dishes, many of which had formerly occupied niches in the walls of the building erected by Shah Abbas the Great[175] (1587–1628). Unfortunately, the conditions were not favourable to photography, and the picture, valuable as it is, only permits a clear view of the nearer objects, the rest being out of focus and represented by mere shadows of themselves. They are, we are told, mainly blue and white, but with a sprinkling of coloured pieces, and it is clear from the picture that they belong to various periods of the Ming dynasty, mostly to the later part. They include, no doubt, presents from the Chinese Court,[176] besides the porcelains which came in the ordinary way of trade, and we recognise a large vase almost identical with the fine Chia Ching specimen on Plate 72: a small-mouthed, baluster-shaped vase, similar in form and decoration to a marked Wan Li specimen in the Pierpont Morgan Collection[177]; a bowl with lotus scrolls in blotchy blue, recalling the style of Plate 67, Fig. 4; a ewer with the curious fountain design described on p. 67; besides a number of the ordinary late Ming export types and some celadon jars and bulb bowls of a slightly earlier period. Some of the pots, we are told, are almost a metre in height. Among the tantalising forms in the indistinct background are some large covered jars with a series of loop-handles on the shoulders, such as are found in Borneo and the East Indies (see vol. i., p. 189).

One of the most attractive types of late Ming export porcelain, and at the same time the most easily recognised, consists of ewers, bowls, and dishes of thin, crisp porcelain with characteristic designs in pale, pure blue of silvery tone; see Plate 77, Fig. 1. The ware is of fine, white, unctuous material with a tendency (not very marked) to turn brown at the foot rim and in parts where the glaze is wanting. The glaze partakes of the faintly greenish tinge common to Ming wares, but it is clear and of high lustre. Here, again, a little sand or grit occasionally adhering to the foot rim and radiating lines lightly scored in the base indicate a summary finish which detracts from the artistic effect no more than the obviously rapid though skilful brushwork of the decoration. Sharply moulded forms and crinkled borders, admirably suited to this thin crisp material, give additional play to the lustrous glaze, and the general feeling of the ware is well expressed by Mr. F. Perzynski[178] in his excellent study of the late Ming blue and white porcelains, in which he remarks that "the artists of this group have used thin, brittle material more like flexible metal than porcelain."

The designs as shown in the illustration are typical of the ware.

Fig. 1

Fig. 2

PLATE 77

Two examples of Ming Blue and White Porcelain in the British Museum

Fig. 1.—Ewer of thin, crisp porcelain with foliate mouth and rustic spout with leaf attachments. Panels of figure subjects and landscapes on the body: "rat and vine" pattern on the neck and a band of hexagon diaper enclosing a cash symbol. Latter half of the sixteenth century. Height 7 inches.

Fig. 2.—Octagonal stand perhaps for artist's colours. On the sides are scenes from the life of a sage; borders of *ju-i* pattern and gadroons. On the top are lions sporting with brocade balls. Painted in deep Mohammedan blue. Mark of the Chia Ching period (1522–1566). Diameter 4¾ inches.

A freely drawn figure of a man or woman usually in garden surroundings, standing before a fantastic rock or seated by a table and a picture-screen often form the leading motive, though this is varied by landscape, floral compositions, spirited drawings of birds (an eagle on a rock, geese in a marsh, a singing bird on a bough), or a large cicada on a stone among plants and grasses. The borders of dishes and the exteriors of bowls are divided into radiating compartments (often with the divisions lightly moulded) filled with figures, plant designs, symbols, and the like, and separated by narrow bands with pendent jewels and tasselled cords, which form perhaps the most constant characteristics of the group. Small passages of brocade diapers with swastika fret, hexagon and matting patterns, are used to fill up the spaces. The finer examples of this group are of admirable delicacy both in colour and design; but the type lasted well into the seventeenth century and became coarse and vulgarised. It appears in a debased form in the large dishes which were made in quantity for the Persian and Indian markets, overloaded with crudely drawn brocade diapers and painted in dull indigo blue, which is often badly fired and verges on black. The central designs on these dishes, deer in a forest, birds in marsh, etc., usually betray strong Persian influence.

I am not aware of any specimens of this group, either of the earlier or the more debased kinds which bear date-marks, but still a clear indication of the period is given by various circumstances. A bowl in the National Museum at Munich is credibly stated to have belonged to William V., Duke of Bavaria (1579–1597),[179] and a beautiful specimen, also a bowl, with silver-gilt mount of about 1585, is illustrated by Mr. Perzynski.[180] The characteristic designs of this ware are commonplace on the Persian pottery of the early seventeenth century, and a Persian blue and white ewer in the British Museum, which is dated 1616, clearly reflects the same style. The shallow dishes with moulded sides are frequently reproduced in the still-life pictures by the Dutch masters of the seventeenth century, from whose work many precious hints may be taken by the student of ceramics. To give one instance only, there are two such pictures[181] in the Dresden Gallery from the brush of Frans Snyders (1579–1657).

We shall have occasion later on to discuss more fully another kind of blue and white porcelain for which the Chinese and American collectors show a marked partiality, and which has received the unfortunate title, "soft paste," from the latter. It has an opaque body, often of earthy appearance, and a glaze which looks soft and is usually crackled, and the ware is usually of small dimensions, such as the Chinese *literatus* delighted to see in his study, and beautifully painted with miniature-like touches, every stroke of the brush clear and distinct. Ming marks—Hsüan Tê, Ch'êng Hua, etc.—are not uncommon on this ware, and there is no doubt that it was in use from the early reigns of the dynasty, but the style has been so faithfully preserved by the potters of the eighteenth century that it is wellnigh impossible to distinguish the different periods. A dainty specimen with the Wan Li mark illustrated in Fig. 2 of Plate 93 will serve to show the delicacy and refinement of this exquisite porcelain. At the same time it should be mentioned that the imitation Ting wares described on p. 96, vol. i., when painted in blue, are included in this group.

Fig. 1

Fig. 2

Fig. 3

Plate 78.—Porcelain with pierced (*ling lung*) designs and biscuit reliefs. Late Ming.

Fig. 1.—Bowl with Eight Immortals and pierced swastika fret. Diameter 3¾ inches. *S. E. Kennedy Collection.*

Fig. 2.—Bowl with blue phœnix medallions, pierced trellis work and characters. Wan Li mark. Height 2¼ inches. *Hippisley Collection.*

Fig 3.—Covered Bowl with blue and white landscapes and biscuit reliefs of Eight Immortals. Height 6½ inches. *Grandidier Collection.*

Two interesting kinds of decoration mentioned in the Wan Li list[182] are frequently found in combination with blue and white; these are relief (*ting chuang* or *tui hua*) and pierced work (*ling lung*). Though both have been seen in various forms on the earlier wares, they occur at this period in a fashion which challenges special attention. I allude particularly to the small bowls with or without covers, decorated on the sides with unglazed (or "biscuit") figures in detached relief, or with delicately perforated fretwork, or with a combination of both. The catalogue[183] of the Pierpont Morgan Collection illustrates two covered bowls of the first type with the Eight Immortals in four pairs symmetrically arranged on the sides, and a "biscuit" lion on the cover doing duty for a handle. A similar bowl, formerly in the Nightingale Collection, had the same relief decoration and painted designs in the typical grey blue of the Wan Li period; and Fig. 3 of Plate 78 represents an excellent example from the Grandidier collection. The Chinese were in the habit of daubing these biscuit reliefs (just as they did the unglazed details of statuettes) with a red pigment which served as a medium for oil gilding, but as neither of these coatings was fired they have worn away or been cleaned off in the majority of cases. In the Rijks Museum, Amsterdam, is a picture[184] by Van Streeck (1632–1678), which shows one of these covered bowls with the biscuit reliefs coloured red, and Mr. Perzynski[185] alludes to another in a still-life by Willem Kalf (1630–1693) in the Kaiser Frederick Museum, Berlin, with the figures both coloured[186] and gilt. An excellent example of the second kind of decoration is illustrated by Fig. 2 of Plate 78, one of a set of four bowls in the Hippisley Collection, with phœnix medallions and other decoration in a fine grey blue, the spaces filled with perforated designs of the utmost delicacy, veritable "devil's work," to borrow a Chinese term for workmanship which shows almost superhuman skill. The small pierced medallions contain the characters *fu, shou, k'ang, ning*[187] (happiness, longevity, peace, and tranquillity), and under the base are the six characters of the Wan Li mark. A line cut in the glaze (before firing) at the lip and on the base-rim seems to have been designed to give a firm hold to a metal mount, a use to which it has been actually put in one case; and in another the glazing of the mark under the base has been omitted with the result that it has come from the kiln black instead of blue. The third kind which combines the reliefs and the pierced ornament is illustrated by Fig. 1 of Plate 78. The reliefs of these medallions are small and very delicately modelled, and the subjects are various, including human and animal figures, birds and floral compositions; the borders are often traced in liquid clay, which is left in unglazed relief. An example in the British Museum has an interior lining washed with blue to serve as a backing for the pierced work, and it is painted inside with dragon designs in Wan Li grey blue. It bears a mark which occurs on other late Ming porcelains, *yü tang chia ch'i* (beautiful vessel for the Jade Hall).[188] Examples of this same pierced and relief work in white, without the supplementary blue designs, though rare, are yet to be seen in several collections. If marked at all they usually bear the apocryphal date of Ch'êng Hua, but an example in the Marsden Perry collection, Providence, U.S.A., has the T'ien Ch'i (1621–1627) date under the base, which no doubt represents the true period of its manufacture. This intricate *ling lung* work, which the Wan Li censor deprecated as too difficult and elaborate, has been perpetuated, though it was probably never more beautifully executed than in the late Ming period. The later examples are mostly characterised by larger perforations, which were easier to manage. There are several references to the pierced and relief decorations in the lists of porcelain supplied to the Court of Wan Li, e.g. "brush rests with sea waves and three dragons in relief over pierced designs, and landscapes," "landscape medallions among pierced work," and "sacred fungus carved in openwork, and figures of ancient cash." In the finer examples of pierced work the most frequent design is the fret or key pattern often interwoven with the four-legged symbol known as the swastika, which commonly serves in Chinese for the character *wan* (ten thousand), carrying a suggested wish for "long life," as expressed in the phrase *wan sui* (Jap. *banzai*), ten thousand years. The pierced patterns are carved out of the porcelain body when the ware has been dried to a "leather-tough" consistency, and the manipulative skill exercised in the cutting and handling of the still plastic material is almost superhuman. Similar *tours de force* distinguish the Japanese Hirado porcelain, and Owen's work in our own Worcester ware exhibits extraordinary skill, but I doubt if anything finer in this style has ever been made than the *ling lung* bowls of the late Ming potters.

Another form of decoration which, if not actually included in the *ling lung* category, is at any rate closely allied to it, is the fretwork cut deeply into the body of the ware without actually perforating it, the hollows of the pattern being generally left without glaze. This ornament is used in borders or to fill the spaces between blue and white medallions after the manner of the pierced fretwork, and it was evidently contemporaneous with the latter, viz. dating from the late Ming period onwards (Plate 68, Fig. 3).

It will be convenient here to consider another type of decoration which was probably in use in the early periods of the Ming dynasty, certainly in the reign of Wan Li, and which has continued to modern times. This is the decoration in white clay varying in thickness from substantial reliefs to translucent brush work in thin slip or liquid clay, which allows the colour of the background to appear through it. The designs are painted or modelled in white against dark or light-coloured grounds of various shades—lustrous coffee brown (*tzŭ chin*), deep blue, slaty blue, lavender, celadon, plain white, and crackled creamy white—and they are usually slight and artistically executed. The process, which is the same in principle as in the modern *pâte sur pâte*, consisted of first covering the ground with colouring matter, then tracing the design in white slip (i.e. liquid clay) or building it up with strips of clay modelled with a wet brush, and finally covering it with a colourless glaze. In this case the white design has a covering of glaze. When a celadon green ground is used the design is applied direct to the biscuit and the celadon glaze covers the whole, but being quite transparent it does not obscure the white slip beneath. Sometimes, however, as in Fig. 3 of Plate 75, the design is unglazed and stands out in a dry white "biscuit." Elaborate and beautiful examples of slip decoration were made in the K'ang Hsi and later periods, and Pére d'Entrecolles, writing in 1722, describes their manufacture, stating that steatite and gypsum were used to form the white slip.[189] The Ming specimens are usually of heavier make and less graceful form, and distinguished by simplicity and strength of design, the backgrounds being usually lustrous brown or different shades of blue. They consist commonly of bottles, jars, flower pots, bulb bowls, dishes, and narghili bowls, and many of them were clearly made for export to Persia and India, where they are still to be found. On rare examples the slip decoration is combined with passages of blue and white.

There is little to guide us to the dating of these wares, and marks are exceptional.[190] There is, however, a flower pot in the British Museum with white design of *ch'i-lin* on a brown ground which has the late Ming mark *yü t'ang chia ch'i*[191]; and a specimen with an Elizabethan metal mount was exhibited at the Burlington Fine Arts Club in 1910.[192] These are, no doubt, of Ching-tê Chên make; but there is a curious specimen in the British Museum which seems to be of provincial manufacture. It is a dish with slaty blue ground and plant designs with curious feathery foliage traced with considerable delicacy. The border of running floral scroll has the flowers outlined in dots, and the whole execution of the piece is as distinctive as the strange coarse base which shows a brown-red biscuit and heavy accretions of sand and grit at the foot rim. The same base and the same peculiarities of design appeared on a similar dish with celadon glaze exhibited by Mrs. Halsey at the Burlington Fine Arts Club in 1910,[193] and in the British Museum there are other dishes clearly of the same make, but with (1) crackled grey white glaze and coarsely painted blue decoration, and (2) with greenish white glaze and enamelled designs in iron red and the Ming blue green. It is clear that we have to deal here with the productions of one factory, and though we have no direct clue to its identity, it certainly catered for the export trade to India and the islands; for the enamelled dishes of this type have been found in Sumatra. Mrs. Halsey's dish came from India, and fragments of the blue and enamelled types were found in the ruins of the palace at Bijapur,[194] which was destroyed by Aurungzebe in 1686. Probably the factory was situated in Fukien or Kuangtung, where it would be in direct touch with the southern export trade, and the style of the existing specimens points to the late Ming as the period of its activity.

The process of marbling or "graining" has been tried by potters all the world over, and the Chinese were no exceptions. The effect is produced either by slips of two or more coloured clays worked about on the surface, or by blending layers of clays in two or more colours (usually brown and white) in the actual body. Early examples of this marbling occur among the T'ang wares, and Mr. Eumorfopoulos has examples of the Ming and later periods. One of these, a figure with finely crackled buff glaze and passages of brown and white marbling in front and on the back, has an incised inscription, stating that it was modelled by Ch'ên Wên-ching in the year 1597.[195]

The use of underglaze red in the Wan Li period has already been mentioned (p. 59), and though Chinese writers classed it as *chi hung* they would not admit it to an equality with the brilliant reds of the fifteenth century.[196] Where red is named in the lists of Imperial porcelains we are left in doubt as to its nature, whether under or over the glaze; but there are two little shallow bowls in the British Museum with a curious sponged blue associated with indifferent underglaze red painting, which bear the late Ming mark *yü t'ang chia ch'i*.[197] A bowl of lotus flower pattern, similar in form to that described on p. 66, but deeper, and painted with similar designs in pale underglaze red, though bearing the Ch'êng Hua mark, seems to belong to the late Ming period.

The Wan Li polychromes will naturally include continuations of the early Ming types, such as the large jars with decoration in raised outline, pierced or carved and filled in with glazes of the *demi-grand feu*—turquoise, violet purple, green and yellow—wares with flat washes of the same turquoise and purple, incised designs filled in with transparent glazes of the three colours (*san ts'ai*), green, yellow and aubergine, and, what is probably more truly characteristic of this period, combinations of the first and last styles. A good example of the transparent colours over incised designs is Fig. 1 of Plate 79, a vase of the form known as *mei p'ing* with green Imperial dragons in a yellow ground and the Wan Li mark. All three of the *san ts'ai* colours were also used separately as monochromes with or without engraved designs under the glaze, a striking example in the Pierpont Morgan Collection being a vase with dragon handles and engraved designs under a brilliant iridescent green glaze, "which appears like gold in the sunlight."[198] But though these types persisted, they would no doubt be gradually superseded by simpler and more effective methods of pictorial decoration in painted outline on the biscuit, filled in with washes of transparent enamels in the same three colours. These softer enamels, which contained a high proportion of lead and could be fired at the relatively low temperature of the muffle kiln, must have been used to a considerable extent in the late Ming period, though their full development belongs to the reign of K'ang Hsi, and there will always be a difficulty in separating the examples of these two periods, whether the colours be laid on in broad undefined washes, as on certain figures and on the "tiger skin" bowls and dishes, or brushed over a design carefully outlined in brown or black pigment. There is one species of the latter family with a ground of formal wave pattern usually washed with green and studded with floating plum blossoms, in which are galloping sea horses or symbols, or both, reserved and washed with the remaining two colours, or with a faintly greenish flux, almost colourless, which does duty for white. This species is almost always described as Ming; and with some reason, for the sea wave and plum blossom pattern is mentioned in the Wan Li lists as in polychrome combined with blue decoration. But the danger of assuming a specimen to be Ming because it exhibits a design which occurred on Ming porcelain is shown by an ink pallet in the British Museum, which is dated in the thirty-first year of K'ang Hsi, i.e. 1692. This important piece (Plate 94, Fig. 2) is decorated in enamels on the biscuit over black outlines with the wave and plum blossom pattern, the same yellow trellis diaper which appears on the base of the vase in Plate 97, and other diaper patterns which occur on so many of the so-called Ming figures. This piece is, in fact, a standing rebuke to those careless classifiers who ascribe all on-biscuit enamel indiscriminately to the Ming period, and I am strongly of opinion that most of the dishes,[199] bowls, ewers, cups and saucers, and vases with the wave and plum blossom pattern and horses, etc., in which a strong green enamel gives the dominating tint, belong rather to the K'ang Hsi period. The same kind of decoration is sometimes found applied to glazed porcelain, as on Fig. 3 of Plate 79, a covered potiche-shaped vase in the British Museum with the design of "jewel mountains and sea waves," with floating blossoms, and *pa pao*[200] symbols in green, yellow and white in an aubergine ground, supplemented by a few plain rings in underglaze blue. The style of this vase and the quality of the paste suggest that it really does belong to the late Ming period.

Plate 79.—Wan Li Polychrome Porcelain.

Fig. 1.—Vase (*mei p'ing*) with engraved design, green in a yellow ground, Imperial dragons in clouds, rock and wave border. Wan Li mark. Height 15 inches. *British Museum.*

Fig. 2.—Bottle with pierced casing, phœnix design, etc., painted in underglaze blue and enamels; cloisonné enamel neck. Height 23 inches. *Eumorfopoulos Collection.*

Fig. 3.—Covered Jar, plum blossoms and symbols in a wave pattern ground, coloured enamels in an aubergine background. Height 15½ inches. *British Museum.*

The use of enamels over the glaze was greatly extended in the Wan Li period, though practically all the types in vogue at this time can be paralleled in the Chia Ching porcelain, and, indeed, have been discussed under that heading. There is the red family in which the dominant colour is an iron red, either of curiously sticky appearance and dark coral tint or with the surface dissolved in a lustrous iridescence. Yellow, usually a dark impure colour, though sometimes washed on extremely thin and consequently light and transparent, and transparent greens, which vary from leaf tint to emerald and bluish greens, occur in insignificant quantity. This red family is well illustrated by a splendid covered jar in the Salting Collection (Plate 80), and by three marked specimens in the British Museum, an ink screen, a bowl, and a circular stand. It also occurs on another significant piece in the latter collection, a dish admirably copying the Ming style but marked *Shên tê t'ang po ku chih*[201] (antique made for the Shên-tê Hall), a palace mark of the Tao Kuang period (1821–1850). It should be added that this colour scheme[202] is frequently seen on the coarsely made and roughly decorated jars and dishes with designs of

- 82 -

lions in peony scrolls, etc., no doubt made in large quantities for export to India and Persia. They are not uncommon to-day, and in spite of their obvious lack of finish they possess certain decorative qualities, due chiefly to the mellow red, which are not to be despised.

But the characteristic polychrome of the period, the *Wan Li wu ts'ai*, combines enamelled decoration with underglaze blue, and this again can be divided into two distinctive groups. One of these is exemplified by Plate 81, an Imperial vase shaped after a bronze model and of the same massive build as its fellow in blue and white, which was described on p. 67. Here the underglaze blue is supplemented by the green, the impure yellow and the sticky coral red of the period, and the subject as on the blue and white example consists of dragons and phœnixes among floral scrolls with borders of rock and wave pattern. The object of the decorator seems to have been to distract the eye from the underlying ware, as if he were conscious of its relative inferiority, and the effect of this close design, evenly divided between the blue and the enamels, is rather checkered when viewed from a distance. But both form and decoration are characteristic of the Wan Li Imperial vases, as is shown by kindred specimens, notably by a tall vase in the Pierpont Morgan Collection, of which the design is similar and the form even more metal-like, having on the lower part the projecting dentate ribs seen on square bronze and cloisonné beakers of the Ming dynasty. Two other marked examples of this colour scheme, from which the absence of aubergine is noteworthy, are (1) a ewer in the British Museum with full-face dragons on the neck supporting the characters *wan shou* (endless longevity) and with floral sprays on a lobed body, and (2) a straight-sided box with moulded six-foil elevation, painted on each face with a screen before which is a fantastic animal on a stand, and a monkey, dog and cat in garden surroundings.

The second—and perhaps the more familiar—group of *Wan Li wu ts'ai* is illustrated by Fig. 1 of Plate 82, on which all the colours, including aubergine, are represented in company with the underglaze blue. There is no longer the same patchy effect, because the blue is more evenly balanced by broader washes of the enamel colours, particularly the greens. The design of this particular example is a figure subject taken from Chinese history (*shih wu*), supplemented by a brocade band of floral scroll work on the shoulder and formal patterns on the neck and above the base. The former and the latter positions are commonly occupied in these vases by a band of stiff leaves and a border of false gadroons, both alternately blue and coloured. The stiff leaves in this instance are replaced by floral sprays, and the coloured designs are outlined in a red brown pigment. The mark under the base is the "hare," which has already been noticed on examples of late Ming blue and white.[203] Another late Ming mark, *yü t'ang chia ch'i*,[204] occurs on a dish in the British Museum, with design of the Eight Immortals paying court to the god of

Longevity (*pa hsien p'êng shou*), painted in the same style but with a predominance of underglaze blue.

PLATE 80

Covered Jar or potiche. Painted in iron red and green enamels, with a family scene in a garden, and brocade borders of *ju-i* pattern, peony scrolls, etc. Sixteenth century.

Height 17½ inches.

Salting Collection (Victoria and Albert Museum).

But it is not necessary to multiply instances, for the type is well known, and must have survived for a long period. Indeed, many competent authorities assign the bulk of this kind of porcelain to the Yung Chêng period (1723–1735); and it is undoubtedly true that imitations of Wan Li polychrome were made at this time, for they are specifically mentioned in the Yung Chêng list of Imperial wares.[205] But I am inclined to think that the number of these late attributions has been exaggerated, and that they do not take sufficiently into account the interval of forty-two years between the reigns of Wan Li and K'ang Hsi. It was a distracted time when the potters must have depended largely upon their foreign trade in default of Imperial orders, and it is probable that much of this ware, characterised by strong, rather coarse make, greyish glaze and boldly executed decoration in the Wan Li colour scheme, belongs to this intermediate period. The vases usually have the flat unglazed base which characterises the blue and white of this time.[206] Two handsome beakers, with figure subjects and borders of the peach, pomegranate and citron, and a beautiful jar with phœnix beside a rock and flowering shrubs, in the British Museum, seem to belong to this period, but there are numerous other examples, many of which are coarse and crude, and obviously made wholesale for the export trade.

Among the various examples of Wan Li polychrome exhibited at the Burlington Fine Arts Club in 1910, there was one which calls for special mention, a box[207] with panels of floral designs surrounded by fruit and diaper patterns in the usual colours of the *wu ts'ai*, with the addition of an overglaze blue enamel. It is true that this blue enamel was clearly of an experimental nature and far from successful, but its presence on this marked and indubitable Wan Li specimen is noteworthy. For it has long been an article of faith with collectors that this blue enamel does not antedate the Ch'ing dynasty, being, in fact, a characteristic feature of the K'ang Hsi *famille verte* porcelain. The rule still remains an excellent one, and this solitary exception only serves to emphasise its general truth, showing as it does that so far the attempts at a blue enamel were a failure. But at the same time the discovery is a warning against a too rigid application of those useful rules of thumb, based on the generalisation from what must, after all, be a limited number of instances.

Marked examples of Wan Li monochromes are rarely seen, but we may assume that the glazes in use in the previous reigns continued to be made— blue, lavender, turquoise, violet and aubergine brown, yellow in various shades, leaf green, emerald green, apple green, celadon, coffee brown, and golden brown—besides the more or less accidental effects in the mottled and *flambé* glazes. The plain white bowls of the period had a high reputation,[208] and a good specimen in the British Museum, though far from equalling the Yung Lo bowl (Plate 59), is nevertheless a thing of beauty. The white wares of the Ting type made at this time have been already discussed.[209] The monochrome surfaces were not infrequently relieved by carved or etched designs under the glaze, but it must be confessed that monochromes are exceedingly difficult to date. Particular colours and particular processes continued in use for long periods, and the distinctions between the productions of one reign and the next, or even between those of the late Ming and the early Ch'ing dynasties, are often almost unseizable. At best these differences consist in minute peculiarities of form and potting, in the texture of the body and glaze, and the finish of the base, which are only learnt by close study of actual specimens and by training the eye to the general character of the wares until the perception of the Ming style becomes instinctive. But something further will be said on this subject in the chapter on Ming technique.

PLATE 81

Beaker-shaped Vase of bronze form, with dragon and phœnix designs painted in underglaze blue, and red, green and yellow enamels: background of fairy flowers (*pao hsiang hua*) and borders of "rock and wave" pattern. Mark of the Wan Li period (1573–1619) in six characters on the neck. An Imperial piece. Carved wood stand with cloud pattern.

Height 18½ inches.

British Museum.

THE LAST OF THE MINGS

T'ai Ch'ang 泰昌 (1620)

T'ien Ch'i 天啓 (1621–1627)

Ch'ung Chêng 崇禎 (1628–1643)

Chinese ceramic history, based on the official records, is silent on the subject of the three last Ming reigns, and we are left to infer that during the death struggles of the old dynasty and the establishment of the Manchu Tartars on the throne work at the Imperial factory was virtually suspended. The few existing specimens which bear the marks of T'ien Ch'i and Ch'ung Chêng (the T'ai Ch'ang mark is apparently unrepresented) are of little merit. A barrel-shaped incense vase with floral scrolls and a large bowl with four-clawed dragons of the former date in the British Museum are painted the one in dull greyish blue, and the other in a bright but rather garish tint of the same colour; both have a coarse body material with blisters and pitting in the glaze, and the painting of the designs is devoid of any distinction. Similarly, a polychrome saucer dish with the same mark and in the same collection, decorated with an engraved dragon design filled in with purple glaze in a green ground, carries on the early tradition of that type of Ming polychrome, but the ware is coarse, the design crudely drawn, and the colours impure.[210] From the same unflattering characteristics another dish in the British Museum, with large patches of the three on-biscuit colours—green, yellow and aubergine—may be recognised as of the T'ien Ch'i make. This is a specimen of the so-called tiger skin ware, of which K'ang Hsi and later examples are known—a ware which, even in the best-finished specimens with underglaze engraved designs, is more curious than beautiful. On the other hand, one of the delicate bowls with biscuit figures in high relief, already described (p. 75), proves that the potters of the T'ien Ch'i period were still capable of skilful work when occasion demanded. A pair of wine cups in the British Museum, with freely drawn designs of geese and rice plants in pale greyish blue under a greyish glaze, are the solitary representatives of the Ch'ung Chêng mark.

In the absence of Imperial patronage, and with the inevitable trade depression which followed in the wake of the fierce dynastic struggle, it was fortunate for the Ching-tê Chên potters that a large trade with European countries was developing. The Portuguese and Spanish had already established trading connections with the Chinese, and the other Continental nations—notably the Dutch—were now serious competitors. The Dutch East India Company was an extensive importer of blue and white porcelain, and we have already discussed one type of blue and white which figures frequently in the Dutch pictures of the seventeenth century.

There is another group of blue and white which can be definitely assigned to this period of dynastic transition, between 1620–1662. A comparative study of the various blue and white types had already led to the placing of this ware in the middle of the seventeenth century, and Mr. Perzynski, in those excellent articles[211] to which we have already alluded, has set out the characteristics of this ware at some length, with a series of illustrations which culminate in a dated example. There will be no difficulty in finding a few specimens of this type in any large collection of blue and white. It is recognised by a bright blue of slightly violet tint under a glaze often hazy with minute bubbles, which suggested to Mr. Perzynski the picturesque simile of "violets in milk." Other more tangible characteristics appear in the designs, which commonly consist of a figure subject—a warrior or sage and attendant—in a mountain scene bordered by a wall of rocks with pine trees and swirling mist, drawn in a very mannered style and probably from some stock pattern. Other common features are patches of herbage rendered by pot-hook-like strokes, formal floral designs of a peculiar kind, such as the tulip-like flower on the neck of Fig. 4 of Plate 82; the band of floral scroll work on the shoulder of the same piece is also characteristic. In many of the forms, such as cylindrical vases and beakers, the base is flat and unglazed, and reveals a good white body, and European influence is apparent in some of the shapes, such as the jugs and tankards.

As for the dating of this group, an early example of the style of painting in the Salting Collection[212] has a silver mount of the early seventeenth century, and a tankard of typical German form in the Hamburg Museum has a silver cover dated 1642.[213] There is, besides, a curious piece in the British Museum, the decoration of which has strong affinities to this group. It is a bottle with flattened circular body and tall, tapering neck, with landscape and figures on one side and on the other a European design copied from the reverse of a Spanish dollar, and surrounded by a strap-work border. The dollar, from a numismatic point of view, might have been made equally well for Philip II. (1556–1598), Philip IV. (1621–1665), or Charles II. (1665–1700), but there can be little doubt from the style of the ware that it belonged to one of the two earlier reigns.

A comparison of the ware and the blue of this group leads to the placing of the fairly familiar type illustrated by Figs. 3 and 5 of Plate 82 in the same intermediate period, and similarly certain specimens of polychrome, with underglaze blue and the usual enamels, display the characteristic body and blue painting, and even some of the decorative mannerisms. These specimens, particularly when of beaker form, are often finished off with a band of ornament engraved under the glaze.

Fig. 1

Fig. 2

Fig. 3   Fig. 4   Fig. 5

Plate 82.—Late Ming Porcelain.

Fig. 1—Jar of Wan Li period, enamelled. Mark, a hare. Height 9 inches. *British Museum.* Fig. 2. Bowl with Eight Immortals in relief, coloured glazes on the biscuit. Height 3¼ inches. *Eumorfopoulos Collection.*

Figs. 3, 4 and 5.—Blue and white porcelain, early seventeenth century. Height of Fig. 5, 17 inches. *British Museum.*

Plate 83.—Vase

With blue and white decoration of rockery, phœnixes, and flowering shrubs.
Found in India. Late Ming period. Height 22 inches. *Halsey Collection.*

CHAPTER VI

THE TECHNIQUE OF THE MING PORCELAIN

Although the processes involved in the various kinds of decoration and in the different wares have been discussed in their several places, a short summary of those employed in the manufacture of the Ching-tê Chên porcelain during the Ming period will be found convenient. The bulk of the materials required were found in the surrounding districts, if not actually in the Fou-liang Hsien. The best kaolin (or porcelain earth) was mined in the Ma-ts'ang mountains until the end of the sixteenth century, when the supply was exhausted and recourse was had to another deposit at Wu-mên-t'o. The quality of the Wu-mên-t'o kaolin was first-rate, but as the cost of transport was greater and the manager of the Imperial factory refused to pay a proportionately higher price, very little was obtained. The material for the large dragon bowls, and presumably for the other vessels of abnormal size, was obtained from Yü-kan and Wu-yüan and mixed with powdered stone (*shih mo*) from the Hu-t'ien district. Other kaolins, brought from Po-yang Hsien and the surrounding parts, were used by the private potters, not being sufficiently fine for the Imperial wares.

The porcelain stone, which combined with the kaolin to form the two principal ingredients of true porcelain, came from the neighbourhoods of Yü-kan and Wu-yüan, where it was pounded and purified in mills worked by the water power of the mountains, arriving at Ching-tê Chên in the form of briquettes. Hence the name *petuntse*,[214] which, like kaolin, has passed into our own language, and the term *shih mo* (powdered stone) used above.

The glaze earth (*yu t'u*) in various qualities was supplied from different places. Thus the Ch'ang-ling material was used for the blue or green (*ch'ing*) and the yellow glazes, the Yi-k'êng for the pure white porcelain, and the T'ao-shu-mu for white porcelain and for "blue and white." This glazing material was softened with varying quantities of ashes of lime burnt with ferns or other frondage. Neither time nor toil was spared in the preparation of the Imperial porcelains, and according to the *T'ung-ya*[215] the vessels were, at one time at any rate, dried for a whole year after they had been shaped and before finishing them off on the lathe. When finished off on the lathe they were glazed and dried, and if there were any inequalities in the covering they were glazed again. Furthermore, if any fault appeared after firing they were put on the lathe, ground smooth, and reglazed and refired.

It was not the usual custom with Chinese potters to harden the ware with a slight preliminary firing before proceeding to decorate and apply the glaze, and consequently such processes as underglaze painting in blue, embossing, etc., were undergone while the body was still relatively soft and required exceedingly careful handling. The glaze was applied in several ways—by dipping in a tub of glazing liquid (i.e. glaze material finely levigated and mixed with water), by painting the glaze on with a brush, or by blowing it on from a bamboo tube, the end of which was covered with a piece of tightly stretched gauze. One of the last operations was the finishing off of the foot, which was hollowed out and trimmed and the mark added (if it was to be in blue, as was usually the case) and covered with a spray of glaze. To the connoisseur the finish of the foot is full of meaning. It is here he gets a glimpse of the body which emerges at the raw edge of the rim, and by feeling it he can tell whether the material is finely levigated or coarse-grained. The foot rim of the Ming porcelains is plainly finished without the beading or grooves of the K'ang Hsi wares, which were evidently designed to fit a stand[216]; and the raw edge discloses a ware which is almost always of fine white texture and close grain (often almost unctuous to the touch), though the actual surface generally assumes a brownish tinge in the heat of the kiln. The base is often unglazed in the case of large jars and vases, rarely in the cups, bowls, dishes, or wine pots, except among the coarser types of export porcelain. A little sand or grit adhering to the foot rim and radiating lines under the base caused by a jerky movement of the lathe are signs of hasty finish, which occur not infrequently on the export wares. The importance of the foot in the eyes of the Chinese collector may be judged from the following extract from the *Shih ch'ing jih cha*[217]:—

"Distinguish porcelain by the vessel's foot. The Yung Lo 'press-hand' bowls have a glazed bottom but a sandy foot; Hsüan ware altar cups have 'cauldron'[218] bottom (i.e. convex beneath) and wire-like foot; Chia Ching ware flat cups decorated with fish have a 'loaf' centre[219] (i.e. convex inside) and rounded foot. All porcelain vessels issue from the kiln with bottoms and feet which can testify to the fashion of the firing."

It is not always easy unaided by illustration to interpret the Chinese metaphors, but it is a matter of observation that many of the Sung bowls, for instance, have a conical finish under the base, and that the same pointed finish appears on some of the early Ming types, such as the red bowls with Yung Lo mark. The "loaf centre" of the Chia Ching bowls seems to refer to the convexity described on p. 35. The blue and white conical bowls with Yung Lo mark (see p. 6) have, as a rule, a small glazed base and a relatively wide unglazed foot rim.

But this digression on the nether peculiarities of the different wares has led us away from the subject of glaze. The proverbial thickness and solidity of the early Ming glazes, which are likened to "massed lard," are due to the piling up of successive coatings of glaze to ensure a perfect covering for the body, and the same process was responsible for the undulating appearance of the surface, which rose up in small rounded elevations "like grains of millet" and displayed corresponding depressions.[220] This uneven effect, due to an excess of glaze, was much prized by the Chinese connoisseurs, who gave it descriptive names like "millet markings," "chicken skin," or "orange peel," and the potters of later periods imitated it freely and often to excess. Porcelain glazes are rarely dead white, and, speaking generally, it may be said that the qualifying tint in the Ming period was greenish. Indeed, this is the prevailing tone of Chinese glazes, but it is perhaps accentuated by the thickness of the Ming glaze. This greenish tinge is most noticeable when the ware is ornamented with delicate traceries in pure white clay or slip under the glaze.

PLATE 84

Vase of baluster form with small mouth (*mei p'ing*). Porcelain with coloured glazes on the biscuit, the designs outlined in slender fillets of clay. A meeting of sages in a landscape beneath an ancient pine tree, the design above their heads representing the mountain mist. On the shoulders are large *ju-i* shaped lappets enclosing lotus sprays, with pendent jewels between: fungus (*ling chih*) designs on the neck. Yellow glaze under the base. A late example of this style of ware, probably seventeenth century.

Height 11 inches.

Salting Collection (Victoria and Albert Museum).

As for the shape of the various Ming wares, much has already been said in reference to the various lists of Imperial porcelains, more particularly with regard to the household wares such as dishes, bowls, wine pots, boxes, etc. No precise description, however, is given in these lists of the actual forms of the vases, and we have to look elsewhere for these. There are, however, extracts from books on vases[221] and on the implements of the scholar's table in the *T'ao shuo* and the *T'ao lu*, in which a large number of shapes are enumerated. Observation of actual specimens shows that bronze and metal work supplied the models for the more elaborate forms which would be made, partly or wholly, in moulds. These metallic forms, so much affected by the Chinese *literatus*, though displaying great cleverness in workmanship and elaboration of detail, are not so pleasing to the unprejudiced Western eye as the simple wheel-made forms of which the Chinese potter was a perfect master. Of the latter, the most common in Ming porcelains are the potiche-shaped covered jar (Plate 80) and the high-shouldered baluster vase with small neck and narrow mouth (Plate 84), which was known as *mei p'ing* or prunus jar from its suitability for holding a flowering branch of that decorative flower. Next to these, the most familiar Ming forms are the massive and often clumsy vases of double gourd shape, or with a square body and gourd-shaped neck, bottles with tapering neck and globular body, ovoid jars, melon-shaped pots with lobed sides, jars with rounded body and short narrow neck, all of which occur in the export wares. These are, as a rule, strongly built and of good white material, and if the shoulders are contracted (as is nearly always the case) they are made in two sections, or more in the case of the double forms, with no pains taken to conceal the seam. Indeed, elaborate finish had no part in the construction of these strong, rugged forms, which are matched by the bold design and free drawing of the decoration. I may add that sets of vases hardly come within the Ming period. They are an un-Chinese idea, and evolved in response to European demands. The mantelpiece sets of five (three covered jars and two beakers) are a development of the mid-seventeenth century when the Dutch traders commanded the market. The Chinese altar-set of five ritual utensils is the nearest approach to a uniform set, consisting as it did of an incense burner, two flower vases, and two pricket candlesticks, often with the same decoration throughout.

The Ming bowls vary considerably in form, from the wide-mouthed, small-footed bowl (*p'ieh*) of the early period to the rounded forms, such as Fig. 1

of Plate 74. In some cases the sides are moulded in compartments, and the rims sharply everted. Others again are very shallow, with hollow base and no foot rim; others follow the shape of the Buddhist alms bowl with rounded sides and contracted mouth; and there are large bowls for gold-fish (*yü kang*), usually with straight sides slightly expanding towards the upper part and broad flat rims, cisterns, hot-water bowls with double bottom and plug hole beneath, square bowls (Plate 66, Fig. 1) for scraps and slops, and large vessels, probably of punch-bowl form, known as "wine seas." The commonest type of Chinese dish is saucer-shaped, but they had also flat plates bounded by straight sides and a narrow rim, which has no relation to the broad, canted rim of the European plate constructed to carry salt and condiments.

The Chinese use porcelain plaques for inlaying in furniture and screens, or mounting as pictures, and there are, besides, many objects of purely native design, such as barrel-shaped garden seats for summer use, cool pillows, and hat stands with spherical top and tall, slender stems. But it was only natural that when they began to cater for the foreign market many foreign forms should have crept in, such as the Persian ewer with pear-shaped body, long elegant handle and spout, the latter usually joined to the neck by an ornamental stay: the hookah bowl: weights with wide base and ball-shaped tops for keeping down Indian mats, etc., when: spread on the ground; and at the end of the Ming period a few European shapes, such as jugs and tankards. In the Ch'ing dynasty European forms were made wholesale.

In considering the colours used in the decoration, we naturally take first the limited number which were developed in the full heat of the porcelain furnace, the *couleurs de grand feu* of the French classification. These were either incorporated in the glazing material or painted on the porcelain body and protected by the glaze. Chief among them was blue, which we have already discussed in its various qualities. The Mohammedan blue—the *su-ni-p'o* of the Hsüan Tê period and the *hui hui ch'ing* of the reigns of Chêng Tê and Chia Ching—was an imported material of pre-eminent quality but of uncertain supply. It was supplemented—and, indeed, usually blended—with the native mineral[222] which was found in several places. Thus the *po-t'ang* blue (so called from a place name) was found in the district of Lo-p'ing Hsien in the Jao-chou Fu; but the mines were closed after a riot in the Chia Ching period, and its place was taken by a blue known as *shih-tzŭ ch'ing* (stone, or mineral, blue) from the prefecture of Jui-chou in Kiangsi. According to Bushell[223] the *po-t'ang* blue was very dark in colour, and it was sometimes known as *Fo t'ou ch'ing* (Buddha's head blue) from the traditional colour of the hair of Buddha. Another material used for painting porcelain was the *hei chê shih* (black red mineral) from Hsin-chien in Lu-ling, which was also called *wu ming tzŭ*. It was evidently a cobaltiferous ore of manganese and a blue-producing mineral, doubtless the same as the *wu ming i* (nameless wonder), which we have already found in use as a name for cobalt.

Much confusion exists, in Chinese works, on the subject of these blues, and it is stated in one place that the "Buddha head blue" was a variety of the *wu ming i*, which would make the *po t'ang* blue and the *wu ming i* and the *wu ming tzŭ* one and the same thing. In effect they were the same species of mineral, and the local distinctions are of no account at the present day except in so far as they explain the variety of tints in the Ming blue and white. It is, however, interesting to learn from a note on Mohammedan blue in the K'ang Hsi Encyclopædia that the native mineral, when carefully prepared, was very like the Mohammedan blue in tint.

All these blues were used either for painting under the glaze or for mixing with the glaze to form ground colours or monochromes, which varied widely in tint, according to the quantity and quality of the cobalt, from dark violet blue (*chi ch'ing*) through pale and dark shades of the ordinary blue colour to slaty blue and lavender. Some of them—notably the lavender and the dark violet blue—are often associated with crackle, being used as an overglaze covering a greyish white crackled porcelain. This treatment of the surface is well illustrated by a small covered jar in the British Museum with a dark violet blue apparently uncracked but covering a crackled glaze. Two lavender blue bowls in the Hippisley Collection with the Chêng Tê mark are similarly crackled. Other Ming blue monochromes are a small pot found in Borneo and now in the British Museum with a dark blue of the ordinary tint used in painted wares, and a wine pot in the same collection with dragon spout and handle of a peculiar slaty lavender tint strewn with black specks, the colour evidently due to a strain of manganese in the cobalt.

Next in importance to the blue is the underglaze red derived from copper, which was discussed at length in connection with the Hsüan Tê porcelains.[224] Its various tints, described as *hsien hung* (fresh red), *pao shih hung* (ruby red), and cinnabar bowls "red as the sun," are, we may be sure, more or less accidental varieties of the capricious copper red. The same mineral produced the *sang de bœuf*, maroon and liver reds, and probably the peach bloom[225] of the K'ang Hsi and later porcelains.

Other colours incorporated in the high-fired glaze in the Ming period are the pea green (*tou ch'ing*) or celadon, and the lustrous brown (*tzŭ chin*) which varied from coffee colour to that of old gold. Both of these groups derived their tint from iron oxide, carried in the medium of ferruginous earth. The use of two or more of these coloured glazes on one piece is a type of polychrome which was doubtless used on the Ming as on the later porcelains.

The glazes fired at a lower temperature, in the cooler parts of the great kiln, and known for that reason as *couleurs de demi-grand feu*, include turquoise (*ts'ui sê*), made from a preparation of old copper (*ku t'ung*) and nitre; bright yellow (*chin huang*), composed of 1⅕ oz. of antimony mixed with 16 oz. of pulverised lead; bright green (*chin lü*), composed of 1⅖ oz. of pulverised copper, 6 oz. of powdered quartz and 16 oz. of pulverised lead; purple (*tzŭ sê*), composed of 1 oz. of cobaltiferous ore of manganese, 6 oz. of powdered quartz and 16 oz. of pulverised lead. These colours, melting as they did at a lower temperature than that required to vitrify the porcelain body, had to be applied to an already fired porcelain "biscuit."[226]

The irregular construction of the Chinese kilns resulted in a great variety of firing conditions, of which the Chinese potter made good use; so that, by a judicious arrangement of the wares, glazes which required a comparatively low temperature were fired in the same kiln as those which needed the same heat as the porcelain body itself. The glazes just enumerated are familiar from the large covered jars, vases, garden seats, etc., with designs raised, carved, or pierced in outline, many of which date from the fifteenth century.[227] Their manufacture continued throughout the Ming period, both in porcelain and pottery, and in the latter, at any rate, continued into the Ch'ing dynasty.

Another group of glazes applied likewise to the biscuit and fired in the temperate parts of the kiln differs from the last mentioned in its greater translucency.[228] These are the *san ts'ai* or three colours, viz. green, yellow and aubergine, all of which contain a considerable proportion of lead, and differ little in appearance from the on-glaze enamels of the muffle kiln. They were used either as monochromes, plain or covering incised designs, or in combination to wash over the spaces between the outlines of a pattern which had been incised or painted on the biscuit.

Finally, the enamels of the *Wan li wu ts'ai*,[229] overglaze colours used in addition to underglaze blue, were composed of a vitreous flux coloured with a minute quantity of metallic oxide. The flux, being a glass containing a high percentage of lead, was fusible at such a low temperature that it was not possible to fire them in the large kiln. Consequently these enamels were painted on to the finished glaze, a process which greatly increased the freedom of design, and fired in a small "muffle" or enameller's kiln, where the requisite heat to melt the flux and fix the colours could be easily obtained.

Though the *T'ao shuo*, in the section dealing with Ming technique, makes a general allusion to painting in colours on the glaze, the only specific reference to any colour of the muffle kiln, excepting gold, is to the red obtained from sulphate of iron (*fan hung sê*). This, we are told, was made with 1 oz. of calcined sulphate of iron (*ch'ing fan*) and 5 oz. of carbonate of lead, mixed with Canton ox-glue to make it adhere to the porcelain before it was fired. This is the iron red, the *rouge de fer* of the French, which varies in tint from orange or coral to deep brick red, and in texture from an impalpable film almost to the consistency of a glaze, according to the quantity of lead flux used with it. On the older wares it is often deeply iridescent and lustrous, owing to the decomposition of the lead flux. This *fan hung* is the colour which the Chia Ching potters were fain to substitute for the underglaze copper red (*chi hung*) when the usual material for that highly prized colour had come to an end, and difficulty was experienced in finding an effective substitute.

The remaining colours of the on-glaze palette are more obviously enamels; that is to say, glassy compounds; and as they were, in accordance with Chinese custom, very lightly charged with colouring matter, it was necessary to pile them on thickly where depth of colour was required.

Hence the thickly encrusted appearance of much of the Chinese enamelled porcelain. The Wan Li enamels consisted of transparent greens of several shades (all derived from copper), including a very blue green which seems to have been peculiar to the Ming palette, yellow (from antimony) pale and clear or brownish and rather opaque, and transparent aubergine, a colour derived from manganese and varying in tint from purple to brown. Two thin dry pigments—one an iron red and the other a brown black colour derived from manganese—were used for drawing outlines; and the brown black was also used in masses with a coating of transparent green to form a green black colour, the same which is so highly prized on the *famille noire* porcelains of the K'ang Hsi period. As for the blue enamel of the K'ang Hsi period, it can hardly be said to have existed before the end of the Ming dynasty.[230]

Gilding, which was apparently in use throughout[231] the Ming period, was applied to the finished porcelain and fired in the muffle kiln. The gold leaf, combined with one-tenth by weight of carbonate of lead, was mixed with gum and painted on with a brush. The effect, as seen on the red and green bowls (Plate 74), was light and filmy, and though the gold often has the unsubstantial appearance of size-gilding, in reality it adheres firmly[232] and is not easily scratched.

Of the other processes described in the *T'ao shuo*,[233] embossed (*tui* 堆) decoration was effected by applying strips or shavings of the body material and working them into form with a wet brush. Some of the more delicate traceries, in scarcely perceptible relief, are painted in white slip. Engraved (*chui* 錐) decoration was effected by carving with an iron graving-tool on the body while it was still soft. And so, too, with the openwork (*ling lung*), which has already been described.[234] All these processes were in use in one form or another from the earliest reigns of the Ming dynasty, and some of them, at any rate, have been encountered on the Sung wares. High reliefs, such as the figures on the bowls described on p. 74, would be separately modelled and "luted" on by means of liquid clay; and, as already noted, these reliefs were often left in the biscuit state, though at times we find them covered with coloured glazes. It is hardly necessary to add that the same processes were applied to pottery, and that the reliefs took many other forms besides figures, e.g. dragon designs, foliage, scrollwork, symbols, etc.

PLATE 85

Vase with crackled greenish grey glaze coated on the exterior with transparent apple green enamel: the base unglazed. Probably sixteenth century.

Height 14 inches.

British Museum.

The crackled glazes of the Sung period were still made, though the Ming tendency was to substitute painted decoration for monochrome; and we have already noted the crackled blue and lavender in which a second glaze is added to a grey white crackle. This process is particularly noticeable in the "apple green" monochromes (Plate 85), both of the Ming and Ch'ing dynasties, in which a green overglaze itself uncrackled is washed on to a crackled stone grey porcelain. The green is often carried down over the slightly browned biscuit of the foot rim, forming a band of brown. But this, so far from being a peculiarity of the Ming technique, is much more conspicuous on the porcelains of the early eighteenth century, when it was the constant practice to dress the foot rim of the crackled wares with a brown ferruginous earth in imitation of the "iron foot" of their Sung prototypes.

The work at the Imperial factory[235] was divided between twenty-three departments, nine of which were occupied with accessories, such as the making of ropes and barrels, general carpentry, and even boat building. Five separate departments were employed in making the large bowls, the wine cups, the plates, the large round dishes, and the tea cups; another in preparing the "paste" or body material, and another in making the "seggars" or fireclay cases in which the ware was packed in the kiln. Five more were occupied in the details of decoration, viz. the mark and seal department, the department for engraving designs, the department for sketching designs, the department for writing, and the department for colouring.

It does not appear that the work of decoration was so minutely subdivided in the Ming period as in later times, when we are told that a piece of porcelain might pass through more than seventy hands; but it is clear, at least, that the outlining and filling in of the designs were conducted in separate sheds. This is, indeed, self-apparent from the Ming blue and white porcelains, the designs of which are characterised by strong and clear outlines filled in with flat washes of colour.

With regard to the actual designs, we are told that in the Ch'êng Hua period they were drawn by the best artists at the Court, and from another passage[236] it is clear that the practice of sending the patterns from the palace continued in later reigns as well. Such designs would no doubt accumulate, and probably they were collected together from time to time and issued in the form of pattern books.[237] Another method in which the painters of Ming blue and white were served with patterns is related in the *T'ao shuo*[238]:—"For painting in blue, the artists were collected each day at dawn and at noon, and the colour for painting was distributed among them. Two men of good character were first selected, the larger pieces of porcelain being given to one, the smaller pieces to the other; and when they had finished their painting, the amount of the material used was calculated before the things were taken to the furnace to be baked. If the results were satisfactory, then the pieces were given as models to the other painters, and in the rest of the pieces painted, the quantity of the colour used and the depth of the tint was required to be in exact accordance with these models." There was little scope for originality or individual effort under this system, where everything, even to the amount of material used, was strictly prescribed. To translate their model with feeling and accuracy was the best that could be expected from the rank and file. But with the manual skill and patient industry for which the Chinese are proverbial, and the good taste which prevailed in the direction of the work, it was a system admirably suited to the task, and it unquestionably led to excellent results.

As to the systems in use in the private factories we have no information, but we may fairly assume that their processes were much the same; and that, not having the benefit of the designs sent from Court, they were more dependent upon the pattern books and stock designs more or less remotely connected with the work of famous painters.

CHAPTER VII

MISCELLANEOUS PORCELAIN FACTORIES

Although from the Ming period onwards our interest is almost entirely centred in Ching-tê Chên, there were other factories which cannot be altogether ignored. A certain number have already been mentioned at the end of the first volume, our scanty information being drawn chiefly from the pottery section of the K'ang Hsi Encyclopædia. The same monumental work includes in another part[239] a discourse on porcelain (*tz'ŭ ch'i*), in which several additional factories are named. The passage in question is prefaced by a quotation from the *Tien hung k'ai wu*, a late-seventeenth century manual, in which we are told that the white earth (*o t'u*[240]) necessary for the manufacture of fine and elegant ware was found in China in five or six places only[241]: viz. at Ting Chou, in the Chên-ting Fu in Chih-li, at Hua-ting Chou in the Ping-liang Fu in Shensi, at P'ing-ting Chou in the T'ai-yüan Fu in Shansi, and at Yü Chou in the K'ai-fêng Fu in Honan, in the north; and at Tê-hua Hsien in the Ch'üan-chou Fu in Fukien, at Wu-yüan Hsien and Ch'i-mên Hsien in the Hui-chou Fu, in Anhui, in the south. As to the wares made in these localities, we are told that the porcelains of the Chên-ting and K'ai-fêng districts were generally yellow and dull and without the jewel-like brilliancy, and that all put together were not equal to the Jao Chou ware. It would appear, then, that the Ting Chou factories so noted in Sung times were still extant, though they had lost their importance. For the rest, the Ch'i-mên district supplied Ching-tê Chên with the raw material, the Tê-hua wares will be discussed presently, and we have no information about the productions (if any) of the other localities.

The province of Fukien apparently contained several factories besides the important centre at Tê-hua. The Annals of Ch'üan-chou Fu (celebrated as a trading port in the Middle Ages), for instance, are quoted with reference to a porcelain (*tz'ŭ ch'i*) manufacture at Tz'ŭ-tsao in the Chin-chiang Hsien, and three other places in the district of An-ch'i are named as producers of white porcelain which was inferior to that of Jao Chou. Similarly, the Annals of Shao-wu Fu, on the north-east border of the province, allude to white porcelain made at three places,[242] the factory at T'ai-ming in An-jen being the best, but all were far from equalling the Jao Chou ware.

The district of Wên-chou Fu (formerly in the south of Fukien but now transferred to northern Chekiang) was noted for pottery in the distant days of the Chin dynasty (265–419 A.D.), and for the "bowls of Eastern Ou."[243] Of its subsequent ceramic history we have no information, but there is an interesting specimen in the British Museum which seems to bear on the question. It is an incense burner in the form of a seated figure of the god of Longevity on a deer, skilfully modelled in strong white porcelain and painted in a good blue in the Ming style; and on the box in which it came was a note to the effect that it is Wên-chou ware. If there is any truth in this legend (and it would be quite pointless if untrue), then a blue and white porcelain in the style of the better class of Ming export ware was made at Wên-chou.

Another interesting specimen in the same museum, which should also be mentioned here, is a bottle with wide straight neck, of fine white ware thickly potted, with soft, smooth-worn glaze painted in a greyish blue with a medley of flowers, fruit, insects, and symbols, completed by borders of *ju-i* heads and stiff leaves. It is marked under the base in a fine violet blue, *fu fan chih ts'ao*, which, rendered "made on the borders of Fukien," might refer to the factories at Shao-wu Fu or even Wên-chou Fu. This is another piece which has many affinities with the late Ming export blue and white.

But the Fukien porcelain *par excellence* is a white ware of distinctive character and great beauty which was and still is made at Tê-hua Hsien, in the central part of the province.[244] This is the *blanc de Chine* of the French writers and the modern Chien yao of the Chinese, but to be carefully distinguished from the ancient Chien yao with mottled black glaze which was made in the Sung dynasty at Chien-yang in the north of the province.[245] The *T'ao lu*[246] informs us that the porcelain industry at Tê-hua began in the Ming dynasty, that the cups and bowls usually had a spreading rim, that the ware was known as *pai tz'ŭ* (white porcelain), that it was rich and lustrous but, as a rule, thick, and that the images of Buddha were very beautiful. This condensed account is supplemented by a few remarks in the K'ang Hsi Encyclopædia,[247] from which we gather that the material for the ware was mined in the hills behind the Ch'êng monastery and that it was very carefully prepared, but if the porcelain was worked thin it was liable to lose shape in the kiln, and if it was too thick it was liable to crack. At first it was very expensive, but by the time of writing (about 1700) it was widely distributed and no longer dear.

Tê-hua porcelain is, in fact, a fine white, highly vitrified material, as a rule very translucent and covered with a soft-looking, mellow glaze which blends so intimately with the body that they seem to be part and parcel of one another. The glaze varies in tone from ivory or cream white to the colour of skim milk, and its texture may be aptly described by the homely comparison with blancmange. When the ivory colour is suffused by a faint rosy tinge, it is specially prized; but I can find no reason for supposing that the cream white and milk white tints represent different periods of the ware. On the contrary, there is good evidence to show that they were made concurrently.

As the ware is with few exceptions plain white or white decorated with incised, impressed, moulded, or applied ornaments of a rather formal and often archaic character, there will always be a difficulty in determining the date of the finer specimens, viz. whether they are Ming or early Ch'ing. The nature of the ware itself is a most uncertain guide, for one of the most beautiful examples of the material which I have seen is a figure of a European soldier which cannot be older than 1650. I need hardly say that owners of Fukien porcelain, particularly of the figures, habitually give themselves the benefit of this ever present doubt, and that these pieces are usually listed in sale catalogues as Ming or early Ming according to taste. This attitude is fundamentally illogical, for the ware is still made at the present day, and the Ming specimens in modern collections are likely to be the exception, and not, as optimistic owners would lead one to suppose, the rule. But in any case it will be more convenient to deal with the ware as a whole in the present chapter than to attempt the difficult task of treating its different periods separately, even though the bulk of our examples belong to the Ch'ing dynasty.

Tê-hua porcelain can be conveniently studied in the British Museum, where there is a fairly representative collection comprising more than a hundred specimens. It includes a number of the figures for which the factories were specially noted, of deities and sages such as Kuan-yin, goddess of Mercy; Kuan-yü, god of War; Bodhidharma, the Buddhist apostle; Manjusri, of the Buddhist Trinity; Hsi-wang-mu, the Taoist queen of the west; the Taoist Immortals; besides small groups representing romantic or mythological subjects such as Wang Chih watching the two spirits of the pole stars playing chess. But the favourite subject of the Tê-hua modeller was the beautiful and gracious figure of Kuan-yin, represented in various poses as standing on a cloud base with flowing robes, seated in contemplation on a rocky pedestal, or enthroned between her two attributes, the dove—which often carries a necklace of pearls—and the vase of nectar, while at her feet on either side stand two diminutive figures representing[248] her follower Lung Nü (the dragon maid), holding a pearl, and the devoted comrade of her earthly adventures Chên Tsai. The Kuan-yin of this group is reputed to have been the daughter of a legendary eastern King named Miao-chuang, but other accounts make the deity a Chinese version of the Buddhist Avalokitesvara, and it is certain that her representations as the Kuan-yin with eleven heads and again with a "thousand" hands reflect Indian traditions. In the latter manifestations the sex of the deity is left in doubt, but there can be no question on that head when she is represented with a babe in her arms as "Kuan-yin the Maternal," to whom childless women pray, a figure strangely resembling our images of the Virgin and Child. Indeed, we are told[249] that the Japanese converts to Christianity in the sixteenth century adopted the Kuan-yin figure as a Madonna, and that there is in the Imperial Museum in the Ueno Park, Tokio, a remarkable collection of these images among the Christian relics. There is, however, another deity with whom this Kuan-yin may easily be confounded, viz. the Japanese Kichimojin, also "the Maternal," the Sanskrit Hâriti, who was once the devourer of infants but was converted by Sakyamuni and was afterwards worshipped as the protector of children. This deity figures in Japanese pictorial art as a "female holding a peach and nursing in her bosom an infant, whose hands are folded in prayer. In front stand two nude children, one of whom grasps a peach, the other a branch of bamboo."[250]

Among the Tê-hua porcelains in the British Museum are no fewer than nine specimens—groups, figures, or ornamental structures—with figures in European costumes which date from the middle to the end of the seventeenth century. One, a soldier apparently Dutch, about 1650, is well modelled in deliciously mellow and translucent cream white porcelain. Most of the others are more roughly designed, and vary in tint from cream to milk white.

It is said that the natives of the Fukien province are among the most superstitious of the Chinese, and Bushell[251] sees a reflection of this religious temperament in the nature of the Tê-hua wares. If this is so, they must have had exalted opinions of their European visitors, whom they often furnish with the attributes of Chinese divinities, representing them in positions and poses which seem to caricature native deities and sages. There is, for instance, an ornament in form of a mountain retreat with a shrine in which is seated a figure in a three-cornered European hat and a Buddha-like attitude. Another group consists of a European mounted on a *ch'i-lin*, posing as an Arhat, and another of a European standing on a dragon's head which would symbolise to the Chinese the attainment of the highest literary honours.

There are, besides, in the British Museum collection figures of animals and birds, the Buddhist lion, the cock, the hawk, or the parrot, mostly fitted with tubes to hold incense sticks; and there are a pair of well modelled figures of Chou dogs.

As for the vessels of Tê-hua porcelain, they consist chiefly of incense vases and incense burners, libation cups shaped after bronze or rhinoceros horn models, brush pots, wine cups, water vessels for the study table and the like (often beautifully modelled in the form of lotus leaves or flowers), boxes, tea and wine pots, cups and bowls, and more rarely vases.

An extensive trade was done with the European merchants, whose influence is apparent in many of the wares, such as coffee cups with handles, mugs of cylindrical form or globular with straight ribbed necks in German style, and "barber-surgeons' bowls" with flat pierced handles copied from silver models. Indeed, the superficially European appearance of some of these pieces has led serious students to mistake them for early Meissen porcelain and even for that nebulous porcelain supposed to have been made by John Dwight, of Fulham, at the end of the seventeenth century. Père d'Entrecolles[252] incidentally mentions the fact that some Ching-tê Chên potters had in the past removed to Fukien in the hope of making profits out of the European traders at Amoy, and that they had taken their plant and even their materials with them, but that the enterprise was a failure.

Conversely, the influence of the Tê-hua wares is obvious in many of the early European porcelains, such as those made at Meissen, St. Cloud, Bow, and Chelsea, which were often closely modelled on the Fukien white. There is, indeed, a striking similarity between the creamy soft-paste porcelain of St. Cloud and the creamy variety of the *blanc de chine*, both having the same mellow, melting appearance in the glaze.

Plate 86.—Fukien Porcelain, Ming Dynasty.

Fig 1.—Figure of Kuan-yin with boy attendant. Ivory white. Height 10¼ inches. *Eumorfopoulos Collection.*

Fig. 2.—Bottle with prunus sprigs in relief, the glaze crackled all over and stained a brownish tint. Height 9⅛ inches. *Eumorfopoulos Collection.*

Fig. 3.—Figure of Bodhidharma crossing the Yangtze on a reed. Ivory white. Height 7½ inches. *Salting Collection (V. & A. Museum).*

Fig. 1

Fig. 2

Fig. 3

Plate 87.—Ivory White Fukien Porcelain.

Fig. 1.—Libation Cup. About 1700. Length 3⅞ inches. *British Museum.*

Fig. 2.—Cup with sixteenth-century mount. Height 2 inches. *Dresden Collection.*

Fig. 3.—Incense Vase and Stand. About 1700. Diameter 6¾ inches. *British Museum.*

It would be possible to guess from these European copies, if we had no other means, the character of the Tê-hua porcelain of the K'ang Hsi period with its quaintly moulded forms, its relief decoration of prunus sprigs, figures of Immortals, deer, etc., the only conspicuously absent type being the incised[253] ornament which was unsuited to the European ware. But there is no lack of actual specimens of the period of active export which extended from about 1650–1750. Naturally they vary greatly in quality, which depends on the purity and translucence of the ware whether it be cream or milk white, and on the soft aspect and rich lustre of the glaze. A large series, which may be taken as representative of the K'ang Hsi period, was collected by Augustus the Strong, and is still to be seen at the Johanneum at Dresden; or, rather, part of it is still there, for much of that historic collection was given away or pilfered from time to time, and many specimens with the Dresden catalogue numbers engraved are now to be found in our own museums. Many of the figures at Dresden have evidently been coated with a kind of black paint, which probably served as a medium for oil gilding, but this unfired colouring has worn away, and only traces now remain.

Occasionally one finds among the Tê-hua wares a specimen with dry appearance and crazed or discoloured glaze, defects due to faulty firing or to burial in damp soil. Such pieces are surprising in a ware with such apparent homogeneity of body and glaze, and the crazed examples might be easily mistaken for one of the *t'u ting* (or earthy Ting ware) types.

As to the history of the factories, it is expressly stated in the *T'ao lu* that they were started in the Ming dynasty. No account need be taken of the few legendary specimens to which tradition assigns an earlier origin than this, such as the so-called flute of Yoshitsune, a twelfth-century hero of Japan, and the incense burner in St. Mark's, Venice, which is reputed to have been brought from China by Marco Polo. The latter is of the same model as Fig. 3 of Plate 87, perhaps from the same mould, and I have seen at least half a dozen others in London. A third piece which was long regarded as a document is the jewelled white plate in the Dresden collection, supposed to have been brought back from Syria by a Crusader in the twelfth century. The story is no doubt apocryphal, but in any case it has no real bearing on the question, for the plate is not Fukien ware but a specimen of white Ching-tê Chên porcelain with a "shop mark" in underglaze blue. It has been set with jewels in India or Persia, like a sixteenth-century bowl in the British Museum, but the "Crusader plate" is probably a century later.

Brinkley[254] asserts, without giving any authority, that the Tê-hua industry was virtually discontinued at the end of the eighteenth century, and revived in recent years. The latter part of the statement is unquestionably true, for we have the eye-witness of a missionary[255] who visited the place about 1880 and describes the manufactory as the most extensive of its kind in Fukien— "pottery, pottery everywhere, in the fields, in the streets, in the shops. In the open air children are painting the cups. Each artist paints with his own colour and his own few strokes, whether a leaf, a tree, a man's dress or beard, and passes it over to his neighbour, who in turn applies his brush to paint what is his share in the decoration." Unfortunately there is no reason to suppose that the writer made his observations with an expert eye which would make a distinction between pottery and porcelain, but in any case it is certain that he found a vast ceramic industry in full blast at Tê-hua.

With reference to the modern ware Brinkley says[256]: "A considerable number of specimens are now produced and palmed off upon unwary collectors. But the amateur can easily avoid such deceptions if he remembers that in genuine pieces of ivory white the ware is always translucid when held up to the light, a property which, if not entirely absent, is only possessed in a comparatively slight degree by the modern product. The general quality of the glaze and the technique of a piece should be sufficient guides, but if any doubt remains an examination of the base of the specimens will probably dispel it. In the old ware the bottom of a vase or bowl, though carefully finished, is left uncovered, whereas the modern potter is fond of hiding his inferior pâte by roughly overspreading it with a coat of glaze."

Probably these observations are in the main correct, but experience shows that relative opacity and glazed bases are by no means confined to modern wares. Still, if the collector aims at acquiring pieces of good colour, whether cream or milk white, with translucent body, pure glaze and sharp modelling, he is not likely to go far astray.

The description quoted above of the painting of modern Fukien ware is interesting in view of the common assertion that the Tê-hua white porcelain was never painted. This assertion is probably based on a passage in the first letter of Père d'Entrecolles: "Celle (i.e. la porcelaine) de Fou-kien est d'un blanc de neige qui n'a nul éclat et qui n'est point mélangé de couleurs." On the other hand, a distinct reference is made to the painting in colours in a modern Chinese work.[257] Unfortunately, the question has been complicated by the existence of many pieces of Fukien white which have been enamelled in Europe. In the first half of the eighteenth century in Holland, Germany, and elsewhere, there were decorators busy enamelling white porcelain of whatever kind they could get, and the *blanc de chine* offered a ready subject for this treatment. The decoration thus added was usually in Oriental taste, and might be confused with indifferent Chinese work. Many of these pieces are in the British Museum. On the other hand, there are in the same collection two cups with roughly painted floral designs in green and red which are obviously Chinese, though they might well have been painted in the mechanical method described by Mr. Dukes, which was probably traditional. Mr. Eumorfopoulos possesses several good examples of this painted Fukien ware, one of which may be described to show the style of painting affected. It is executed in leaf green, lustrous red, and the turquoise green which we associate with the Wan Li period, and the form—a double-bottomed bowl— is likewise reminiscent of the Ming dynasty.

The Japanese, whose traditions have often proved most misleading, have frequently classed the Fukien white as Corean porcelain (*haku-gorai* or white Corean), probably because specimens reached them from the Corean ports. In the British Museum, for instance, there is a beautiful white incense vase, formerly in the collection of Mr. Ninagawa of Tokio, and labelled by him as "Corean porcelain, 500 years old." It has all the characteristics of the finest cream white Fukien ware of late Ming or K'ang Hsi period, and if this piece is Corean, then I do not believe that even the subtle perception of the Japanese could find any difference between Corean and Fukien white. It is only right to add that other Japanese experts have pronounced it Chinese. Incidentally, I may mention that the base of this vase is glazed.

Marks were occasionally used by the Tê-hua potters, either incised or stamped in seal form,[258] on the bottoms of cups and other vessels, and on the backs of figures. Reign marks are rare, but apocryphal dates of the Hsüan Tê period occasionally occur, as on a figure of Li T'ieh-kuai in the British Museum. Others consist of potters' marks too often illegible because the thick glaze has filled up the hollows of the stamps, fanciful seal marks, frets, whorls, and occasionally the swastika symbol. A few examples are given in vol. i., p. 222.

CHAPTER VIII

THE CH'ING 清 DYNASTY, 1644–1910

The reigns of the Manchu chieftains T'ien Ming, T'ien Tsung, and Ts'ung Tê (1616–1643) are included in the chronology of the Ch'ing or Pure Dynasty, but it is more usual to reckon that period from 1644, when the Emperor Shun Chih 順治 was firmly established on the throne after the suicide of the last of the Mings. Little is known of the ceramic history of the seventeen years during which Shun Chih occupied the throne. The official records which deal only with the Imperial factory are almost silent, and when they do speak it is merely to chronicle failures. It is clear, however, that the Imperial factory at Ching-tê Chên had again been opened; for orders were sent in 1654 for a supply of large "dragon bowls" for the palace gardens. They were to be 2½ feet high, 3½ feet in diameter, 3 inches thick at the sides, and 5 inches at the bottom. For four years the potters wrestled with this difficult order without success. This time there was no "divine T'ung" to purchase success by a holocaust of himself; and eventually the Emperor was persuaded to withdraw the command. No better fortune attended an order given in 1659 for oblong plaques (3 feet by 2½ feet, and 3 inches thick) which were intended for veranda partitions.

Beyond these two negative items there is no information of the reign of Shun Chih in the Chinese books, and the porcelain itself is scarcely more illuminating, for authentic marked examples of this period are virtually unknown. A figure already mentioned as bearing the date 1650 belongs rather to the pottery section, but it shows that the traditions of the Ming glazes of the *demi-grand feu* were still kept alive. The blue and white and the polychrome made in the private factories at this time have been discussed with the transition wares (pp. 89 and 90), and for the rest we can only assume that the Shun Chih porcelains are not to be distinguished from those of the last Ming reigns on the one hand, and those of the early years of K'ang Hsi on the other.

Reflecting on the insignificance of the Shun Chih porcelains, one is tempted to ask how it is that the celebrated Lang T'ing-tso, whose name is usually associated with the beautiful Lang yao of the K'ang Hsi period, did not succeed in raising the wares of this period to a more conspicuous level. Lang T'ing-tso was governor of Kiangsi from 1654 and viceroy of Kiangsi and Kiangnan from 1656–1661 and again from 1665–1668. His name is mentioned (according to Bushell,[259] at any rate, for I have not been able to verify the statement) in connection with the efforts to make the dragon bowls for the palace in 1654; but we shall return to this point in discussing the Lang yao.

Meanwhile, we pass to the reign of K'ang Hsi 康熙(1662–1722), the beginning of what is to most European collectors the greatest period of Chinese porcelain, a period which may be roughly dated from 1662–1800. Chinese literary opinion gives the preference to the Sung and Ming dynasties, but if monetary value is any indication the modern Chinese collector appreciates the finer Ch'ing porcelains as highly as the European connoisseur. These latter wares have, at any rate, the advantage of being easily accessible to the Western student, and they are not difficult to obtain provided one is ready to pay the high price which their excellence commands. It will be no exaggeration to say that three quarters of the best specimens of Chinese porcelain in our collections belong to this prolific period, and they may be seen in endless variety in the museums and private galleries of Europe and America, nowhere perhaps better than in London itself.

PLATE 88

Two examples of the underglaze red (*chi hung*) of the K'ang Hsi period (1662–1722), sometimes called *lang yao*

Fig. 1.—Bottle-shaped Vase of dagoba form with minutely crackled *sang-de-bœuf* glaze with passages of cherry red. The glaze ends in an even roll short of the base rim, and that under the base is stone-coloured and crackled. Height 8½ inches.

British Museum.

Fig. 2.—Bottle-shaped Vase with crackled underglaze red of deep crushed strawberry tint. The glaze under the base is pale green, crackled. Height 10¾ inches.

Alexander Collection.

With regard to the porcelains made in the early years of K'ang Hsi there is very little information, and their special excellence has been assumed mainly on the supposition that the Viceroy Lang T'ing-tso exercised a beneficent influence on the wares of this period. He is reputed to have been sponsor of the Lang yao, which in the ordinary acceptation of the term[260] includes the beautiful *sang de bœuf* red, an apple green crackle, and perhaps a cognate crackled green glaze on which are painted designs in *famille verte* enamels. The explanation of the term *lang yao* is far from clear, and, as already hinted, the connection of the viceroy Lang T'ing-tso with this or any other of the K'ang Hsi porcelains is by no means established. Bushell[261] accepted the derivation of Lang yao from the first part of the viceroy's name as representing the best of several Chinese theories, and on the supposition that "the ceramic production of this time has retained the name of the viceroy, in the same way as the names of Ts'ang Ying-hsüan, Nien Hsi-yao, and T'ang Ying, who were in turn superintendents of the Imperial potteries, were afterwards given to the *Ts'ang yao*, *Nien yao*, and *T'ang yao*." There are many objections to this reasoning. In the first place, Lang T'ing-tso was viceroy of the two provinces of Kiangsi and Kiangnan for three or four years only (1665–1668) during the reign of K'ang Hsi, and it was only in his capacity as viceroy of Kiangsi that he would have been concerned with Ching-tê Chên, even supposing that the man who had charge of two large provinces could find time to devote himself to the details of ceramic manufactures. Secondly, it is nowhere recorded that Lang T'ing-tso was concerned in any way with the direction of the potteries, so that there is in this respect no parallel between him and the directors Ts'ang, Nien, and T'ang. Thirdly, the history of Ch'ing-tê Chên as given in the *T'ao lu*, and the history of Chinese porcelain as given in the *T'ao shuo*, make no mention whatever of *lang yao* or of Lang T'ing-tso, while the former takes special notice of the wares of Ts'ang, Nien, and T'ang, and the latter discusses T'ang's work at some length. Had so important a person as the viceroy of two provinces been connected with the invention or perfection of such celebrated wares as the *lang yao*, the occurrence would hardly have escaped the notice of the Chinese chronicler.

There are other attempts to explain the name *lang yao*. In the catalogue of Mr. A. B. Mitford's collection[262] it is stated that "the Lang family were a family of famous potters who possessed the secret of this peculiar glaze and paste. They became extinct about the year 1610." Bushell[263] dismisses this with the comment that "the family is apocryphal and the porcelain antedated," and in the same passage gives an alternative theory, viz. "this name has been derived by some Chinese of less weight from that of Lang Shih-ning, an artist protégé of the Jesuits,[264] who also lived in the reign of K'ang Hsi, and whose pictures are still appreciated."

The evidence for all these versions seems to be equally defective. They are, in fact, mere assertions, and the reader can take his choice of any of them, provided he does not insist on Mr. Mitford's date (anterior to 1610), for all authorities are now agreed that the *lang yao* is a K'ang Hsi production. The fact is that the name has been handed down without any explanation, and the current theories are of comparatively modern construction. The secret of the *lang yao* consisted in the first instance in the knowledge of means to produce a brilliant red glaze from copper oxide. It was not a new discovery, but merely a revival of the wonderful "precious stone" red of the early Ming period.[265] The supplies of some essential ingredient for this colour had failed in the Chia Ching period,[266] and the secret of the true colour had been temporarily lost. This secret was now recovered probably by a potter of the name of Lang, and that name has been associated with it ever since. So far from the *lang yao* being limited to the early part of the reign of K'ang Hsi or to the few years when Lang T'ing-tso might have been concerned with it, there can be little doubt that the *sang de bœuf* red or red *lang yao* is the special colour described in detail by Père d'Entrecolles in 1712, and again in 1722 under the significant name of *yu li hung*, or "red in the glaze." The reader can judge for himself from the description given in the second letter[267]: "This red *inside the glaze* is made with granulated red copper and the powder of a certain stone or pebble of a reddish colour. A Christian doctor told me that this stone was a kind of alum, used in medicine. The whole is pounded in a mortar and mixed with a boy's urine and the ordinary porcelain glaze; but I have not been able to ascertain the quantities of the ingredients, for those in possession of the secret take good care not to divulge it. This mixture is applied to the porcelain before it is fired and no other glaze is used; but care has to be taken that the red colour does not run to the bottom of the vase during the firing. They tell me that when they intend to apply this red to porcelain they do not use porcelain stone (*petuntse*) in the body, but they use in its place, mixed with the porcelain earth (*kaolin*), a yellow clay prepared in the same manner as the *petuntse*. Probably it is a kind of clay specially suited to receive this colour." Would that the worthy father had named the possessors of the secret! Had it been a Jesuit family, is it likely that he would not have said so? But here, at any rate, is not only such an accurate description of the manufacture of the *sang de bœuf* red that little need be added to it, but also a valuable commentary on the obscure passages in which the allusion is made to the brilliant red of the Hsüan Tê and other early Ming periods. For what is the reddish stone or pebble but the "red precious stone from the West," which played a mysterious part in the *pao shih hung* of the Hsüan Tê period? Chinese tradition has imagined this stone to have been the ruby, on the impossible assumption that the red colour of the glaze was derived from the red of the ruby. But it was, in all probability, cornaline (the *ma nao* used in the Sung porcelain of Ju Chou) or amethystine quartz, and its only function would have been to increase the brilliancy and transparence of the glaze, the red colour being entirely due to copper oxide. It is interesting, too, to note that the composition of the porcelain body was varied to suit this red colour, and that a yellow clay was substituted for the porcelain stone, in view of the alleged difficulties in obtaining the proper "earth for the fresh red (*hsien hung*)" in the Chia Ching period. In a similar manner a more earthy composition was found to be more sympathetic than the pure white porcelain to some of the other monochromes, as may be observed in existing specimens of turquoise blue.

The *lang yao*, then, is the *chi hung* of the K'ang Hsi period, the brilliant blood red commonly known by the French name *sang de bœuf*, and to-day it is one of the most precious monochromes. A choice example illustrated on Plate 88 shows the changing tints from a brilliant cherry red below the shoulder to the massed blood red where the fluescent glaze has formed thickly above the base. The colour flowing down has left an even white band round the mouth, and has settled in thick coagulations on the flat parts of the shoulders and again above the base; but in spite of its apparent fluidity the glaze has stopped in an even line without overrunning the base. The glaze under the base is of pale buff tone and crackled, and a careful examination of the surface generally shows that a faint crackle extends over the whole piece. The glaze, moreover, is full of minute bubbles and consequently much pinholed, and the red colour has the appearance of lying on the body in a dust of minute particles which the glaze has dragged downward in its flow and spread out in a continuous mass, but where the colour and the glaze have run thick the particles reappear in the form of a distinct mottling or dappling.

To obtain the best colour from the copper oxide in this glaze it was necessary to regulate the firing to a nicety, the margin between success and failure being exceedingly small. Naturally, too, the results varied widely in quality and tone; but the permanent characteristics of the K'ang Hsi *sang de bœuf* are (1) a brilliant red varying in depth and sometimes entirely lost in places,[268] but always red and without any of the grey or grey blue streaks which emerge on the *flambé* red and the modern imitations of the *sang de bœuf*; (2) the faint crackle of the glaze; (3) the stopping of the glaze at the foot rim. The colour of the glaze under the base and in the interior of vases varied from green or buff crackle to plain white. The secret of this glaze, which Père d'Entrecolles tells us was carefully guarded, seems to have been lost altogether about the end of the K'ang Hsi period. Later attempts to obtain the same effects, though often successful in producing large areas of brilliant red, are usually more or less streaked with alien tints such as grey or bluish grey, and are almost invariably marred by the inability of the later potters to control the flow of the glaze which overruns the foot rim and consequently has to be ground off. But it is highly probable that the modern potter will yet surmount these difficulties, and I have actually seen a large bowl of modern make in which the ox-blood red was successfully achieved on the exterior (the interior was relatively poor), and the flow of the glaze had been stopped along the foot rim except in one or two small places where the grinding was cleverly masked. So that it behoves the collector to be on his guard.

Fig. 2 of Plate 88 shows another type of red, also classed as *lang yao*, which has the same peculiarities of texture as the *sang de bœuf*, but the colour is more of a crushed-strawberry tint, and has in a more marked degree that thickly stippled appearance which suggests that the colour mixture has been blown on to the ware through gauze. This is probably the *ch'ui hung* or *soufflé* red mentioned by Père d'Entrecolles in connection with the *yu li hung*. The same glaze is often found on bowls, the colour varying much in depth and the base being usually covered with a crackled green glaze beneath. This crackled green is a very distinctive glaze, highly translucent and full of bubbles, like the red *lang yao*, and it is sometimes found covering the entire surface of a vase or bowl and serving as a background for paintings in *famille verte* enamels. It seems, in fact, to be the true green *lang yao*, and one is tempted to ask if it was not in reality intended to be a *sang de bœuf* red glaze from which a lack of oxygen or some other accident of the kiln has dispelled all the red, leaving a green which is one of the many hues produced by copper oxide under suitable conditions. These conditions might well be present in such an enclosed space as the foot of a bowl; and if they happened to affect the whole of the piece, what more natural than to trick out the failure with a gay adornment of enamel colours?

On the other hand, what is commonly known as green *lang yao* is the brilliant emerald or apple green crackle which has already been discussed on p. 102. But why this colour should be connected in any way with the Lang or any particular family is a mystery. The method of producing it is transparently obvious—a green enamel laid over a stone-coloured crackle; and there are examples of all periods from the Ming down to modern times. Indeed, the modern specimens are only distinguished with the greatest difficulty from the old.

To return to the history of the period from which we digressed to discuss the *lang yao*, the progress of the reviving industry suffered a rude set-back between 1674–1678 when the Imperial factory was destroyed during the rebellion of Wu San-kuei, viceroy of Yunnan. It is improbable that up to this time any notable development had taken place in the manufacture of porcelain, and those who think to flatter a specimen by suggesting that it is "*very* early K'ang Hsi" are likely to be paying a doubtful compliment. When, however, peace was restored and the factory rebuilt, a veritable renaissance of the porcelain industry began. In 1680[269] an official of the Imperial household was sent to reside at the factory and to superintend the work; and we are told in the *T'ao shuo*[270] that "previously to this the first-class workmen had been levied from the different districts of Jao Chou; but now all this forced labour was stopped, and as each manufactory was started the artisans were collected and materials provided, the expenses being defrayed from the Imperial exchequer and the money paid when due, in accordance with the market prices. Even the expenses for carriage were not required from the different districts. None of the proper duties of the local officers were interfered with; both the officials and the common people enjoyed the benefit, and the processes of manufacture were all much improved."

The success of this new movement was assured by the appointment in 1682 of Ts'ang Ying-hsüan 臧應選 to the control of the Imperial works. We are not told how long this distinguished person retained the directorship, but his merits are clearly indicated in the encomiums of a subsequent director, the celebrated T'ang Ying. In his "History of the God of the Furnace Blast," the latter states that when Ts'ang was in charge of the factory the god laid his finger on the designs and protected the porcelain in the kiln, so that it naturally came out perfect. Unfortunately, the notice of Ts'ang's work in the *T'ao lu*[271] is in the conventional style, and extremely meagre. The earth used, we are told, was unctuous, the material lustrous and thin. Every kind of colour was made, but the snake-skin green (*shê p'i lü*), the eel yellow (*shan yü huang*), the (?) turquoise (吉翠 *chi ts'ui*), and the "spotted yellow" (黃斑點 *huang pan tien*) were the most beautiful. The monochrome (*chiao*)[272] yellow, the monochrome brown or purple (*tzǔ*), the monochrome green, the *soufflé* (*ch'ui*) red and the *soufflé* blue, were also beautiful. The Imperial factory under the administration of T'ang-ying imitated these glaze colours.

Most of these colours explain themselves. The *soufflé* red is no doubt the same as the *ch'ui hung* described by Père d'Entrecolles and discussed above with the so-called *lang yao*. The *soufflé* blue will be no other than the familiar "powder blue." But the "spotted yellow" is an ambiguous term, for the Chinese *huang pan tien*[273] might mean a yellow glaze spotted with some other colour, a mottled yellow, or even a glaze with yellow spots like that of a rare vase in the Eumorfopoulos Collection, which has a brown black glaze flecked with greenish yellow spots.

Bushell identified the spotted yellow glaze with the "tiger skin," with its patches of green, yellow and aubergine glazes applied to the biscuit, which in the finer specimens is etched with dragon designs.[274]

This is practically all the direct information which the Chinese annals supply on the K'ang Hsi period, but in contrast with this strange reticence we have a delightful account of the industry at Ching-tê Chên during this important time in the two oft-quoted letters[275] written by the Jesuit father, d'Entrecolles, in 1712 and 1722. The worthy father's work lay among the potters themselves, and his information was derived from first-hand observation and from the notes supplied by his potter converts, with whatever help he was able to extract from the Annals of Fou-liang and similar native books. No subsequent writer has enjoyed such a favoured position, and as his observations have been laid under heavy contribution ever since, no apology is necessary for frequent reference to them in these pages.

CHAPTER IX

K'ANG HSI BLUE AND WHITE

Western collectors have agreed to give the place of honour to the K'ang Hsi blue and white. The Ming wares of the same kind, mainly from lack of adequate representation, have not yet been fully appreciated; and in the post-K'ang Hsi periods the blue and white took an inferior status, owing to the growing popularity of enamelled wares. The peculiar virtues of the K'ang Hsi blue and white are due to simple causes. Blue was still regarded as the best medium for painted designs, and the demand for it, both in China and abroad, was enormous. The body material was formed of carefully selected clay and stone, thoroughly levigated and freed from all impurities. No pains were spared in the preparation of the blue, which was refined over and over again until the very quintessence had been extracted from the cobaltiferous ore. Naturally this process was costly, and the finest cobalt was never used quite pure; even on the most expensive wares it was blended with a proportion of the lower grades of the mineral, and this proportion was increased according to the intended quality of the porcelain. But the choicest blue and white of this period was unsurpassed in the purity and perfection of the porcelain, in the depth and lustre of the blue, and in the subtle harmony between the colour and the white porcelain background; and the high standard thus established served to raise the quality of the manufacture in general.

Vast quantities of this blue and white were shipped to Europe by the Dutch and the other East India companies, who sent extensive orders to Ching-tê Chên. It need hardly be said that this export porcelain varied widely in quality, but it included at this time wares of the highest class. Indeed, in looking through our large collections there are surprisingly few examples of the choice K'ang Hsi blue and white which cannot be included in the export class, as indicated by the half-Europeanised forms of plates, jugs, tankards, and other vessels, and by the fact that the vases are made in sets of five. But considering that it was made to suit purchasers of such varied tastes and means, it is surprising how little of this K'ang Hsi porcelain is bad. Even the roughest specimens have a style and a quality not found on later wares, and all have an unquestionable value as decoration.

It would be futile to attempt to describe exhaustively the different kinds of K'ang Hsi blue and white and the innumerable patterns with which they are decorated. We must confine our descriptions to a few type specimens, but first it will be useful to give the points of a choice example. Such a vessel, whatever its nature, will be potted with perfect skill, its form well proportioned and true. The surface will be smooth, because the material is thoroughly refined and the piece has been carefully trimmed or finished on the lathe, and finally all remaining inequalities have been smoothed away with a moist feather brush before the glazing. The ware will be clean and white, and the glaze[276] pure, limpid, and lustrous, but with that faint suspicion of green which is rarely absent from Chinese porcelain. The general effect of the body and glaze combined is a solid white like well set curds. The base, to which the connoisseur looks for guidance, is deeply cut and washed in the centre with glaze which reaches about half-way down the sides of the foot rim. This patch of glaze is usually pinholed, as though the nemesis of absolute perfection had to be placated by a few flaws in this inconspicuous part. The rim itself is carefully trimmed, and in many cases grooved or beaded, as though to fit a wooden stand,[277] and the unglazed edge reveals a smooth, close-grained biscuit whose fine white material is often superficially tinged with brown in the heat of the furnace. The decoration is carefully painted in a pure sapphire blue of great depth and fire, and singularly free from any strain of red or purple—a quality of blue only obtained by the most elaborate process of refining. The designs, as on the Ming porcelains, are first drawn in outline; but, unlike the strong Ming outlines, these are so faint as to be practically unobserved; and the colour is filled in, not in flat washes, as on the Ming blue and white, but in graded depths of pulsating blue. This procedure is clearly shown by two interesting bowls in the British Museum. They are identical in form and were intended to match in pattern; but in one the design (the Eight Immortals of the Wine Cup) is completed, while on the other it remains in outline only, giving us a wonderful illustration of the beautiful firm touch with which the artists traced these faint outlines. The work of decoration was systematically subdivided in the Chinese factory, and Père d'Entrecolles tells us that "one workman is solely occupied with the ring which one sees on the border of the ware; another outlines the flowers, which a third paints; one does the water and the mountains, another the birds and animals."[278] Whatever the advantages and disadvantages of this divided labour, the designs on the blue and white were admirably chosen to show off the fine qualities of the colour; and it is to the blue that the collector looks first. The distinction between the various qualities of blue hardly admit of verbal definition. It can only be learnt by comparing the actual specimens, and by training the eye to distinguish the best from the second best.

The patterns are not always blue on a white ground. Many of the most beautiful results were obtained by reserving the design in white in a blue ground, and both styles are often combined on the same piece. The second is fairly common on the K'ang Hsi porcelains, being specially suited to the lambrequins, arabesques, and formal patterns which were a favourite decoration at this time. See Plates 89 and 91.

Fig. 1   Fig. 2   Fig. 3

PLATE 89

Three examples of K'ang Hsi Blue and White Porcelain in the British Museum

Fig. 1.—Ewer with leaf-shaped panels of floral arabesques, white in blue, enclosed by a mosaic pattern in blue and white: stiff plantain leaves on the neck and cover. Silver mount with thumb-piece. Height 7⅛ inches.

Fig. 2.—Deep bowl with cover, painted with "tiger-lily" scrolls. Mark, a leaf. Height 7½ inches.

Fig. 3.—Sprinkler with panels of lotus arabesques, white in blue, and *ju-i* shaped border patterns. A diaper of small blossoms on the neck. Mark, a leaf. Height 7⅛ inches.

The choicest materials were lavished on the porcelains with these formal designs, which consisted now of bands of *ju-i* shaped lappets[279] filled with arabesque foliage, forming an upper and lower border, between which are floral sprays, now of a belt of three or four palmette-like designs, similarly ornamented, and linked together round the centre of a vase or bottle; of large, stiff, leaf-shaped medallions borrowed, like the patterns which fill them, from ancient bronzes, and of ogre-head designs from a similar source; of successive belts of arabesque scrolls and dragon designs covering cylindrical jars; of a mosaic of small blossoms, or of network diapers recalling the pattern of a crackled porcelain. The white on blue process is constant in a well known decoration in which archaic dragons, floral arabesques, roses or peonies are arranged in "admired disorder" over the whole surface of a cylinder vase or a triple gourd, as on Plate 91. Sometimes the roses occupy the greater part of the design, and among them are small oval or round blank medallions, which have earned for the pattern the name of "rose and ticket."

This type of ware is represented in almost every variety in the Dresden collection, and there are examples of the "rose and ticket" jars in the *Porzellan-zimmer* of the Charlottenburg Palace. Both these collections are mainly composed of the export porcelain sent from China in the last decades of the seventeenth century, and the latter is practically limited to the presents made by the English East India Company to Queen Sophia Charlotte of Prussia (1688–1705). The white on blue patterns are also freely used in combination with blue and white to form borders and to fill in the ground between panels.

As for the blue on white designs, they are legion. There are the old Ming favourites such as the Court scenes, historical and mythological subjects, pictorial designs, such as ladies looking at the garden flowers by candlelight.[280] There are landscapes after Sung and Ming paintings, the usual dragon and phœnix patterns, animal, bird, and fish designs, lions and mythical creatures, the familiar group of a bird (either a phœnix or a golden pheasant) on a rock beside which are peony, magnolia, and other flowering plants. Panel decoration, too, is frequent, the panels sometimes petal-shaped and emphasised by lightly moulded outlines, or again mirror-shaped, circular, fan-shaped, leaf-shaped, oval, square, etc., and surrounded by diapers and "white in blue" designs. The reserves are suitably filled with figure subjects from romance, history, or family life, mythical subjects such as the adventures of Taoist sages, the story of Wang Chi watching the game of chess, Tung-fang So and his peaches, or, if numerical sequences are needed, with the Four Accomplishments (painting, calligraphy, music and chess), the flowers of the Four Seasons, the Eight Taoist Immortals, the Eight Immortals of the Wine Cup, etc. Another favourite panel design is a group of vases, furniture, and symbolical objects from the comprehensive series known as the Hundred Antiques.[281] Sometimes the whole surface of a vase is divided into rows of petal-shaped compartments filled with floral designs, figure subjects, birds and flowers or landscapes. Plate 91, Fig. 3, from a set of five, is one of the large vases in the Dresden collection which, tradition says, were obtained by Augustus the Strong from the King of Prussia in exchange for a regiment of dragoons. It is decorated with panels illustrating the stories of the Twenty-four Paragons of Filial Piety.

Some of the purely floral patterns strike perhaps a more distinctive note. The "aster pattern," for instance, is a design of stiff, radiating, aster-like flowers usually in a dark tone of blue and displayed on saucer dishes or deep covered bowls. Some of the specimens of this class appear to be a little earlier than K'ang Hsi. The so-called "tiger-lily" pattern illustrated by Fig. 2 of Plate 89 is usually associated with deep cylindrical covered bowls of fine material and painted in the choicest blue. A beaker (Plate 91, Fig. 2) shows a characteristic treatment of the magnolia, parts of the blossoms being lightly sculptured in relief and the white petals set off by a foil of blue clouding. It evidently belongs to a set of five (three covered jars and two beakers) made as a *garniture de cheminée* for the European market.

The squat-bodied bottle (Plate 92, Fig. 1) illustrates a familiar treatment of the lotus design, with a large blossom filling the front of the body.

But perhaps the noblest of all Chinese blue and white patterns is the prunus design (often miscalled hawthorn) illustrated by Plate 90, a covered vase once in the Orrock Collection and now in the Victoria and Albert Museum. The form is that of the well-known ginger jar, but these lovely specimens were intended for no banal uses. They were filled with fragrant tea or some other suitable gift, and sent, like the round cake boxes, by the Chinese to their friends at the New Year, but it was not intended that the jars or boxes should be kept by the recipients of the compliment.

The New Year falls in China from three to seven weeks later than in our calendar, and it was seasonable to decorate these jars with sprays and petals of the flowering prunus fallen on the ice, which was already cracked and about to dissolve. The design is symbolic of the passing of winter and the coming of spring; and the vibrating depths of the pure sapphire blue broken by a network of lines simulating ice cracks form a lovely setting for the graceful prunus sprays reserved in the pure curd-like white of the ware.

The prunus pattern has been applied to every conceivable form, whether to cover the whole surface or to serve as secondary ornament in the border of a design or on the rim of a plate, and the prunus jar appears in all qualities of blue and on porcelain good and bad, old and new. The graceful sprays have become stereotyped and the whole design vulgarised in many instances; and in some cases the blossoms are distributed symmetrically on a marbled blue ground as a mere pattern. But nothing can stale the beauty of the choice K'ang Hsi originals, on which the finest materials and the purest, deepest blue were lavished. The amateur should find no difficulty in distinguishing these from their decadent descendants. The freshness of the drawing, the pure quality of the blue, and the excellence of body, glaze, and potting are unmistakable. The old examples have the low rim round the mouth unglazed where the rounded cap-shaped cover fitted, and the design on the shoulders is finished off with a narrow border of dentate pattern. The original covers are extremely rare, and in most cases have been replaced with later substitutes in porcelain or carved wood.

There are, besides, a number of types specially prevalent among the export porcelains, some purely Chinese in origin, others showing European influence. Take, for example, the well-known saucer dish with mounted figures of a man and a woman hunting a hare—a subject usually known as the "love chase"—a free and spirited design, rather sketchily painted in pale silvery blue. The porcelain itself is scarcely less characteristic, a thin, crisp ware, often moulded on the sides with petal-shaped compartments, and in many ways recalling the earlier type described on p. 70. It is, however, distinguished from the latter class by slight differences in tone and finish which can only be learnt by comparison of actual specimens. It is, moreover, almost always marked with a *nien hao* in six characters, whereas marks on the other type are virtually unknown. The *nien hao* is usually that of Ch'êng Hua, but an occasional example with the K'ang Hsi mark gives the true date of the ware.

A quantity of this porcelain was brought up by divers from wrecks of old East Indiamen in Table Bay, among which was the *Haarlem*, lost in 1648,[282] though most of the ships were wrecked at later dates. It is a thin and sharply moulded ware, often pure eggshell, and the blue varies from the pale silvery tint to vivid sapphire. The usual forms are of a utilitarian kind—plates, saucer dishes, cups and saucers, small vases and bottles, jugs, tankards, and the like—and the designs are not confined to the "love chase," but include other figure subjects (e.g. a warrior on horseback carrying off a lady,[283] and various scenes from romance and family life), floral designs, deer, phœnixes, fish, birds, etc., and perhaps most often the tall female figures, standing beside flowering shrubs or pots of flowers, which are vulgarly known as "long Elizas," after the Dutch *lange lijsen* (see Plate 92, Fig. 2).

Graceful ladies (*mei jên*) are familiar motives in Chinese decoration, but this particular type, usually consisting of isolated figures in small panels or separated from each other by a shrub or flowerpot, and standing in a stereotyped pose, are, I think,[284] peculiar to the export wares of the last half of the seventeenth century.

This same type of thin, crisply moulded porcelain was also painted with similar designs in *famille verte* enamels over the glaze. It has a great variety of marks, the commonest being the apocryphal Ch'êng Hua date-mark, while others are marks of commendation,[285] such as *ch'i chên ju yü* (a rare gem like jade), *yü* (jade), *ya* (elegant), and various hall-marks.

PLATE 90

Covered Jar for New Year gifts, with design of blossoming prunus (*mei hua*) sprays in a ground of deep sapphire blue, which is reticulated with lines suggesting ice cracks: dentate border on the shoulders

Height 10 inches.

Victoria and Albert Museum.

Yet another group of superior quality is obviously connected with the European trade by a peculiar mark (see vol. i., p. 228) resembling the letter C or G. It is most commonly represented by pairs of bottles with globular body and tall, tapering neck, decorated with flowing scrolls of curious rosette-like flowers, a design stated with much probability to have been copied from Dutch delft. As the Dutch design in question had evidently been based on a Chinese original, the peculiar nature of the flowers explains itself. There are other instances of patterns bandied in this way between the Far East and the West. The same peculiar floral scroll appears in *famille verte* associated with the same mark; and the same G mark occurs on two rare bottles in the collection of Mr. J. C. J. Drucker, which have blue and white painting on the neck and *famille verte* designs in the finest enamels on the body. A deep bowl in the Eumorfopoulos collection with *famille verte* panels of symbols from the Hundred Antiques, and a ground of green "prunus" pattern, bears the same mark. Neither of these last examples can be even remotely connected with Dutch influence, so that we may dismiss the suggestion that the letter in the mark is intended to be a D, standing for D(elft), for this reason quite apart from the fact that such a mark on Delft ware is non-existent. I imagine that the true explanation is that this peculiar mark is a merchant's sign placed by order on the goods made for some particular trader.

A close copy of the "wing handles" of Venetian glass on certain blue and white bottles (Plate 92, Fig. 3), the appearance of Prince of Wales's feathers in the border of a plate and of an heraldic eagle in the well of a salt cellar, no less than many forms obviously Western in origin, further emphasise the close relations between the Ching-tê Chên potters and European traders.[286] An immense quantity of indifferent blue and white was made for the European table services, and summarily decorated with baskets of flowers, the usual flowering plant designs, close patterns of small blossoms, floral scrolls with large, meaningless flowers, ivy scrolls, passion flowers, and numerous stereotyped designs, such as dragons in sea waves, prunus pattern borders, pine tree and stork, a garden fence with rockery and flowering shrubs, groups from the Hundred Antiques, a parrot on a tree stump, etc. The blue of these pieces is usually rather dull and heavy, but the ware has the characteristic appearance of K'ang Hsi porcelain, and was evidently made for the most part about the year 1700. If marked at all, the marks are usually symbols, such as the double fish, the lozenge, the leaf, a tripod vase, and a strange form of the character *shou* known as the "spider mark" (see vol. i., p. 225). The plates are often edged with lustrous brown glaze to prevent that chipping and scaling to which the Chinese glaze was specially liable on projecting parts of the ware.[287]

Something has already been said[288] of another very distinctive class of blue and white for which the misleading name of "soft paste" has been widely adopted. The term is of American origin and has been too readily accepted, for it is not only inaccurate as a description, but is already current in Europe for a totally different ware, which it describes with greater exactitude, viz. the artificial, glassy porcelains made at Sèvres and Chelsea and other factories, chiefly in France and England, in the middle of the eighteenth century. In actual fact the Chinese ware to which the term "soft paste" is applied has an intensely hard body. The glaze, however, which is softer than that of the ordinary porcelain, contains a proportion of lead, and if not actually crackled from the first becomes so in use, the crackle lines being usually irregular and undecided.

A detailed description of the manufacture of this ware is given by Père d'Entrecolles,[289] though he is probably at fault in supposing that its chief ingredient was a recent discovery in 1722. It was made, he says, with a mineral called *hua shih* (in place of kaolin), a stone of glutinous and soapy nature, and almost certainly corresponding to the steatite or "soapy rock" which was used by the old English porcelain makers at Bristol, Worcester and Liverpool. "The porcelain made with *hua shih*," to quote Père d'Entrecolles, "is rare and far more expensive than the other porcelain. It has an extremely fine grain; and for purposes of painting, when compared with ordinary porcelain, it is almost as vellum to paper. Moreover, this ware is surprisingly light to anyone accustomed to handle the other kinds; it is also far more fragile than the ordinary, and there is difficulty in finding the exact temperature for its firing. Some of the potters do not use *hua shih* for the body of the ware, but content themselves with making a diluted slip into which they dip their porcelain when dry, so as to give it a coating of soapstone before it is painted and glazed. By this means it acquires a certain degree of beauty." The preparation of the *hua shih* is also described, but it is much the same as that of the kaolin, and the composition of the steatitic body is given as eight parts of *hua shih* to two of porcelain stone (*petuntse*).

There are, then, two kinds of steatitic porcelain, one with the body actually composed of *hua shih* and the other with a mere surface dressing of this material. The former is light to handle, and opaque; and the body has a dry, earthy appearance, though it is of fine grain and unctuous to touch. It is variously named by the Chinese[290] *sha-t'ai* (sand bodied) and *chiang-t'ai* (paste bodied), and when the glaze is crackled it is further described as *k'ai pien* (crackled).

The painting on the steatitic porcelain differs in style from that of the ordinary blue and white of this period. It is executed with delicate touches like miniature painting, and every stroke of the brush tells, the effects being produced by fine lines rather than by graded washes. The ware, being costly to make, is usually painted by skilful artists and in the finest blue. Fig. 3, of Plate 93, is an excellent example of the pure steatitic ware, an incense bowl in the Franks collection, of which the base and a large part of the interior is unglazed and affords a good opportunity for the study of the body material. The glaze is thin and faintly crackled, and the design—Hsi Wang Mu and the Taoist Immortals—is delicately drawn in light, clear blue.

The second type, which has only a dressing of steatite over the ordinary body, has neither the same lightness nor the opacity of the true steatitic ware, but it has the same soft white surface, and is painted in the same style of line drawing.

There are, besides, other opaque and crackled wares painted in underglaze blue, which are also described as "soft paste," and, indeed, deserve the name far more than the steatitic porcelain. The creamy, crackled copies of old Ting wares, for instance, made with *ch'ing tien* stone,[291] are occasionally enriched with blue designs; and the ordinary stone-coloured crackle with buff staining is also painted at times with underglaze blue,[292] or with blue designs on pads of white clay in a crackled ground.

On the other hand, there are numerous wares of the Yung Chêng and Ch'ien Lung periods which are probably composed in part, at least, of steatite. They are usually opaque, and the surface is sometimes dead white, sometimes creamy and often undulating like orange peel, and in addition to blue decoration, enamel painting is not infrequent on these later types. The purely steatitic porcelains are generally of small size, which was appropriate to the style of painting as well as to the expensive nature of the material. The furniture of the scholar's table, with its tiny flower vases for a single blossom, its brush washers and water vessels of fanciful forms, its pigment boxes, etc., were suitable objects for the material, and many of these little crackled porcelains are veritable gems. Snuff bottles are another appropriate article, and a representative collection of snuff bottles will show better than anything the great variety of these mixed wares and so-called "soft pastes."

It has been already observed that crackled blue and white porcelain of the steatitic kind is found with the date marks of Ming Emperors, and there can be little doubt that it was made from early Ming times, but as the style of painting seems to have known no change it will be always difficult to distinguish the early specimens. It is safe to assume that almost all the specimens in Western collections belong to the Ch'ing dynasty, a few to the K'ang Hsi period, but the bulk of the better examples to the reigns of Yung Chêng and Ch'ien Lung. Modern copies of the older wares also abound.

Fig. 1   Fig. 2   Fig. 3

Plate 91.—Blue and White K'ang Hsi Porcelain.

Fig. 1.—Triple Gourd Vase, white in blue designs of archaic dragons and scrolls of season flowers. Height 36½ inches. *Dresden Collection.*

Fig. 2.—Beaker, white magnolia design slightly raised, with blue background. Height 18 inches. *British Museum.*

Fig. 3.—"Grenadier Vase," panels with the Paragons of Filial Piety. Height 44 inches. *Dresden Collection.*

Plate 92.—Blue and White K'ang Hsi Porcelain.

Fig. 1.—Sprinkler with lotus design. Height 6¼ inches. *British Museum.*

Fig. 2.—Bottle with biscuit handles, design of graceful ladies (*mei jen*). Height 11 inches. *Fitzwilliam Museum (formerly D. G. Rosetti Collection).*

Fig. 3.—Bottle with handles copied from Venetian glass. Height 6¼ inches. *British Museum.*

Fig. 1

Fig. 2

Fig. 3

Plate 93.—Blue and White Porcelain.

Fig. 1.—Tazza with Sanskrit characters. Ch'ien Lung mark. Height 4¼ inches. *British Museum.*

Fig. 2.—Water Pot, butterfly and flowers, steatitic porcelain. Wan Li mark. Height 1⅞ inches. *Eumorfopoulos Collection.*

Fig. 3.—Bowl, steatitic porcelain. Immortals on a log raft. K'ang Hsi period. Diameter 5¾ inches. *British Museum.*

Fig. 1

Fig. 2

Plate 94.—Porcelain decorated in enamels on the biscuit.

Fig. 1.—Ewer in form of the character *Shou* (Longevity); blue and white panel with figure designs. Early K'ang Hsi period. Height 8¾ inches. *Salting Collection.*

Fig. 2.—Ink Palette, dated 31st year of K'ang Hsi (1692 A.D.). Length 5¼ inches. *British Museum.*

An interesting passage in the first letter[293] of Père d'Entrecolles describes a curious kind of porcelain, of which the secret had already been lost. It was known as *chia ch'ing* or "blue put in press," and it was said that the blue designs on the cups so treated were only visible when the vessel was filled with water.

The method of the manufacture is described as follows: "The porcelain to be so decorated had to be very thin; when it was dry, a rather strong blue was applied, not to the exterior in the usual manner, but on the interior to the sides. The design usually consisted of fish, as being specially appropriate to appear when the cup was filled with water. When the colour was dry a light coating of slip, made with the body material, was applied, and this coating enclosed the blue between two layers of clay. When this coating was dry, glaze was sprinkled inside the cup, and shortly afterwards the porcelain was placed on the wheel. As the body had been strengthened on the interior, the potter proceeded to pare it down outside as fine as possible without actually penetrating to the colour. The exterior was then glazed by immersion. When completely dry it was fired in the ordinary furnace. The work is extremely delicate, and requires a dexterity which the Chinese seem no longer to possess. Still, they try from time to time to recover the secret of this magical painting, but without success. One of them told me recently that he had made a fresh attempt, and had almost succeeded."

No example of this mysterious porcelain is known to exist, and it is probable that the whole story is based on some ill-grounded tradition. It is true that water will bring out the faded design on certain old potteries, but this is due to the action of the water in restoring transparency to a soft decayed glaze. But how the water or any other liquid could affect the transparency of a hard, impenetrable porcelain glaze, still less influence the colour concealed beneath a layer of clay and glaze, is far from clear. Indeed, the whole story savours of the "tall tales" quoted in chap. x. of vol. i.

But perhaps it will not be inappropriate to mention here another peculiar type of blue and white, which, if we may judge by the early date mark usually placed upon it, throws back to some older model. The design, usually a dragon, is delicately traced with a needle point on the body of the ware, and a little cobalt blue is dusted into the incisions.[294] The glaze is then applied, and when the piece is fired and finished the dragon design appears faintly "tattooed" in pale blue. The effect is light and delicate, but of small decorative value, and the few examples which I have seen are redeemed from insignificance by a peculiarly beautiful body of pure glassy porcelain. They bear an apocryphal Ch'êng Hua mark, but evidently belong to the first half of the eighteenth century, to the Yung Chêng, or perhaps the late K'ang Hsi period.

CHAPTER X

K'ANG HSI POLYCHROME PORCELAINS

Broadly speaking, the polychrome porcelains of the Ming and K'ang Hsi periods are the same in principle, though they differ widely in style and execution. The general types continued, and the first to be considered is that in which all the colours are fired in the high temperature of the large kiln, comprising underglaze blue and underglaze red, and certain slips and coloured glazes. Conspicuous among the last is a pale golden brown commonly known as Nanking yellow, which is found in narrow bands or in broad washes, dividing or surrounding blue designs, and is specially common on the bottles, sprinklers, gourd-shaped vases, and small jars exported to Europe in the last half of the seventeenth century. The golden brown also darkens into coffee brown, and in some cases it alternates in bands with buff crackle and pale celadon green.

A deep olive brown glaze is sometimes found as a background for ornament in moulded reliefs which are touched with underglaze blue and red. A fine vase of this type is in the Salting Collection, and a good example was given by Mr. Andrew Burman to the British Museum. Both seem to be designed after bronze models.

But the central colour of this group is undoubtedly the underglaze red. Derived from copper it is closely akin to the red of the *chi hung* glaze, and both were conspicuous on the Hsüan Tê porcelain, both fell into disuse in the later Ming periods, and both were revived in the reign of K'ang Hsi.

I have seen two examples of this colour in combination with underglaze blue bearing the hall mark *chung-ho-t'ang*, and cyclical dates corresponding to 1671 and 1672 respectively. In neither of these pieces, however, was the red very successful, and probably the better K'ang Hsi specimens belong to a later period of the reign. It was, however, always a difficult colour to fire, and examples in which the red is perfectly developed are rare. As a rule, it tends to assume a maroon or dark reddish brown tint.

Nor is the method of its application always the same. Sometimes it is painted on in clean, crisp brush strokes; at others it is piled up in thick washes which flow in the firing and assume some of the qualities and the colour of *sang de bœuf* red, even displaying occasional crackle; on other pieces again a "peach bloom" tint is developed.[295] On two of the best examples in the Franks Collection, where a deep blood red is combined with a fine quality of blue, it is noteworthy that the surface of the white glaze has a peculiar dull lustre. This, I understand, is due to "sulphuring" in the kiln, a condition which, whether accidental or intentional, is certainly favourable to the red colour. It is also noticeable that the red is particularly successful under a glaze which is faintly tinged with celadon green such as is often used on imitations of Ming porcelains, and it was no doubt this consideration which led to the frequent use of celadon green in this group. The celadon is used either as a ground colour for the whole piece or in parts only of the design, and the addition of white slip further strengthened the palette. With these colours some exquisite effects have been compassed in such designs as birds on prunus boughs and storks among lotus plants, the main design being in blue, the blossoms in white slip slightly raised and touched with red, and the background plain white, celadon green (Plate 115), and sometimes pale lavender blue. The celadon and pale lavender vases with this decoration were favourites with the French in the eighteenth century, and many sets of vases and beakers in this style have been furnished with sumptuous ormolu mounts by the French goldsmiths.

The painting in underglaze red, which was revived in the K'ang Hsi period, continued with success in the succeeding reigns of Yung Chêng and Ch'ien Lung (indeed it has not ceased to this day), but the bulk of the finer examples in our collections seem to belong to the late K'ang Hsi and the Yung Chêng periods. The underglaze red is used alone as well as in combination, and some of its most successful effects are found on small objects like colour boxes and snuff bottles.

The black or brown pigment used for outlining designs under the softer enamel colours such as green and yellow, though in one sense an underglaze colour, does not belong to this group.

From this group of polychrome porcelain we pass to another in which the colour is given by washes of various glazes. A few of the high-fired glazes are employed for this purpose, especially blue in combination with celadon green and white, and a few clay slips, of which the commonest is a dressing of brown clay applied without any glaze and producing an iron-coloured surface. The most familiar members of this group are small Taoist figures of rough but vivacious modelling with draperies glazed blue, celadon and white,[296] and the base unglazed and slightly browned in the firing. Collectors are tempted to regard these figures as late or modern productions, but examples in the Dresden collection prove that this technique was employed in the K'ang Hsi period. In the same collection there are numbers of small toy figures, such as monkeys, oxen, grotesque human forms, etc., sometimes serving as whistles or as water-droppers. They are made of coarse porcelain or stoneware with a thin dressing of brown ferruginous clay, and touches of high-fired glazes. The appearance of these, too, is so modern that we realise with feelings of surprise that they formed part of the collection of Augustus the Strong.

The polychrome porcelain coloured with glazes of the *demi-grand feu* (i.e. glazes fired in the more temperate parts of the large kiln) has been discussed in the chapters on the Ming period.[297] The group characterised by green, turquoise and aubergine violet, semi-opaque, and minutely crackled is not conspicuous among K'ang Hsi porcelains; indeed it seems to have virtually ceased with the Ming dynasty. The individual colours, however, were still used as monochromes; in combination they are chiefly represented by aubergine violet and turquoise in broad washes on such objects as peach-shaped wine pots, Buddhist lions with joss-stick holders attached, parrots, and similar ornaments.

The other three-colour group, composed of transparent green, yellow and aubergine purple glazes, usually associated with designs finely etched with a metal point on the body, were freely used in the K'ang Hsi and Yung Chêng periods in imitation of Ming prototypes. Such specimens are often characterised by extreme neatness of workmanship and technical perfection of the ware. The best-known examples are thin, beautifully potted rice bowls, with slightly everted rim, and a design of five-clawed Imperial dragons traced with a point and filled in with a colour contrasting with that of the ground, e.g. green on yellow, or green on aubergine, all the possible changes being rung on the three colours. Being Imperial wares these bowls are usually marked with the *nien hao* of their period, but such is the trimness of their make that collectors are tempted to regard them as specimens of a later reign. But here again the Dresden collection gives important evidence, for it contains a bowl of this class with dragons in a remarkable purplish black colour (probably an accidental variety of the aubergine) in a yellow ground. It bears the mark of the K'ang Hsi period.

The application of similar plumbo-alcaline glazes to a commoner type of porcelain is described by Père d'Entrecolles[298]:—"There is a kind of coloured porcelain which is sold at a lower rate than the enamelled ware just described.... The material required for this work need not be so fine. Vessels which have already been baked in the great furnace without glaze, and consequently white and lustreless, are coloured by immersion in a bowl filled with the colouring preparation if they are intended to be monochrome. But if they are required to be polychrome like the objects called *hoam lou houan*,[299] which are divided into kinds of panels, one green, one yellow, etc., the colours are laid on with a large brush. This is all that need be done to this type of porcelain, except that after the firing a little vermilion is applied to certain parts such as the beaks of birds, etc. This vermilion, however, is not fired, as it would evaporate in the kiln, and consequently it does not last. When the various colours have been applied, the porcelain is refired in the great furnace with the other wares which have not yet been baked; but care is taken to place it at the bottom of the furnace and below the vent-hole where the fire is less fierce; otherwise the great heat would destroy the colours."

Fig. 1   Fig. 2

PLATE 95

Two examples of Porcelain painted with coloured enamels on the biscuit, the details of the designs being first traced in brown. K'ang Hsi period (1662–1722)

Fig. 1.—One of a pair of Buddhistic Lions, sometimes called Dogs of Fo. This is apparently the lioness, with her cub: the lion has a ball of brocade under his paw. On the head is the character *wang* (prince) which is more usual on the tiger of Chinese art. Height 18 inches. *S. E. Kennedy Collection.*

Fig. 2.—Bottle-shaped Vase and Stand moulded in bamboo pattern and decorated with floral brocade designs and diapers. Height 8¾ inches. *Cope Bequest (Victoria & Albert Museum).*

In this interesting passage, written in 1722, we have a precise account of the manufacture of one of the types of porcelain which have been indiscriminately assigned to the Ming period. This on-biscuit polychrome was undoubtedly made in the Ming dynasty, but in view of d'Entrecolles' description it will be safe to assume that, unless there is some very good evidence to the contrary, the examples in our collections are not older than K'ang Hsi. The type is easily identified from the above quotation, and there is a little group of the wares in the British Museum, mostly small figures and ornaments with washes of green, brownish yellow and aubergine purple applied direct to the biscuit, and on some of the unglazed details the unfired vermilion still adheres. These coloured glazes are compounded with powdered flint, lead, saltpetre, and colouring oxides, and the porcelain belongs to the comprehensive group of *san ts'ai* or three-colour ware, although the three colours—green, yellow and aubergine—are supplemented by a black formed of brown black pigment under one of the translucent glazes and a white which d'Entrecolles describes[300] as composed of ⅔ ounce of powdered flint to every ounce of white lead. This last forms the thin, iridescent film often of a faintly greenish tinge, which serves as white on these three-colour porcelains. In rare cases also a violet blue enamel is added to the colour scheme.

A characteristic of this particular type is the absence of any painted outlines. The colours are merely broad washes bounded by the flow of the glaze, and this style of polychrome is best suited to figures and moulded ornamental pieces, in which the details of the design form natural lines of demarcation for the glazes. On a flat surface this method of coloration is only suited to such patchy patterns as the so-called tiger skin and the tortoiseshell wares.

The Dresden collection is peculiarly rich in this kind of *san ts'ai*, but though two or three of the specimens (Plate 71, Figs. 1 and 2) differing considerably from the rest, are clearly of the Ming period, the great majority are undoubtedly contemporaneous with the forming of the collection, viz. of the K'ang Hsi period. The latter include numerous figures, human and animal, and ornaments such as the junk on Plate 98, besides some complicated structures of rocks and shrines and grottos, peopled with tiny images and human figures. To this group belong such specimens as the "brinjal bowls," with everted rim and slight floral designs engraved in outline and filled in with coloured glaze in a ground of aubergine (brinjal) purple. There are similar specimens with green ground, and both types are frequently classed with Ming wares. Some of them may indeed belong to the late Ming period,[301] but those with finer finish are certainly K'ang Hsi. They are usually marked with rough, undecipherable seal marks in blue, which are commonly known as shop marks.

Some of the figures of deities, birds and animals, besides the small ornamental objects such as brush-washers in the form of lotus leaves and little water vessels for the writing table are of very high quality, skilfully modelled and of material far finer than that described by d'Entrecolles. Fig. 2, Plate 99, a statuette of Ho Hsien-ku, one of the Eight Immortals, is an example. The flesh is in white biscuit, showing the fine grain of the porcelain, white to-day, though possibly it was originally coloured with unfired pigment and gilt as was often the case. The glazes on this finer quality of ware, especially the green and the aubergine, are peculiarly smooth and sleek, and the yellow is fuller and browner than on the kindred ware, enamelled on the biscuit, which we now proceed to investigate.

The French term, *émaillé sur biscuit*, is used somewhat broadly to cover the coloured glazes just described, as well as the enamels proper of the muffle kiln. We shall try to confine the expression, "on-biscuit enamels," to the softer, verifiable enamels which are fired at a lower temperature and in a smaller kiln or muffle. These are, in fact, the same enamels as are used in the ordinary *famille verte* porcelain painted over the finished glaze, but when applied direct to the biscuit they have a slightly darker and mellower tone, the background of biscuit reflecting less light than the glittering white glaze.

PLATE 96

Vase of baluster form painted in coloured enamels on the biscuit. The design, which is outlined in brown, consists of a beautifully drawn prunus (*mei hua*) tree in blossom and hovering birds, beside a rockery and smaller plants of bamboo, etc., set in a ground of mottled green. Ch'êng Hua mark but K'ang Hsi period (1662–1722)

Height 16¾ inches.

British Museum.

Though the colour scheme of this group is substantially the same as that of the *san ts'ai* glazes, and though the enamels when used in wide areas are not always easily distinguished from the glazes, the former do, in fact, differ in containing more lead, being actually softer and more liable to acquire crackle and iridescence, and in some cases there are appreciable differences in tint. The yellow enamel, for instance, is as a rule paler, and even when of a dark tint it has a muddy tone wanting in the fullness and strength of the yellow glaze; the green enamel varies widely in tone from the glaze, and includes, besides, several fresh shades, among which is a soft apple green of great beauty; and the aubergine is less claret coloured and often of a decidedly pinkish tone.

But perhaps the most distinctive feature of this *san ts'ai* of the muffle kiln is the careful tracing of the design in a brown black pigment on the biscuit. The transparent enamels are washed on over these black outlines, and give appropriate colours without obscuring the design which is already complete in itself.[302] The same brown black pigment[303] is also used over wide areas, laid on thickly and washed with transparent green to form the fine green black which is so highly prized. Like so much of the porcelain with coloured ornament applied to the biscuit this large group has been indiscriminately assigned to the Ming dynasty. The lack of documentary evidence has made it difficult to combat this obvious fallacy, obvious because the form and style of decoration of the finest specimens are purely K'ang Hsi in taste and feeling; but, while fully recognising that the scheme of decoration was not a new one, but had been in use in the Ming porcelains, I would point a warning finger again[304] to the ink slab in the British Museum with its design of aubergine plum blossoms on conventional green waves, its borders of lozenge and hexagon diaper, all enamelled on the biscuit, and in the characteristic style habitually described as Ming in sale catalogues, but actually dated 1692. Another consideration is the quantity of these pieces in the Dresden collection which consists mainly of K'ang Hsi wares, and the presence of several examples (e.g. bamboo vases such as Fig. 2 of Plate 95) in the rooms of the Charlottenburg Palace, which were furnished mainly with presents made by the British East India Company to Queen Sophia Charlotte (1668–1705).

Marks are rare on this group, as a whole, though they occur fairly frequently on the large vases, the commonest being the date mark of the Ch'êng Hua period. No one would, however, seriously argue a fifteenth century date from this mark which is far more common than any other on K'ang Hsi porcelain; and I have actually seen the K'ang Hsi mark on one or two specimens which appeared to be perfectly genuine. Curiously enough the K'ang Hsi mark is more often a sign of a modern imitation, but this in view of the perverse methods of marking Chinese porcelain is in itself evidence that the modern copyist regards the reign of K'ang Hsi as the best period of manufacture for this style of ware.

PLATE 97

Square Vase with pendulous body and high neck slightly expanding towards the top: two handles in the form of archaic lizard-like dragons (*chih lung*), and a pyramidal base. Porcelain painted with coloured enamels on the biscuit, with scenes representing Immortals on a log raft approaching Mount P'êng-lai in the Taoist Paradise. K'ang Hsi period (1662–1722)

Height 20½ inches.

British Museum.

The noblest examples of this group, and perhaps the finest of all Chinese polychromes, are the splendid vases with designs reserved in grounds of green black, yellow or leaf green. Plates 96, 97 and Frontispiece will serve to illustrate the colours and at the same time some of the favourite forms[305] of these sumptuous pieces, the baluster vase, and the square vase with pendulous body, pyramidal base, and two handles usually of archaic dragon form. The favourite design for the decoration of these forms is the flowering prunus tree, beside a rockery with a few bright plumaged birds in the branches, one of the most familiar and at the same time most beautiful of Chinese patterns (see Plate 96). The flowers of the four seasons—peony, lotus, chrysanthemum and prunus—form a beautiful decoration for the four sides of another favourite form, a tall vase of square elevation with sides lightly tapering downwards, rounded shoulders, arid circular neck, slightly flaring at the mouth. The specimens illustrated are in the British Museum, but there is a wonderful series of these lordly vases in the Salting Collection, and in the Pierpont Morgan and Altmann Collections in New York. To-day they are rare, and change hands at enormous prices. Consequently all manner of imitations abound, European and Oriental, the modern Chinese work in this style being often highly successful. But the most insidious copies are the deliberate frauds in which old K'ang Hsi vases are stripped of a relatively cheap form of decoration, the glaze and colour being removed by grinding, and furnished with a cleverly enamelled design in colours on the biscuit. The actual colours are often excellent, and as the ware seen at the base is the genuine K'ang Hsi porcelain even the experienced connoisseur may be deceived at first, though probably his misgivings will be aroused by something in the drawing which betrays the copyist, and a searching examination of the surface will reveal some traces of the sinister treatment to which it has been subjected or the tell-tale marks, such as black specks or burns, left on the foot rim by the process of refiring. There is much truth besides in the saying that things "look their age," and artificial signs of wear imparted by friction and rubbing with sand or grit are not difficult for the experienced eye to detect.

As already noted, the black of the precious black-ground vases, the *famille noire* as they are sometimes called, is formed by overlaying a dull black pigment with washes of transparent green enamel. The result is a rich greenish black, the enamel imparting life and fire to the dull pigment; and as the green is fluxed with lead it tends to become iridescent, giving an additional green *reflet* to the black surface. The modern potters have learnt to impart an iridescence to their enamels, and one often sees a strong lustre on specimens which are clearly "hot from the kiln"; but these enamels have a sticky appearance differing widely from the mellow lustre which partial decay has spread over the K'ang Hsi colours. It will be found, besides, that the shapes of the modern copies are wanting in the grace and feeling of the originals.

This type of porcelain enamelled on the biscuit is particularly well suited to statuettes and ornamental objects of complex form. The details of the biscuit remain sharp and clear, and there is no thick white glaze to soften the projections and fill up the cavities, for the washes of transparent enamel are too slight to obscure the modelling. Consequently we find in this style of ware all the familiar Chinese figures, the Buddhist and Taoist deities, demigods, and sages, which, like our own madonnas and saints, mostly conform to well established conventions, differing mainly in their size, the quality of their finish, the form of their bases or pedestals, and the details of the surface colouring. Of these the figures of Kuan-yin[306] are the most frequent and the most attractive, the compassionate goddess with sweet pensive face, mounted on a lotus pedestal or a rocky throne and sometimes canopied with a cloak which serves as a hood and a covering for her back and shoulders. She has moreover a long flowing robe open at the neck, and displaying a jewelled necklace on her bare bosom. There are, besides, the god of Longevity: the Eight Immortals: Tung-fang So with his stolen peaches: the star-gods of Longevity, Rank, and Happiness: the twin genii of Mirth and Harmony: Kuan-ti, the god of War, on a throne or on horseback: Lao-tzŭ on his ox: the demon-like Kuei Hsing, and the dignified Wên Ch'ang, gods of Literature; and all the throng. There are a few animal forms such as the horse, the ox, the elephant, the mythical *ch'i-lin*, and most common of all the Buddhist lions (sometimes called the dogs of Fo), usually in pairs, one with a cub, and the other playing with a ball of brocade, mounted on an oblong base, to which is attached, in the smaller sizes at any rate, a tube for holding incense sticks. Other familiar objects are four-footed or tripod stands for manuscript rolls, boxes for brushes colours, etc., ink screens, water pots of fanciful shape for the writing table, picture plaques (Plate 100), supper sets made up of a number of small trays which fit together in the form of a lotus flower[307] or a rosette, perforated boxes and hanging vases for fragrant flowers (Fig. 2 of Plate 98), "butterfly cages," and "cricket boxes." Another well-known specimen represents the famous T'ang poet, Li T'ai-po, the Horace of China, reclining in drunken stupor against a half overturned wine jar, the whole serving as a water vessel for the writing table.

Instances of the combination of on-glaze and on-biscuit enamels in the same piece also occur. Thus on the splendid black-ground potiche in the Franks Collection (Frontispiece) passages of white glaze have been inserted to receive the coral red colour which apparently could not be applied to the biscuit. And conversely in the ordinary *famille verte* decoration on the glaze there are sometimes inserted small areas of on-biscuit enamels on borders, handles, base ornaments, etc. Such combinations give an excellent opportunity for observing the contrast between the softer, fuller tints on the biscuit and the brighter, more jewel-like enamels on the white glaze. In rare instances we find passages of blue and white decoration associated with the on-biscuit enamels as on the curious ewer illustrated by Fig. 1 of Plate 94. Blue and white is similarly combined with decoration in coloured glazes on the biscuit in a late Ming jar in the Victoria and Albert Museum (Case 9, No. 4396–57).

Fig. 1   Fig. 2

Fig. 3

Plate 98.—K'ang Hsi Porcelain with on-biscuit decoration.

Dresden Collection.

Fig. 1.—Teapot in form of a lotus seed-pod, enamels on the biscuit. Height 2¾ inches.

Fig. 2.—Hanging Perfume Vase, reticulated, enamels on the biscuit. Height 3½ inches.

Fig. 3.—Ornament in form of a junk, transparent *san ts'ai* glazes. Height 11½ inches.

Fig. 1   Fig. 2   Fig. 3

Plate 99.—K'ang Hsi Porcelain with on-biscuit decoration.

Fig. 1.—Ewer with black enamel ground, lion handle. Height 8¾ inches. *Cope Bequest (V. & A. Museum)*.

Fig. 2.—Figure of the Taoist Immortal, Ho Hsien Ku, transparent *san ts'ai* glazes. Height 10⅛ inches. *S. E. Kennedy Collection*.

Fig. 3.—Vase and Stand, enamelled on the biscuit. Height 8¾ inches. *Cope Bequest*.

Plate 100.—Screen with Porcelain Plaque, painted in enamels on the biscuit.

Light green background. K'ang Hsi period (1662–1722). Total height 22½ inches.

In the Collection of the Hon. E. Evan Charteris.

Plate 101.—Vase with panels of landscapes and *po ku* symbols in *famille verte* enamels

In a ground of underglaze blue trellis pattern. K'ang Hsi period (1662–1722). Height 32 inches. *Dresden Collection.*

Fig. 1

Fig. 2

Plate 102.—Two Dishes of *famille verte* Porcelain in the *Dresden Collection.* K'ang Hsi period (1662–1722).

Fig. 1.—With birds on a flowering branch, brocade borders. Artist's signature in the field. Diameter 16 inches.

Fig. 2.—With ladies on a garden terrace. Diameter 21 inches.

The familiar phrase, *famille verte*, was first used by Jacquemart as a class name for the enamelled porcelains on which green plays a leading part. According to this definition it should include the *Wan li wu ts'ai*, the Ming enamelled porcelain, as well as much of the on-biscuit enamelled wares, in addition to the typical K'ang Hsi enamelled porcelain to which usage has specially consecrated the term. A direct descendant of the *Wan li wu ts'ai*, the *famille verte* includes the combinations of underglaze blue with the translucent on-glaze enamels green, yellow, and aubergine, and the coral red (derived from iron), the French *rouge de fer*, which is so thin that it resembles a pigment rather than a vitreous enamel. Add to these the brown black pigment, which is used to trace the outlines of the design and with a covering of green to form the green black, and we have one type of *famille verte* which differs in no essential from the Wan Li prototype. It is, in fact, no easy matter to find the line which divides the two groups. The nature of the ware and the style of the painting are the best guides; and the study of the K'ang Hsi blue and white will be a great help in this delicate task.

But the real K'ang Hsi *famille verte*, which we might call the *K'ang hsi wu ts'ai*, is distinguished by the addition of an overglaze blue enamel which enhanced the brilliancy of the colour scheme, and at the same time removed the necessity of using underglaze and overglaze colours together.[308] It is not to be supposed, however, that the underglaze blue disappeared entirely from the group. The old types were always dear to the Chinese mind, and there were frequent revivals of these in addition to the special wares,[309] such as the "Chinese Imari," in which this kind of blue was essential. There are indeed examples of both blues on the same pieces.

The history of this overglaze blue enamel has already[310] been partially discussed, and evidence has been given of its tentative use in the Wan Li porcelain. A passage in the second letter of Père d'Entrecolles[311] actually places its invention about the year 1700, but the worthy father's chronology (based no doubt chiefly on hearsay) is often at fault. It is fairly certain, however, that the blue enamel was not used to any extent before the Ch'ing dynasty, owing no doubt to the fact that it had not been satisfactorily made until that date.

A beautiful enamel of violet blue tone, it is an important factor of the *famille verte* decoration, and the merits of a vase or dish are often decided on the purity and brilliance of this colour alone. There is, however, something in the nature of the enamel which seems to affect the surrounding glaze; at any rate, it is often ringed about by a kind of halo of dull lustre, reflecting faint rainbow tints to a distance of perhaps an inch from the edge of the blue. It is as though an exhalation from the blue enamel deposited a thin film of lustre on the glaze, and it is a very frequent occurrence, though not always in the same conspicuous degree. Collectors who are ever looking for a sign have been tempted to hail its presence as a sure proof of antiquity. But it is by no means constant on the old *famille verte*, and it has yet to be proved that the same enamel will not produce a similar effect on the modern glaze.

In view of the appreciation of *famille verte* porcelain at the present day a contemporary criticism will be of interest. D'Entrecolles in his first letter,[312] referring to "porcelain painted with landscapes in a medley of almost all the colours heightened with gilding," says: "They are very beautiful, if one pays a high price, but the ordinary wares of this kind are not to be compared with blue and white." And again,[313] following an exact description of painting with enamel colours on the finished glaze and of the subsequent refiring of the ware, we read: "Sometimes the painting is intentionally reserved for the second firing; at other times they only use the second firing to conceal defects in the porcelain, applying the colours to the faulty places. This porcelain, which is loaded with colour, is not to the taste of a good many people. As a rule one can feel inequalities on the surface of this kind of porcelain, whether due to the clumsiness of the workmen, to the exigencies of light and shade in the painting, or to the desire to conceal defects in the body of the ware."

The tenor of these criticisms will not be endorsed by the modern collector of K'ang Hsi porcelain. *Famille verte* porcelain is enthusiastically sought, and even indifferent specimens command a high price, while the really choice examples can only be purchased by the wealthy. As to the inequalities on the surface, the second of the three reasons hazarded by d'Entrecolles is nearest the truth. The enamels used by the Chinese porcelain painter contain a remarkably small percentage of colouring oxide, and one of the characteristics of *famille verte* colours is their transparency. To obtain full tones and the contrast between light and shade (even to the limited extent to which the Chinese use this convention) it was necessary to pile up the layers of colour at the risk of unduly thickening the enamel. But the connoisseur of to-day finds nothing amiss in these jewel-like incrustations of colour, so long as the enamels are pure and bright, and have not scaled off or suffered too severely from the wear to which their prominent surface is exposed.

It seems[314] that when the porcelain was destined to receive on-glaze enamels (without any underglaze blue) a special glazing mixture was used in which only one part of the softening element[315] was combined with thirteen of the ordinary glazing fluid. This glaze was very white and strong, and too opaque to do justice to an underglaze blue.

There is a reference in the first letter of Père d'Entrecolles to a white colour which was used on the "porcelain painted in various colours." It was fluxed with lead like the other enamel colours, and it was also used mixed with the latter to modify their tint. In fact there can be little doubt that it was arsenical white, an opaque white familiar on the Yung Chêng and Ch'ien Lung porcelains, and prominent in the *famille rose* palette, but not usually suspected of such an early appearance as 1712, the date of the letter in question.

The designs of the *famille verte* porcelain, like those on the blue and white, are first traced in outline and then filled in with washes of colour. The outlines are in a dry dull pigment of red or brown black tint, inconspicuous in itself, but acquiring prominence when covered with transparent enamel. M. Grandidier tried to formulate certain rules for these outlines which, if reliable, would simplify greatly the task of dating the porcelains. On Ming ware, he said, the outlines were blue; on K'ang Hsi wares the face and body outlines were red, those of the vestments and other objects black. Unfortunately the first of these generalisations is wholly wrong, and the second pointless, because only partly right.

Omitting the underglaze blue as foreign to this particular group of *famille verte* under discussion, the colours consist of dark leaf green often of a mottled appearance, a beautiful light apple green, which is characteristic of the K'ang Hsi wares just as the blue green is of the sixteenth century polychrome, an aubergine colour (derived from manganese) which varies from purple brown to rosy purple, a yellow of varying purity and usually of brownish tone, a green black formed of the brown black pigment under washes of transparent green, a blue enamel of violet tone, and the thin iron red. The blue enamel and the red are sometimes omitted, leaving a soft harmony of green, aubergine and yellow in which green plays the chief part. A little gilding is often used to heighten parts of the design.

As for the shapes of the *famille verte* porcelain, they are substantially the same as those of the blue and white and call for no further comment. The designs, too, of the painted decoration are clearly derived from the same sources as those in the blue and white, viz. books of stock patterns, pictures, illustrations of history and romance, and of such other subjects as happened to be specially appropriate or of general interest.

To take a single instance of a pictorial design, the familiar rockery and flowering plants (peony, magnolia, etc.) and a gay-plumaged pheasant lends itself to effective treatment in enamel colours. It is taken from a picture, probably Sung in origin, but there are many repetitions of it in pictorial art, one of which by the Ming painter Wang-yu is in the British Museum collection.[316] The original is said to have been painted by the Emperor Hui Tsung in the beginning of the twelfth century. Another familiar design— quails and millet—is reputed to have been painted by the same Imperial artist.

A good instance of the kind of illustrated book which supplied the porcelain decorator with designs is the *Yü chih kêng chih t'u* (Album of Ploughing and Weaving, compiled by Imperial order), which deals with the cultivation of rice and silk in some forty illustrations. It was first issued in the reign of K'ang Hsi, and there are copies of the original and of several later editions in the British Museum. A specimen of *famille rose* porcelain in the Franks Collection is decorated with a scene from this work, and in the Andrew Burman Collection there are two *famille verte* dishes with designs from the same source. In the Burdett Coutts Collection, again, there is a polygonal bowl with subjects on each side representing the various stages of cotton cultivation, evidently borrowed from an analogous work.

PLATE 103

Club-shaped (*rouleau*) Vase finely painted in *famille verte* enamels with panel
designs in a ground of chrysanthemum scrolls in iron red; brocade borders.
Last part of the K'ang Hsi period (1662–1722)

Height 17 inches.

Salting Collection (Victoria and Albert Museum).

Signatures and seals of the artist usually attached to a stanza of verse, or a
few phrases which allude to the subject, are often found in the field of the
pictorial designs. Fig. 1 of Plate 102, for instance, belongs to a series of
beautiful dishes in the Dresden collection, which display the same seal—
apparently[317] *wan shih chü* (myriad rocks retreat), the studio name not, I think,
of the porcelain painter but of the artist whose picture was copied on the
porcelain. There are numerous examples of similar seals in the field of the
design, and we shall return to the subject later in a place where important
issues turn on the solution of the problem which it raises.[318]

The types of *famille verte* porcelain are extremely numerous, almost as varied
as those of the blue and white (p. 136). Like the latter they include much that
was obviously made for European consumption, and most of the groups

which were singled out from the mass of blue and white for special description can be paralleled in the *famille verte*. The thin, crisp, moulded ware with petal-shaped panels and lobed borders, the group with the "G" mark, and many other types are found with the same peculiarities of paste and glaze, and even the same design painted in on-glaze enamels. As in the case of the blue and white, the quality of this export ware varies widely, and the individual specimens will be judged by the drawing of the designs and the purity and fire of the enamels.

A few of the more striking types are illustrated on Plates 103 and 104. Perhaps the most sumptuous effects of this colour scheme are displayed in the vases decorated with panel designs surrounded by rich diapers borrowed from silk brocades. A favourite brocade pattern consists of single blossoms or floral sprays woven into a ground of transparent green covering a powder of small brown dots. This dotted green ground is commonly known as "frog's spawn," and another diaper of small circles under a similar green enamel is easily recognised under the name of "fish roe." But the variety of these ground patterns is great, and in spite of their prosaic nomenclature they render in a singularly effective manner the soft splendour of the Chinese brocades.

In dating the *famille verte* porcelains the collector will find his study of the blue and white of great assistance. There is, for instance, the well-known type of export ware—sets of vases with complex moulding, and dishes and plates, etc., with petal-shaped lobes on the sides or borders. The central design of the decoration commonly consists of *ch'i lin*, and phœnix, sea monsters (*hai shou*), storks or ducks beside a flowering tree or some such familiar pattern; and the surrounding petal-shaped panels are filled each with a growing flower, or a vignette of bird and plant, plant and insect, or even a small landscape. These bright but often perfunctorily painted wares are paralleled in the early K'ang Hsi blue and white. They are among the first Chinese polychrome porcelains to be copied by the European potters. See Plate 107.

In the purely native wares the early Ch'ing *famille verte* is distinguished by strong and rather emphatic colouring, the energy of the drawing and the breadth of design which recall the late Ming polychromes. The zenith of this style of decoration was reached about 1700, say between 1682 and 1710. This is the period of the magnificent vases with panel designs in brocaded grounds, or with crowded figure subjects, Court scenes, and the like, filling large areas of the surface, such vases as may be seen in the splendid series of the Salting Collection or in the Grandidier Collection in the Louvre. They are probably children of the great renaissance which began under the auspices of Ts'ang Ying-hsüan. Dated examples are extremely rare, and consequently the square vase on Plate 104 assumes unusual importance on account of the cyclical date which occurs in the long inscription, "the 29th day of the 9th moon of the *kuei mo* year," which we can hardly doubt is 1703. Incidentally another side of this vase illustrates the celebrated scene of the wine cups started from the "orchid arbour to float down the nine-bend river."[319]

Another example with a cyclical date (the year *hsin mao*, and no doubt 1711) is a globular water bottle "of the highest quality and technique, decorated with transparent luminous enamels of great beauty and delicacy," in the Pierpont Morgan Collection.[320] But in this case the date is attached to a verse in the field of the decoration, and it may belong to the design rather than to the porcelain.

Plate 104.—Three Examples of K'ang Hsi *famille verte* Porcelain.

Fig. 1.—Square Vase with scene of floating cups on the river; inscription with cyclical date 1703 A.D.; *shou* characters on the neck. Height 18⅜ inches. *Hippisley Collection.*

Fig. 2.—Lantern with river scenes. Height 13¾ inches. *Dresden Collection.*

Fig. 3.—Covered Jar of *rouleau* shape, peony scrolls in iron red ground, brocade borders. Height 22 inches. *Dresden Collection.*

Plate 105.—Covered Jar painted in *famille verte* enamels

With brocade ground and panel with an elephant (the symbol of Great Peace). Lion on cover. K'ang Hsi period (1662–1722). Height 21¼ inches. *Dresden Collection.*

Plate 106.—K'ang Hsi *famille verte* Porcelain. *Alexander Collection.*

Fig. 1.—Dish with rockery, peonies, etc., birds and insects. Diameter 16¼ inches.

Fig. 2.—"Stem Cup" with vine pattern. Height 5¾ inches.

Plate 107.—*Famille verte* Porcelain made for export to Europe. K'ang Hsi period (1662–1722). *British Museum.*

Fig. 1.—Vase with "sea monster" (*hai shou*).

Fig. 2.—Dish with basket of flowers. Mark, a leaf. Diameter 11 inches.

Fig. 3.—Covered Jar with *ch'i-lin* and *fêng-huang* (phœnix).

The lateness of this latter date and the use of the word "delicacy" in the description of the piece lead us naturally to that peculiarly refined type of late *famille verte* in which the ware is of eggshell thinness, the painting extremely dainty and delicate, and the colours rather pale but of perfect purity. Such are the well-known "birthday plates" with the reign mark of K'ang Hsi on the back and the birthday salutation in seal characters on the border: *wan shou wu chiang*—"a myriad longevities without ending!" They are reputed to have been made for the Emperor's sixtieth birthday which fell in the year 1713, but the story is supported by no evidence of any kind, and they would have been equally appropriate for any Imperial birthday. The character of these wares is more suggestive of the Yung Chêng period, and it is probable that they belong to the extreme limit of the long reign of K'ang Hsi. To this period then we shall assign these and the whole group of kindred porcelains, the plates with designs similar to those of the "birthday plates," but without the inscribed border, the small eggshell plates with one or two figures painted in the same delicate style, others with a single spray of some flowering shrub almost Japanese in its daintiness, and occasional bowls and vases with decoration of the same character. See Plate 113.

For extreme delicacy of treatment is by no means a feature of the K'ang Hsi *famille verte* in general, in which the Ming spirit with its boldness and vigour still breathed. It is rather a late development in the decadence of the ware, heralding the more effeminate beauty of the *famille rose*, and were it not for the evidence of the birthday plates I believe many connoisseurs would be tempted to ascribe these delicate porcelains to a much later reign.

Such, however, is the evolution of the *famille verte* during the sixty years of the K'ang Hsi period, from the strong colours and forceful Ming-like designs of the earlier specimens to the mature perfection of the splendid wares made about 1700, and thence by a process of ultra-refinement to the later types in which breadth of treatment gives place to prettiness and the strong thick enamels to thinner washes of clear, delicate tints. These thin transparent colours continued in use; indeed, they are a feature of a special type of enamelling which will be discussed with the Yung Chêng wares; but the pure *famille verte* may be said to have come to an end with the last years of the reign of K'ang Hsi. Later reproductions of course exist, for no style of decoration is ever wholly extinct in Chinese art, but they are merely revivals of an old style, which even before the end of the K'ang Hsi period had reached the stage of transition to another family. The opaque enamels of the *famille rose* palette had already begun to assert themselves. Timid intruders at first—a touch of opaque pink, a little opaque yellow and arsenical white breaking in upon the old harmony of transparent tints—they gradually thrust the *famille verte* enamels into a subsidiary position, and in the succeeding reigns rose pinks entirely dominate the field.

A word must be said of the use of the *famille verte* painting in combination with other types of decoration, in the subordinate position of border patterns or more prominently in panel designs. Exquisite effects are obtained by the latter in a ground of coral red, or where a brilliant powder blue field is broken by shapely panels with flowering plants and birds and other familiar vehicles for *famille verte* colouring. Occasionally we find the enamels actually painted over a powder blue or an ordinary blue glaze, but the combination is more peculiar than attractive; for the underlying colour kills the transparent enamels, and the enamels destroy the lustre of the blue ground. Indeed, it is probable that in many cases these freak decorations were intended to hide a faulty background.

A similar painting over the crackled green *lang yao* glaze has already been described, and it occurs over the grey white crackles, and rarely but with much distinction, over a pale celadon glaze. But perhaps the most effective combination of this kind is that in which a pale lustrous brown or Nanking yellow is the ground colour. The quiet and refined effects of this union are well exhibited by a small group of vases, bowls, and dishes in the Salting Collection.

Something has already been said of the use of underglaze blue in combination with *famille verte* enamels. The blue is either an integral part of the general design as in the Wan Li "five colour" scheme, or it forms a distinct decoration by itself, apart from the enamels, though sharing the same surface. The latter use is exemplified by a pair of bottles in the Salting Collection which have blue patterns on the neck and *famille verte* decoration on the body, consisting of landscape panels surrounded by brocade patterns.[321] But the great drawback to this union of underglaze and overglaze colours is usually apparent. The blue was liable to suffer in the subsequent firings necessitated by the enamels, even though those firings took place at a relatively low temperature. Probably the potter would not expose his finest blue to such risks, but at any rate the blue of this mixed decoration is rarely of first-rate quality.

PLATE 108

Dish painted in underglaze blue and *famille verte* enamels. In the centre, a five-clawed dragon rising from waves in pursuit of a pearl. Deep border in "Imari" style with cloud-shaped compartments with chrysanthemum and prunus designs in a blue ground, separated by close lotus scrolls reserved in an iron red ground in which are three book symbols. K'ang Hsi period (1662–1722)

Diameter 19½ inches.

There is one group of porcelain which combines the underglaze blue with on-glaze enamels, and which deserves special notice if only because it has been recently favoured with particular attention by collectors. This is what we are pleased to call "Chinese Imari." Our ceramic nomenclature has never been noted for its accuracy, and like good conservatives we hold firmly to the old names which have been handed down from days when geography was not studied, and from ancestors who were satisfied with old Indian china, or Gombroon ware, as names for Chinese porcelain. So Meissen porcelain is still Dresden, the blue and white of Ching-tê Chên is Old Nanking, Chinese export porcelain painted at Canton with pink roses is Lowestoft, and the ware made at Arita, province of Hizen, in Japan, is Imari, because that is the name of the seaport from which it was shipped. In fact, there are many shops where you cannot make yourself understood in these matters unless you call the wares by the wrong name.

The Arita porcelain in question, this so-called Imari, was made from the middle of the seventeenth century onwards, and it must have competed seriously with the export wares of Ching-tê Chên. At any rate, it was brought to Europe in large consignments by the Dutch traders, who enjoyed the privilege of a trading station on the island of Deshima, after the less politic Portuguese had been driven out of Nagasaki in 1632. For the moment we are specially concerned with two types of Arita ware. The first is distinguished by slight but artistic decoration in vivid enamels of the *famille verte*, supplemented by gilding and occasionally by underglaze blue. Favourite designs are a banded hedge, prunus tree, a Chinese boy and a tiger or phœnix; two quails in millet beside a flowering prunus; simple flowering sprays or branches coiled in circular medallions; or only a few scattered blossoms. Whatever the nature of the design, it was artistically displayed, and in such a manner as to enhance without concealing the fine white porcelain. This is what the old catalogues call the *première qualité coloriée de Japon*, and a very popular ware it was in eighteenth century Europe, when it was closely copied on the early productions of the St. Cloud, Chantilly, Meissen, Chelsea, and other porcelain factories. To-day it is commonly known as Kakiemon ware, because its very distinctive style of decoration is traditionally supposed to have been started by a potter named Kakiemon, who, with another man of Arita, learned the secret of enamelling on porcelain from a Chinese merchant about the year 1646.

The second type was made entirely for the European trade, and it is distinguished by large masses of dark, cloudy blue set off by a soft Indian red (derived from oxide of iron) and gilding. These colours are supplemented by touches of green, yellow, and aubergine enamels, and occasionally by a brownish black. The ware itself is heavy, coarse and greyish, but its rough aspect is well concealed by irregular and confused designs of asymmetrical panels surrounded by mixed brocade patterns. The panels often contain Chinese figures, phœnixes, lions, floral designs of chrysanthemums, peony and prunus, a basket of flowers, rough landscapes or garden views. They are medleys of half-Chinese, half-Japanese motives, a riot of incoherent patterns, but not without broad decorative effect thanks to the bold masses of red, blue and gold. Such is the typical "Old Imari." There is, however, a finer and more Japanese variety of the same group which is distinguished by free use of the chrysanthemum rosette, and the Imperial kiri (paulonia imperialis), and by panels of diaper pattern and floral designs alternating and counter-changed in colour, the grounds now red, now blue, and now gold. The same colour scheme prevailed in this sub-group, and the dark blue was usually netted over with gold designs.

It was no doubt the success which these wares met in European commerce that induced the Chinese to take a lesson from their pupils, and to adopt the "Imari" style. At any rate, they did copy all these types, sometimes very closely, sometimes only in part. Thus in some cases the actual Japanese patterns as well as the colour scheme are carefully reproduced, in others the Japanese colour scheme is employed on Chinese patterns or vice versa, and, again, there are cases in which passages of Japanese ornament are inserted in purely Chinese surroundings. But whether pure or diluted the Japanese style is unmistakable to those who have once learnt to know its peculiarities, of which masses of blue covered with gilt patterns and the prominence of red and gold are the most conspicuous.

There will, of course, always be a few specimens the nationality of which will be difficult to decide, but to anyone familiar with Chinese and Japanese porcelain the distinction between the Chinese "Imari" and its island prototype is, as a rule, a simple matter. The Chinese porcelain is thinner and crisper, its glaze has the smooth oily sheen and faintly greenish tint which are peculiar to Chinese wares, and the raw edge of the base rim is slightly browned. The Japanese porcelain, on the other hand, is whiter in the Kakiemon ware, greyer and coarser in the "Old Imari," and the glaze in both cases has the peculiar bubbled and "muslin-like" texture which is a Japanese characteristic. The Japanese underglaze blue is dark and muddy in tone, the Chinese bright, and purer, and the other colours differ, though not perhaps so emphatically. The iron red of the Chinese, for instance, is thinner and usually lighter in tone than the soft Indian red or thick sealing-wax colour of the Japanese; and to those who are deeply versed in Oriental art there is always the more subtle and less definable distinction, the difference between the Chinese and Japanese touch and feeling.

Plate 108 is a fine specimen which shows the blend of Chinese motives and the Japanese colouring.

The general character of the Chinese "Imari" is that of the K'ang Hsi period, to which most of the existing specimens will be assigned; but it is clear that the Chinese continued to use Japanese models in the succeeding reign, for the last three items in the Imperial list of porcelain made in the Yung Chêng period comprise wares "decorated in gold and in silver in the style of the Japanese."[322]

CHAPTER XI

K'ANG HSI MONOCHROMES

In passing to the K'ang Hsi monochromes we enter a large field with boundaries ill defined. Many of the colours are legacies from the Ming potters, and most of them were handed on to after generations; some indeed have enjoyed an unbroken descent to the present day. Consequently there are few things more difficult in the study of Chinese porcelain than the dating of single-colour wares.

In some cases the origin of a particular glaze has been recorded, and within certain limits the style of the piece will guide us in assessing its age; but how often must we be content with some such non-committal phrase as "early eighteenth century," which embraces the late K'ang Hsi, the Yung Chêng and the early Ch'ien Lung periods? On the other hand, the careful student observes certain points of style and finish, certain slight peculiarities of form which are distinctive of the different periods, and on these indefinite signs he is able to classify the doubtful specimens. To the inexpert his methods may seem arbitrary and mysterious, but his principles, though not easy to enunciate, are sound nevertheless.

Plate 109.—Figure of Shou Lao, Taoist God of Longevity.

Porcelain painted with *famille verte* enamels. K'ang Hsi period (1662–1722). Height 17¼ inches. *Salting Collection* (*V. & A. Museum*).

We have already had occasion to discuss a few of the K'ang Hsi monochromes in dealing with the question of *lang yao*. But besides the *sang de bœuf* there is another rare and costly red to which the Americans have given the expressive name of "peach bloom." Since their first acquaintance with this colour in the last half of the nineteenth century,[323] American collectors have been enamoured of it, and as they have never hesitated to pay vast sums for good specimens, most of the fine "peach blooms" have found their way to the United States, and choice examples are rare in England. "The prevailing shade," to quote from Bushell's description, "is a pale red, becoming pink in some parts, in others mottled with russet spots, displayed upon a background of light green celadon tint. The last colour occasionally comes out more prominently, and deepens into clouds of bright apple green tint." The Chinese, in comparing the colour, have thought of the apple rather than the peach; it is *p'in-kuo hung* (apple red), and the markings on it are *p'in-kuo ch'ing* (apple green), and *mei kuei tzŭ* (rose crimson). Another Chinese name for the colour is *chiang-tou hung* (bean red), in allusion to the small Chinese kidney-bean with its variegated pink colour and brown spots.

It is generally supposed that, like the *sang de bœuf*, the "peach bloom" owes its hue to copper oxide, and that all the accessory tints, the russet brown and apple green, are due to happy accidents befalling the same colouring medium in the changeful atmosphere of the kiln.[324] This precious glaze is usually found on small objects such as water pots and brush washers for the writing table (see Plate 111[325]), and snuff bottles, and a few small elegantly formed flower vases of bottle shape, with high shoulders and slender neck, the body sometimes moulded in chrysanthemum petal design, or, again, on vases of slender, graceful, ovoid form, with bodies tapering downwards, and the mouth rim slightly flaring. In every case the bottom of the vessel shows a fine white-glazed porcelain with unctuous paste, and the K'ang Hsi mark in six blue characters written in a delicate but very mannered calligraphy, which seems to be peculiar to this type of ware, and to a few choice *clair de lune* and celadon vases of similar form and make.

The colour in the peach bloom glaze, as in the *sang de bœuf*, is sometimes fired out and fades into white or leaves a pale olive green surface with only a few spots of brown or pink to bear witness to the original intention of the potter. The glaze is sometimes crackled and occasionally it runs down in a thick crystalline mass at the base of the vessel.

Needless to say this costly porcelain has claimed the earnest attention of the modern imitator. The first real success was achieved by a Japanese potter at the end of the last century. He was able to make admirable copies of the colour, but failed to reproduce adequately the paste and glaze of the originals. I am told that he was persuaded to transfer his secret to China, and with the Chinese body his imitations were completely successful. The latter part of the story is based on hearsay, and is given as such; but it is certain that there are exceedingly clever modern copies of the old peach blooms in the market; otherwise how could an inexpert collector in China bring home half a dozen peach blooms bought at bargain prices?

The copper red used in painting underglaze designs[326] will sometimes develop a peach bloom colour, and there is a vase in the British Museum with parti-coloured glaze in large patches of blue, celadon, and a copper red which has broken into the characteristic tints of the peach bloom vases.

Another red of copper origin allied to the *sang de bœuf* and the peach bloom, and at times verging on both, is the maroon red, which ranges from crimson to a deep liver colour. There are wine cups of this colour whose glaze clouded with deep crimson recalls the "dawn red" of the wine cups made by Hao Shih-chiu.[327] Sometimes the red covers part only of the surface, shading off into the white glaze. The finer specimens have either a crimson or a pinkish tinge, but far more often the glaze has issued from the kiln with a dull liver tint.

Naturally the value of the specimens varies widely with the beauty of the colour. The pinker shades approach within measurable distance of the pink of the peach bloom, and they are often classed with the latter by their proud owners; but the colour is usually uniform, and lacks the bursts of russet brown and green which variegate the true peach bloom, and the basis of the maroon is a pure white glaze without the celadon tints which seem to underlie the peach bloom. It may be added that the maroon red glaze is usually uncrackled.

As to the overglaze red, which is known by the names of *mo hung* (painted red) and *ts'ai hung* (enamel red), it is the colour derived from iron, and it was used both as one of the enamels of the *famille verte* palette and as a monochrome. In both capacities it figured on Ming porcelain, and was fully discussed in that connection. On K'ang Hsi wares it varied in tone from dark brick red to a light orange, according to the density of the pigment, and in texture from a thin dry film to a lustrous enamel, according to the quantity of fluxing material[328] combined with it. Among the richly fluxed varieties is a fine tomato colour of light, translucent tone. Sometimes the iron red is found as sole medium for painted designs, as on a rouleau vase in the Salting collection, but more commonly it serves as a ground colour between panels of enamelled ornament (Plate 103), or in border passages. In these last two positions it is usually of a light orange shade, and broken by floral scrolls reserved in white. A dark shade of the same pigment is also used in diapers of curled scrolls, forming a groundwork for enamelled decoration. There are besides beautiful examples of a pure red monochrome formed of this colour, but I have only met with these among the later wares.

The blue monochromes include a large number of glazes varying in depth and shade with the quality and quantity of the cobalt which is mingled with the glazing material. These are *chiao ch'ing* (blue monochrome glazes), and they are all high-fired colours. They include the *chi ch'ing*[329] or deep sky blue, whose darker shades are also named *ta ch'ing* (*gros bleu*), the slaty blue, the pale clear blue,[330] the dark and light lavender shades, and the faintly tinted *clair de lune* or "moon white" (*yüeh pai*), in which the amount of cobalt used must have been infinitesimal. But it would be useless to attempt to catalogue the innumerable shades of blue, which must have varied with every fresh mixture of colour and glaze and every fresh firing.

There is, however, another group materially different from the ordinary blue glazes. In this the colour was applied direct to the body, as in blue and white painting, and a colourless glaze subsequently added, with the natural result that the blue seems to be incorporated with the body of the ware rather than with the glaze. There were several ways of applying the colour, each producing a slightly different effect. The cobalt powder could be mixed with water, and washed on smoothly with a brush, or dabbed on with a sponge to give a marbled appearance, or it could be projected on to the moistened surface in a dry powder, through gauze stretched across the end of a bamboo tube.

The result of the last process was an infinity of minute specks of blue, a massing of innumerable points of colour. This is the well-known "powder blue," the *bleu soufflé*, or blown blue described by Père d'Entrecolles in his second letter[331]: "As for the *soufflé* blue called *tsoui tsim* (*ch'ui ch'ing*), the finest blue, prepared in the manner which I have described, is used. This is blown on to the vase, and when it is dry the ordinary glaze is applied either alone or mixed with *tsoui yeou* (*sui yu*), if crackle[332] is required." We are further told that as on the blue and white a glaze softened with a considerable proportion of lime was necessary for the perfection of the colour.

The "powder blue" seems to have been a new invention in the K'ang Hsi period. Under the name of *ch'ui ch'ing* (blown blue) it figures in the *T'ao lu*[333] among the triumphs of Ts'ang Ying-hsüan's directorate. It is certainly a singularly beautiful colour effect, and worthy of the homage it has received from collectors and ceramic historians. Though the blue used was as a rule of the finest quality, it varied much in intensity and tone with the nature of the cobalt and amount applied. Probably the majority of collectors would give the palm to the darker shades, but tastes differ, and the lighter tones when the blue is pure sapphire have found whole-hearted admirers. A notable feature of the powder blue is its surprising brilliancy in artificial light, when most other porcelain colours suffer eclipse.

Fig. 1   Fig. 2

PLATE 110

Two examples of "Powder Blue" (*ch'ui ch'ing*) Porcelain of the K'ang Hsi period (1662–1722), in the Victoria and Albert Museum

Fig. 1.—Bottle of gourd shape with slender neck: powder blue ground with gilt designs from the Hundred Antiques (*po ku*) and borders of *ju-i* pattern, formal flowers and plantain leaves. Height 7½ inches.

Fig. 2.—Bottle-shaped Vase with *famille verte* panels of rockwork and flowers reserved in a powder blue ground. Height 7 inches. *Salting Collection.*

It was used indifferently as a simple monochrome or as a ground in which panel decoration was reserved, the panels painted in *famille verte* enamels or in blue and white; and in both cases the blue surface was usually embellished with light traceries in gold. Plate 110 illustrates both types. Both are highly prized by collectors, and change hands at high prices when of the good quality which is usual on the K'ang Hsi specimens. We have already noted[334] the occasional decoration of the powder blue ground with designs in *famille verte* enamels, and Père d'Entrecolles[335] records another process of ornamentation which was applied to all the blue grounds of this group, viz. the washed, the sponged, and the powder blues: "There are workmen who trace designs with the point of a long needle on this blue whether *soufflé* or otherwise; the needle removes as many little specks of dry blue as are necessary to form the design; then the glaze is put on." From this precise description it is easy to recognise this simple but effective decoration. There are two examples in the British Museum with dragon designs etched in this fashion, the one in a washed blue, and the other in a sponged blue ground. The pattern appears in white outline where the blue has been removed by the needle and the porcelain body exposed.

Long usage has given sanction to the term "mazarine blue." It was applied to the dark blue ground colour of eighteenth century English porcelain, and in the contemporary catalogues the name "mazareen" was given to any kind of deep blue from the mottled violet of Chelsea to the powdery *gros bleu* of Worcester. In reference to Chinese porcelain it is used to-day with similar freedom for the *ta ch'ing* or dark sky blue and for the powder blue. Assuming that the phrase derives from the famous Cardinal Mazarin, it cannot in its original sense have had any reference to powder blue, for the Cardinal died in 1661, and, if he had a weakness for blue monochrome, it must have been for some variety of the *chiao ch'ing* or blue glazes proper which were current at the end of the Ming and the beginning of the Ch'ing dynasties. At the present day it is impossible to guess the true shade of mazarine blue, and we must be content to regard it as a phrase connoting a deep blue monochrome the exact definition of which has gone beyond recall.[336]

The K'ang Hsi mark is sometimes found on porcelain coated with a very dark purplish blue glaze with soft looking surface and minute crackle. It is apparently one of those glazes which are fired in the temperate parts of the kiln, and its use is more frequent on porcelains of a slightly later period.

Finally, the turquoise blue, variously named *fei ts'ui* (kingfisher blue) and *k'ung ch'iao lü* (peacock green), was freely used as a monochrome on figures and ornamental wares. It is a colour which descends from Ming times, and whose use has continued unchecked to the present day, so that it is often extremely difficult to give a precise date to any particular specimen, especially if the object happens to be of archaic form, a copy of an old bronze or the like. Its nature has already been discussed[337] among the Ming glazes, and one can only say that the K'ang Hsi pieces have all the virtues of the K'ang Hsi manufacture—fine material, good potting, shapely form, and beautiful quality of colour. The tint varies widely from the soft turquoise blue of kingfisher feathers to a deep turquoise green, and some of the most attractive specimens are mottled or spotted with patches of greenish black. The glaze is always minutely crackled, and has sufficient transparency to allow engraved or carved designs on the body to be visible. It is a colour which develops well on an earthen body, and the potters often mixed coarse clay with the ware which was intended to receive the turquoise glaze; but this, I think, was mainly practised after the K'ang Hsi period, and the K'ang Hsi specimens will, as a rule, be found to have a pure white porcelain basis.

As in the Ming wares, the turquoise sometimes shares the field with an aubergine purple of violet tone, both colours being of the *demi-grand feu*. The purple is also used as a monochrome. There are, in fact, two aubergine purple monochromes, the one a thick and relatively opaque colour sometimes full of minute points as though it had been blown on like the powder blue, the other a thin transparent (and often iridescent) glaze of browner tone. Both are derived from cobaltiferous ore of manganese, both have descended from the Ming period, and have already been discussed as monochromes and as colours applied to the biscuit.

Fig. 1

Fig. 2

PLATE 111

Two examples of Single-colour Porcelain in the Salting Collection (Victoria and Albert Museum)

Fig. 1.—Bottle-shaped Vase of Porcelain with landscape design lightly engraved in relief under a turquoise blue glaze. Early eighteenth century. Height 8½ inches.

Fig. 2.—Water Vessel for the Writing Table of the form known as *T'ai-po tsun* after the poet Li T'ai-po. Porcelain with faintly engraved dragon medallions under a peach bloom glaze; the neck cut down and fitted with a metal collar. Mark in blue of the K'ang Hsi period (1662–1722) in six characters. Height 2¾ inches.

The cobaltiferous ore of manganese is the same material which is used to give a blue colour, but in this case the manganese is removed, and the cobalt rendered as pure as possible. For the manganese if in excess produces a purplish brown, and its presence in however small a quantity gives the blue a purple or violet strain. By the simple method of graduating the amount of manganese which was allowed to remain with the cobalt the potters were able to obtain many intermediate shades between dark blue and purple for their monochrome glazes.

The green monochromes are scarcely less numerous than the blue. There are the transparent greens of apple or leaf green shades whether even or mottled, which have been described among the glazes applied to the biscuit and among the enamels of the *famille verte*. These were used as monochromes and ground colours; and closely akin to them are (1) the cucumber green (*kua p'i lü*), in which a yellowish leaf green is heavily mottled with darker tints, and (2) the snake skin green (*shê p'i lü*), a deep transparent green with iridescent surface, one of the colours for which the directorate of Ts'ang Ying-hsüan was celebrated. There are good examples of both in the Salting Collection, but it would be useless to reproduce them except in colour.

There are the apple and emerald green crackles (in both cases a green glaze overlying a grey or stone-coloured crackle), but these have already been discussed.[338] A somewhat similar technique characterises the series of semi-opaque and crackled green glazes of camelia leaf, myrtle, spinach, light and dark sage, dull emerald and several intermediate tints. These are soft-looking glazes with small but very regular crackle,[339] and their surface often has a "satiny" sheen which recalls the Yi-hsing glazes. They are evidently glazes of the *demi-grand feu*, and the colouring agent is doubtless copper, though apparently modified with other ingredients. How far this particular group was used in the K'ang Hsi period is hard to say. Most of the specimens which I have seen give me the impression of a later make, but as there are a few which might come within the K'ang Hsi limits I have taken this opportunity to discuss them.

There is one specimen of a rare green in the British Museum to which I cannot recall a parallel. It is a bowl with the ordinary white glaze, but covered on the exterior with a very bright yellowish green, like the young grass with the sun shining on it. It is, perhaps, rather in the nature of an enamel than a glaze, but the ware has the appearance of age and should belong to the early part of the K'ang Hsi period.

Most of the green glazes are low fired, melting in the temperature of the *demi-grand feu* and the muffle kiln. The high-fired greens are those of celadon class. There is the *lang yao*[340] green, which has been discussed under that heading, a crackled glaze, in colour intermediate between apple green and the sea green celadon, and with a surface texture hazy with bubbles like the *sang de bœuf*, to which it is a near relation. This soft and beautiful colour has been described as a "copper celadon," and though Dr. Bushell refuses his blessing on the name it seems to me a particularly happy expression. For the colour apparently results from the same copper medium which under slightly different firing conditions produces the *sang de bœuf* red and at the same time its tint approaches very nearly to the typical celadon green.

The true celadon glaze was freely employed on the early Ch'ing porcelains, especially on those of K'ang Hsi and Yung Chêng periods. It is a beautiful pale olive or sea green colour, made light by the pure white porcelain beneath which its transparent nature permits to shine through. Compared with the Sung celadons as we know them,[341] the Ch'ing dynasty ware is thinner in material and glaze, wanting in the peculiar solidity of appearance of the ancient wares; the body is whiter and finer, and the base is usually white with the ordinary porcelain glaze. There is, moreover, no "brown mouth and iron foot," unless indeed this feature has been deliberately added by means of a dressing of ferruginous clay, a make-up which is too obvious to deceive the initiated. There were, however, some careful imitations of the ancient celadons made at this time and got up with the appearance of antiquity, but these were exceptional productions.[342]

Père d'Entrecolles, writing in 1722, alludes to the K'ang Hsi celadon in the following terms[343]:—"I was shown this year for the first time a kind of porcelain which is now in fashion; its colour verges on olive and they call it *long tsiven*. I saw some which was called *tsim ko (ch'ing kuo)*, the name of a fruit which closely resembles the olive." The *long tsiven* is clearly a transliteration of the characters which we write *Lung-ch'üan*, the generic name of the old celadons; but it is odd that Père d'Entrecolles should not have seen copies of this glaze before 1722, for its use must have been continuous at Ching-tê Chên from very early times, and we have found reference to it in various periods of the Ming dynasty. It is evident, however, that the colour was enjoying a fresh burst of popularity just at this time. D'Entrecolles gives a few further notes which concern its composition. His recipe is substantially the same as that given in Chinese works, viz. a mixture of ferruginous earth, which would contribute a percentage of iron oxide, with the ordinary glaze.[344] He also states that *sui yu* (crackle glaze) was added if a crackled surface was required, and there are numerous examples of this kind of ware to be seen. The most familiar are the vases with crackled celadon or grey green glaze interrupted by bands of biscuit carved with formal patterns and stained to an iron colour with a dressing of ferruginous earth. Monster heads with rings (loose or otherwise) serve as twin handles on these vases, which are designed after bronze models. These crackled celadons are evidently fashioned after an old model, but they have been largely imitated in modern times, and almost every pawnbroker's window displays a set of execrable copies (often further decorated in underglaze blue) which are invariably furnished with the Ch'êng Hua mark incised on a square brown panel under the base.

The yellow monochromes of the K'ang Hsi period are mostly descendants of the Ming yellows. There is the pale yellow applied over a white glaze reproducing the yellow of "husked chestnuts," for which the Hung Chih (q.v.) porcelains were celebrated; and there is a fuller yellow, usually of browner shade, applied direct to the biscuit. Yellow is one of the Imperial colours, the usual tint being a full deep colour like the yolk of a hen's egg, and the Imperial wares are commonly distinguished by five-clawed dragons engraved under the glaze. Other glazes[345] used on the services made for the Emperor are the purplish brown (aubergine) and the bright green of camelia leaf tint, which with the yellow make up the *san ts'ai* or three colours. In fact the precise shades of these colours are those used on finer types of three-colour porcelain[346] with transparent glazes fired in the temperate part of the great kiln. All these glazes tend to become iridescent with age.

The colouring medium of the pale yellow is antimony combined with a proportion of lead, and iron oxide is added to give the glaze an orange or brown tinge.[347] It is noticeable that the yellow applied to the biscuit is usually browner in tone. This is the nature, if we may judge from the excellent coloured illustrations in the Walters catalogue,[348] of the eel yellow (*shan yü huang*), a brownish colour of clouded smoky appearance, and one of the few glazes named in the *T'ao lu* as a speciality of the directorate of Ts'ang Ying-hsüan. The other yellow associated with the name of Ts'ang is the "spotted yellow" (*huang pan t'ien*), discussed on p. 127. Its identification is uncertain, and Brinkley describes it as "stoneware with a dark olive green glaze with yellow speckles," while Bushell (*O. C. A.*, p. 317) regards it as a "tiger skin" glaze with large patches of yellow and green enamel, the same as the *huang lü tien* (yellow and green spotted), which he quotes from another context.

All these varieties belong to the *couleurs de demi-grand feu*; but there are besides several varieties of yellow enamels fired in the muffle kiln. Of these the transparent yellow was used as a ground colour in the K'ang Hsi period, but the opaque varieties, such as the lemon yellow, etc., belong rather to a later period. Among the latter I should include the crackled mustard yellow, though examples of it have often been assigned to the K'ang Hsi and even earlier reigns. There is, for instance, a bottle-shaped vase with two elephant handles in the Victoria and Albert Museum, which Bushell[349] regarded as a specimen of the old *mi-sê* ("millet colour") glaze of the Sung dynasty. A careful examination shows that this crackled brownish yellow is made in much the same fashion as the apple green and the sage green crackles, viz. a yellow glaze or enamel overlying a stone-coloured crackle. This is not a Sung technique, but rather an imitative method belonging perhaps to the Yung Chêng period, when old glazes and archaic shapes were reproduced with wonderful skill and truth.

There is a solitary specimen of a high-fired glaze of pale buff yellow colour in the British Museum, which perhaps should be ranked with the yellow monochromes, though its appearance suggests an exceptional effect of the pale *tzŭ chin* or "Nanking yellow" glaze. And a rare vase in the Peters Collection has a minutely crackled brownish yellow glaze clouded with dark olive in bold markings like those of tortoiseshell.

Another Ming monochrome freely used in the K'ang Hsi period is the lustrous brown (*tzŭ chin*), formed like the celadon by mixing ferruginous earth called *tzŭ chin shih* with the ordinary glaze. Presumably the quantity of this material was greater in the brown glaze than in the celadon. Père d'Entrecolles describes this glaze in its diverse shades of bronze, coffee and dead-leaf brown, but he makes the curious error of proclaiming it a new invention in 1722.[350] He also refers to its use on the exterior of white cups and as a ground colour in which white panels were reserved. "On a cup or vase," he tells us, "which one wished to glaze with brown, a round or square of damped paper was applied in one or two places; after the glaze had been laid on, the paper was peeled off, and the unglazed space was painted in red or blue. This dry, the usual glaze was applied to the reserve by blowing or by some other method. Some of the potters fill the blank spaces with a ground of blue or black, with a view to adding gilt designs after the first firing."

There were other methods of decorating these panels, and perhaps the most familiar is that in which the early *famille rose* enamels were employed. This combination of brown ground with panels of floral designs in thick opaque rose red, yellow, white and green was a favourite with the Dutch exporters. In fact this ware is still called Batavian, the old catalogue name derived from the Dutch East Indian settlement of Batavia, which was an entrepot for far-Eastern merchandise. The date of the Batavian porcelain is clearly indicated by the transition enamels as late K'ang Hsi.

The *tzŭ chin* brown was used as a monochrome in all its various shades from dark coffee colour to pale golden brown, and the lighter and more transparent shades were sometimes laid over engraved decoration. In the British Museum there are two candlesticks, the stems of which with dragon designs in full relief are in an intensely dark *tzŭ chin* glaze, so dark, indeed, that the tops have been exactly matched in the deep brown ware made by Böttger of Dresden about 1710, the latter polished on the lathe to simulate the lustrous surface of the Chinese glaze. In the same collection are two saucer dishes of dark *tzŭ chin* glaze of fine quality painted with slight floral designs in silver.[351] This kind of decoration must have been singularly effective in its original state, but the silver does not stand the test of time, and though it still firmly adheres its surface has turned black. An unusual effect is seen on a vase in the Peters collection which has a lustrous coffee brown glaze passing into olive and clouded with black; and a very rare specimen in the same collection has a "leopard skin" glaze of translucent olive brown with large mottling of opaque coffee brown. The latter piece bears the Wan Li mark.

The lightest shade of this colour is what has been described as Nanking yellow.[352] It is used as a monochrome or as a ground colour with panels usually of *famille verte* enamels, and sometimes with enamelled decoration applied over the brown glaze itself. It is clear that the *sui yu* or crackle glaze was sometimes mixed with the *tzŭ chin*, for we find many examples of beautiful lustrous brown crackle. They have, however, in many cases an adventitious tinge of grey or green, for which the crackle glaze is perhaps responsible.

A near relation to the *tzŭ chin* (brown gold) glaze is the *wu chin* (black gold), a lustrous black glaze obtained by mixing a little impure cobaltiferous ore of manganese (or coarse blue material[353]) with the *tzŭ chin* glaze. Like the latter the black is an intensely hard glaze fired in the full heat of the great kiln, and it has a lustrous metallic surface which earned for it the name of "mirror black."[354] This glaze seems to have really been a K'ang Hsi innovation,[355] and possibly it was a confusion with this fact which led d'Entrecolles into his erroneous statement about the date of the lustrous brown.

Plate 112.—Three figures of Birds, late K'ang Hsi Porcelain, with coloured enamels on the biscuit.

Fig. 1.—Stork. Height 17¼ inches. *British Museum.*

Fig. 2.—Hawk. Height 10 inches. *S. E. Kennedy Collection.*

Fig. 3.—Cock. Height 13½ inches. *British Museum.*

Fig. 1

Plate 113.—Porcelain delicately painted in thin *famille verte* enamels. About 1720.

Fig. 1.—Dish with figures of Hsi Wang Mu and attendant. Ch'êng Hua mark. Diameter 6¾ inches. *Hippisley Collection.*

Fig. 2.—Bowl with the Eight Immortals. Diameter 8⅞ inches. *S. E. Kennedy Collection.*

Plate 114.—Hanging Vase with openwork sides, for perfumed flowers. *Cumberbatch Collection.*

Porcelain painted in late *famille verte* enamels. About 1720. Blackwood frame. Total height 17 inches.

The mirror black is usually a monochrome tricked out with gilt traceries, but as in the case of the powder blue the light Chinese gilding is usually worn away, and often its quondam presence can now only be detected by a faint oily film which appears when the porcelain is held obliquely to the light. It is a common practice to have this lost gilding replaced by modern work.

There are several large vases of triple-gourd form in the Charlottenburg Palace with the upper and lower lobes coated with gilt mirror black, and the central bulb enamelled with *famille verte* colours; and another use of the glaze as panel decoration in a lustrous brown ground has already been noted in an extract from Père d'Entrecolles; it is also found on rare specimens as a background for panels of *famille verte* enamelling. But its most effective use is as a pure monochrome only relieved by faint gilding, and some of the choicest K'ang Hsi specimens have soft brown reflexions in the lustre of the surface. Another and probably a later type of mirror black is a thick lacquer-like glaze with signs of minute crackle.

There is a type of glaze which, though variegated with many tints, still belongs to the category of monochromes. This is the *flambé*, to use the suggestive French term which implies a surface shot with flame-like streaks of varying colour. This capricious colouring, the result of some chance action of the fire upon copper oxide in the glaze, had long been known to the Chinese potters. It appeared on the Chün Chou wares of the Sung and Yüan dynasties, and it must have occurred many times on the Ming copper monochromes; but up to the end of the K'ang Hsi period it seems to have been still more or less accidental on the Ching-tê Chên porcelain, if we can believe the circumstantial account written by Père d'Entrecolles in the year 1722[356]:—"I have been shown one of the porcelains which are called *yao pien*, or transmutation. This transmutation takes place in the kiln, and results from defective or excessive firing, or perhaps from other circumstances which are not easy to guess. This specimen which, according to the workman's idea, is a failure and the child of pure chance, is none the less beautiful, and none the less valued. The potter had set out to make vases of *soufflé* red. A hundred pieces were entirely spoilt, and the specimen in question came from the kiln with the appearance of a sort of agate. Were they but willing to take the risk and the expense of successive experiments, the potters would eventually discover the secret of making with certainty that which chance has produced in this solitary case. This is the way they learnt to make porcelain with the brilliant black glaze called *ou kim (wu chin)*; the caprice of the kiln determined this research, and the result was successful."

It is interesting to read how this specimen of *flambé* resulted from the misfiring of a copper red glaze, no doubt a *sang de bœuf*; for in the most common type of *flambé* red (see Plate 123, Fig. 1) passages of rich *sang de bœuf* emerge from the welter of mingled grey, blue and purple tints. The last part of d'Entrecolles' note was prophetic, for in the succeeding reigns the potters were able to produce the *flambé* glaze at will.

There are, besides, many other strangely coloured glazes which can only be explained as misfired monochromes of the *grand feu*, those of mulberry colour, slaty purple, and the like, most of which were probably intended for maroon or liver red, but were altered by some caprice of the fire. But it would be useless to enumerate these erratic tints, which are easily recognised by their divergence from the normal ceramic colours.

The French have always been partial to monochrome porcelains. In the eighteenth century they bought them eagerly to decorate their hotels and châteaux, and enshrined them in costly metal mounts. But as the style of the mounting, rococo in the early part of the century, neo-classical in the latter part, was designed to match the furniture of the period, the oriental shapes were often sacrificed to the European fashion. Dark blue and celadon green were favourite colours, if we may judge by surviving examples, and to-day enormous prices are paid for Chinese monochromes fitted with French ormolu mounts by the Court goldsmiths, such as Gouthière, Caffieri, and the rest.[357] But these richly mounted pieces have more interest as furniture and metal work, and the ceramophile regards them askance for their foreign and incongruous trappings, which disturb the pure enjoyment of the porcelain.[358]

It remains to consider the white porcelain, that is to say the porcelain which was intended to remain white and undecorated with any form of colouring. White was the colour used by the Court in times of mourning, and large services of white porcelain were made for the Emperor on these occasions. But it is not to be supposed that all the beautiful white wares were made solely for this purpose.[359] They have always been highly esteemed by the Chinese from the early Ming times, when the Yung Lo bowls and the white altar cups of Hsüan Tê were celebrated among porcelains, down to the present day. Many exquisite whites were made in the early reigns of the Ch'ing dynasty, and as with so many of the perennial monochromes their exact dating is full of difficulty. We are not concerned here with the *blanc de chine* or white porcelain of Tê-hua in Fukien, which has already been discussed, but with the white of Ching-tê Chên, the glaze of which is distinguished from the former by its harder appearance, and its bluish or greenish tinge.

The latter was made to perfection in the K'ang Hsi period. Having no colours to distract the eye from surface blemishes, nothing short of absolute purity could satisfy the critic. In choice specimens the paste was fine, white and unctuous, the glaze clear, flawless, and of oily lustre,[360] the form was elegant and the potting true. Such pieces without blemish or flaw are the very flower of porcelain, whether they be of eggshell thinness (*t'o t'ai*), half eggshell (*pan t'o t'ai*), or of the substance of ordinary wares.

But though innocent of colour the white porcelain was rarely without decoration. The finest Imperial services were usually delicately etched under the glaze with scarcely visible dragon designs. Other kinds have the ornament strongly cut, such as the eggshell cups and saucers with patterns of hibiscus, lotus, or chrysanthemum petals firmly outlined, or the vases with full-bodied designs in low relief obtained by carving away the ground surrounding the pattern.[361] Others have faint traceries or thickly painted patterns in white slip, in steatite,[362] or in fibrous gypsum under the glaze. A fuller relief was obtained by pressing in deeply cut moulds or by applying strips and shavings of the body clay, and working them into designs with a wet brush after the manner of the modern *pâte sur pâte*. There are still higher reliefs in K'ang Hsi porcelain, figures, and symbolical ornaments, formed separately in moulds and "luted" on to the ware with liquid clay, but these generally appeared on the enamelled wares, and are themselves coloured. The applied reliefs on the white wares are usually in unglazed biscuit, and there are, besides, pierced and channelled patterns, but these processes have been fully described among the late Ming wares,[363] and nothing further need be said of them, except that they were employed with supreme skill and refinement by the K'ang Hsi potters. Père d'Entrecolles[364] alludes to these perforated wares in the following passage:—"They make here (i.e. at Ching-tê Chên) another kind of porcelain which I have never yet seen. It is all pierced *à jour* like fretwork, and inside is a cup to hold the liquid. The cup and the fretwork are all in one piece." Wares of various kinds with solid inner lining and pierced outer casing are not uncommon in Chinese porcelain and pottery. Sometimes, however, the cups are completed without the inner shell, like Fig. 2, of Plate 78, which could be fitted with a silver lining if required to hold liquid.

Objects entirely biscuit are exceptional. There are, however, two small Buddhistic figures, and two lions of this class in the British Museum, and curiously enough both are stamped with potter's marks, which is itself a rare occurrence on porcelain. The former bear the name of Chang Ming-kao and the latter of Ch'ên Mu-chih (see vol. i., page 223). Bushell[365] tells us that the Chinese call biscuit porcelain *fan tz'ŭ* (turned porcelain), a quaint conception which implies that the ware is turned inside out, as though the glaze were inside, and the body out; and this illusion is occasionally kept up by applying a touch of glaze inside the mouth of the unglazed vessel.

Biscuit porcelain is specially suitable for figure modelling, because the sharpness of the details remains unobscured by glaze. It has been largely employed in European porcelain factories for this purpose, but the Chinese seem to have been prejudiced against this exclusive use of the material. As a rule they reserve it for the fleshy parts of their figures, giving the draperies a coating of glaze or of enamel or both. A rare example of the use of biscuit is illustrated in the catalogue of the Walters Collection (*O. C. A.*, Plate XXIX.), a white bottle with a dragon carved out of the glaze and left in biscuit.

The white wares so far described were made of the ordinary porcelain body and glaze, but there is another group of whites which is ranked with the so-called "soft pastes." This is a creamy, opaque and often earthy-looking ware, the glaze of which is almost always crackled. It is in fact an imitation of the old Ting yao (q.v.), and its soft-looking surface and warm creamy tone are seen to perfection in small vases, snuff bottles, and ornamental wares. Indeed, the elegantly shaped and finely potted vessels of this soft, ivory crackle are among the gems of the period.

Crackle is a feature which is common to many of the monochromes, and incidental mention has frequently been made of it in the preceding pages. It is essentially a Chinese phenomenon, dating back to the Sung dynasty, and there are various accounts of the methods employed to produce it. We are speaking of the intentional crackle which is clearly defined and usually accentuated by some colouring matter rubbed into the cracks, as opposed to the accidental crazing which appears sooner or later on most of the glazes of the *demi grand feu*, and on many low-fired enamels. One crackling process used by the Sung potters has been described on p. 99, vol. i. Another method is mentioned in the K'ang Hsi Encyclopædia,[366] viz. to heat the unglazed ware as much as possible in the sun, then plunge it into pure water. By this means a crackle was produced on the ware after the firing.

But the normal process in the Ch'ing dynasty seems to have been to mix a certain ingredient with the glaze which produced a crackle when fired. There are constant references to this ingredient under the name of *sui yu* (crackle glaze) in the letters of Père d'Entrecolles in connection with various monochromes, and in the first letter,[367] the following definite account appears:—"It is to be observed that when no other glaze but that composed of white pebbles[368] is added to the porcelain, the ware turns out to be of a special kind known as *tsoui ki* (*sui ch'i* = crackled ware). It is marbled all over and split up in every direction into a infinite number of veins. At a distance it might be taken for broken porcelain, all the fragments of which have remained in place. It is like mosaic work. The colour produced by this glaze is a slightly ashen white."

The effect of this ingredient of the glaze whatever its composition may have been is easily understood. All porcelain and pottery undergoes a considerable amount of contraction—from loss of moisture, etc.—in the kiln, and to obtain a perfectly even glaze it is necessary that the contraction of the glaze should be the same as that of the body. Clearly this ingredient caused the glaze to contract to a greater extent than the body, and so to split up into minute fissures. The Chinese were able to control to a great extent the size and nature of the crackle, as is shown by the appearance of alternate bands of large and small crackle on the same piece. The methods of colouring the crackle include rubbing red ochre, ink, and decoction of tea leaves into the cracks before the ware was quite cool. Another method is described by Bushell (*O. C. A.*, p. 511) by which a white crackled ware was stained pink or crimson. The vessel was held in the fire in an iron cage until thoroughly heated, and then water mixed with gold-pink colouring matter was blown on to it. This, however, is a later process. Most of the monochrome glazes are occasionally crackled, but the most characteristic colours of the crackle glazes are the greyish white (the *blanc un peu cendré* of Père d'Entrecolles), and light buff, which were probably intended to recall the ash colour (*hui sê*) and the millet colour (*mi sê*) of the Sung *Ko yao*. Some of the light buff or "oatmeal" crackles of the early Ch'ing period are peculiarly refined and beautiful.

Though this has seemed a favourable opportunity for discussing crackle glazes it is not to be supposed that they were a speciality of the K'ang Hsi period. They are common to every age since the Sung dynasty, and probably they were never made in such abundance and with such care as in the Yung Chêng and early Ch'ien Lung periods.

CHAPTER XII

YUNG CHÊNG 雍正PERIOD (1723–1735)

The Emperor, K'ang Hsi, was succeeded by his son, who reigned from 1723–1735 under the title Yung Chêng. The interest which the new ruler had taken as a prince in ceramic manufactures is proved by a passage in the first letter (written in 1712) of Père d'Entrecolles in which he instances among remarkable examples of the potter's skill a "great porcelain lamp made in one piece, through which a torch gave light to a whole room. This work was ordered seven or eight years ago by the Crown Prince." We are further told that the same prince had ordered the manufacture of various musical instruments in porcelain. These could not all be made, but the most successful were flutes and flageolets, and a set of chimes made of nine small, round and slightly concave plaques, which hung in a frame, and were played with drum-sticks. Apparently the Emperor continued to take an intimate interest in the industry after he had ascended the throne, for he commanded his brother the prince of Yi to announce personally to T'ang Ying his appointment at Ching-tê Chên in 1728.

At the beginning of the reign the direction of the Imperial factory was in the hands of Nien Hsi-yao,[369] who, in his capacity of inspector of customs at Huai-an Fu,[370] dispensed the funds for the Imperial porcelain. A brief note in the *T'ao lu*,[371] under the heading "Nien ware of the Yung Chêng period," sums up in the usual compressed style of Chinese ceramic writers the character of the porcelain made at this time. The duty of Nien, inspector of customs at Huai-an Fu, we read, was to select the materials, and to see that the porcelain was furnished to the Imperial orders. The ware was extremely refined and elegant. The coloured porcelains were sent twice monthly to Nien at the Customs, and forwarded by him to the Emperor. Among the vases (*cho ch'i*) many were of egg colour, and of rounded form, lustrous and pure white like silver. They combined blue and coloured decoration, and some had painted, engraved, etched, or pierced ornament all ingeniously fashioned. Imitation of the antique and invention of novelties, these were truly the established principles of Nien.

The interesting list of wares made at the Imperial factory which is given in detail on pp. 223–226 supplies a full commentary on this meagre notice, illustrating the types which are merely hinted in the *T'ao lu* and specifying the particular kinds of antiques which were reproduced and many of the new processes invented in this reign. With regard to the last, however, it appears that the chief credit was due to Nien's gifted assistant, T'ang Ying. Most of the actual processes, such as carving, engraving, piercing *à jour*, embossing in high and low relief, blowing on of the glazes, painting in enamels, in gold and in silver,[372] have already been described in previous chapters. Indeed we may assume that all the science of the K'ang Hsi potters was inherited by their successors in the Yung Chêng period, and we need only concern ourselves with the novelties and the specialities of the period.

A few words should be said first about the ware itself. Necessary variations in the appearance of the Ching-tê Chên porcelain, which were due to purely natural causes such as the use of clays of varying qualities or those from different localities, have been noted from time to time. These differences are generally quite obvious and they explain themselves. But apart from these there are numerous instances in which the potters have deliberately departed from the normal recipes in order to obtain some special effect. Thus we saw that the *ch'ing-tien* stone was introduced into the body in imitations of the opaque and rather earthy-looking white Ting Chou ware; *hua shih* (steatite) was used for another type of opaque porcelain which offered a vellum-like surface to the blue painter; and coarse, impure clays were found of great service in the imitation of the dark-coloured body of the antique wares.

Many other modifications appear in the porcelain of the first half of the eighteenth century. There is, for instance, a very dead white ware, soft looking, but translucent, which occurs on some of the choicer examples of armorial porcelain.[373] There are several specimens of this in the British Museum, one of which bears the early date, 1702, while others belong to the Yung Chêng period. Again there is the highly vitreous ware evolved by T'ang Ying to imitate the opaque glass of *Ku-yüeh-hsüan*; but that will be discussed later.[374] These special bodies were mainly employed for articles of small size and ornamental design, and they can be studied in all their varieties in a representative collection of snuff bottles. The Chinese potters lavished all their skill on these dainty little objects. Not only do they include every kind of ware, crackled or plain, translucent or opaque, but they illustrate in miniature every variety of decoration—monochrome, painted, carved, moulded, incised, pierced and embossed. Probably the choicest snuff bottles were made in the Yung Chêng and Ch'ien Lung periods; but the Chinese have never ceased to delight in them, and many beautiful examples were manufactured in the nineteenth century, particularly in the Tao Kuang period.

The ordinary Yung Chêng porcelain differs but little from that of the previous reign, though it tends to assume a whiter appearance, and the green tinge of the glaze is less marked. Moreover, a change is noticeable in the finish of the base rim of vases and bowls. Bevelling of the edge is less common, and gives place to a rounded or angular finish, the foot rim being often almost **V**-shaped; while the slight tinge of brown around the raw edge, which is usual on K'ang Hsi wares, is often entirely absent. The actual potting of the porcelain displays a wonderful degree of manipulative skill, and the forms, though highly finished, are not lacking in vigour. They are, in fact, a happy mean between the strong, free lines of the K'ang Hsi and the meticulous finish of the later Ch'ien Lung porcelains. The verdict of the *T'ao lu*, "extremely refined and elegant," is fully justified by the porcelain itself no less than by its decoration.

Not the least deserving of this praise, though mainly made for export, is the important group discussed on page 209, viz. the saucer dishes, plates, tea and coffee wares, etc., of delicate white porcelain, painted, apparently at Canton, in the *famille rose* enamels. It is an "eggshell" porcelain, white, thin, and beautifully finished, and the dainty little conical or bell-shaped tea cups, though without handles, are the perfection of table ware. This kind of "eggshell" is easily distinguished from the Ming type, which is greener in tone and has the appearance of melting snow by transmitted light.

The Yung Chêng period is not conspicuous for blue and white porcelain. The perfection of the *famille rose* colours and the growing demand for enamelled wares seem to have withdrawn the attention of the potters from their old speciality. Marked examples of Yung Chêng blue and white are so uncommon that it is difficult to estimate the merits of the ware from them. A saucer dish in the British Museum shows the familiar pattern of a prunus spray reserved in white in a marbled blue ground; but though the ware itself preserves much of the K'ang Hsi character, the blue is dull and grey, and wanting in the vivacity and depth of the old models. One would say that little care had been spent on the refining of the blue, and without the old perfection of material the K'ang Hsi style, with its broad washes of colour, was doomed to failure. Considerations of this sort may have led the painters to abandon the washes in favour of pencilling in fine lines, a method apparent on the armorial porcelain which can be dated to this period. Such a treatment of the blue was admirably suited to small objects. Indeed it was the usual style of decoration on the steatitic porcelain, of which many excellent examples belonging to this time are to be found among the snuff bottles, vermilion boxes, and the small, artistic furniture of the writing table. On large specimens the effect is thin and weak.

On the other hand the Yung Chêng potters, who excelled in reproducing the antique, were most successful in their imitation of the old Ming blue and whites. The Imperial list[375] includes such items as "reproductions of the pale blue painted designs of Ch'êng Hua," and of the dark blue of Chia Ching. An interesting example of a Ming reproduction is a bowl in the British Museum, which is painted on the exterior with the old design of ladies walking in a garden by candle light.[376] In spite of its Yung Chêng mark this piece is obviously a copy of a Ming model. The porcelain is white and thick, and the glaze, which is of greenish tint, has a peculiar soft-looking surface, while the blue design inside is of characteristic Ming colour, though that of the exterior is scarcely so successful.

Another type much copied at this period as well as in the succeeding reign is that in which the blue is mottled and blotched with darker spots, a type discussed among the early Ming wares.[377] And similarly such specimens as Fig. 2 of Plate 116, which bears a Hsüan Tê mark, doubtless belong to this period of imitative manufacture. It is of thick, solid build with smooth, soft-looking glaze, whose bubbled texture gives the blue a hazy appearance.

Painting in underglaze red alone, or in combination with underglaze blue, was freely practised in the reign of Yung Chêng, and probably most of the fine examples of this type in our collections belong to this and the succeeding reign (Fig. 1, Plate 117). There is a good example with the Yung Chêng mark in the British Museum, a vase of "pilgrim-bottle" form with central design of the three emblematic fruits—peach, pomegranate, and finger citron, symbols of the Three Abundances of Years, Sons and Happiness. The fruits are in a soft underglaze red, verging on the peach-bloom tint, and the foliage, together with the borders and accessory designs, are pencilled in dark blue.

The Imperial list alludes to this decoration under the heading of "red in the glaze" (*yu li hung*), including (1) red used alone for painted designs, and (2) red foliage combined with blue flowers.[378] Examples of both these styles are frequent in large and small objects, and especially in the decoration of snuff bottles, which often bear the Yung Chêng mark. They are, however, by no means confined to the Yung Chêng period, but have continued in uninterrupted use to the present day.

PLATE 115

Vase of baluster form with ornament in white slip and underglaze red and blue in a celadon green ground: rockery and birds on a flowering prunus tree. Yung Chêng period (1723–1735)

Height 15½ inches.

Alexander Collection.

Other references in the list[379] to underglaze red painting include designs of three fishes,[380] three fruits, three funguses, and five bats (for the five blessings) in the Hsüan Tê style, red in a white ground; and the same red designs in a celadon green ground, the latter combination being a novelty of the previous reign. Plate 115 is a choice example of the underglaze colours in a celadon ground; and similar designs in a pale lavender blue ground, besides other combinations of the same colours, coloured slips, and high-fired glazes which form the polychrome decoration of the *grand feu* have been already discussed on p. 146. They belong to the Yung Chêng and Ch'ien Lung periods no less than to the K'ang Hsi.

Of the other kinds of polychrome, the porcelain with glazes of the *demi-grand feu*, and enamels of the muffle kiln in the three colours, green, yellow, and aubergine, was still made. It is hardly likely that the manufacture[381] which Père d'Entrecolles describes in 1722 ceased immediately, and we know that the finer types with engraved designs and transparent glazes in the three colours were made to perfection at the Imperial factory. Fig. 1 of Plate 116 illustrates a bowl of this kind with the Yung Chêng mark and, to judge from its exquisite quality, an Imperial piece. The ornament is in green, in a full yellow ground. This type of decoration is a legacy from the Ming dynasty, and doubtless many of the saucer dishes, bowls, etc., with Chêng Tê marks, but with all the trimness and neatness of the Yung Chêng wares, belong to the latter period. One variety is actually specified in the Imperial list[382] viz. "reproductions of porcelain with incised green decoration in a monochrome yellow ground."

As for the on-glaze enamels of the muffle kiln the old *famille verte* colour scheme was to a great and increasing extent supplanted by the *famille rose*. It survived, however, in certain modified forms—in the delicately painted wares, for example, usually of eggshell thinness and decorated in thin, clear, transparent enamels, such as were described in connection with the late K'ang Hsi "birthday plates " (see Plate 113). And again the same colours were employed in a special type of decoration which seems to have originated in the Yung Chêng period, though it was freely used in later reigns. In this the design was carefully traced in pale blue outlines under the glaze, and filled in with light uniform washes of transparent enamels on the glaze. The effect is delicate and refined, though somewhat weak in comparison with the full, iridescent colours and broad washes of the older *famille verte*.

Possibly this style of decoration was intended to reproduce the traditional refinement of the Ch'êng Hua cups. The Imperial list[383] includes "reproductions of Ch'êng Hua polychrome (*wu ts'ai*)," and four exquisite eggshell wine cups in the Hippisley Collection which bear the Ch'êng Hua mark, are painted in this fashion.[384] Similarly in the Bushell collection there are some beautiful reproductions of the Ch'êng Hua "stem-cups," with grape vine patterns, etc., which are no doubt of the same origin. Larger work in the same style is illustrated by a fine vase in the Victoria and Albert Museum with a phœnix design which suggests an Imperial destination (Plate 117).

Fig. 1

Fig. 2

Plate 116.—Yung Chêng Porcelain.

Fig. 1.—Imperial Rice Bowl with design of playing children (*wa wa*), engraved outlines filled in with green in a yellow ground, transparent glazes on the biscuit. Yung Chêng mark. Diameter 6 inches. *British Museum.*

Fig. 2.—Blue and white Vase with fungus (*ling chih*) designs in Hsüan Tê style. Height 7½ inches. *Cologne Museum.*

Plate 117.—Yung Chêng Porcelain.

Fig. 1.—Vase with prunus design in underglaze red and blue. Height 15 inches. *C. H. Read Collection.*

Fig. 2.—Imperial Vase with phœnix and peony design in pale *famille verte* enamels over underglaze blue outlines. Height 25⅝ inches. *V. & A. Museum.*

Plate 118.—Early Eighteenth Century Enamels.

Fig.1—Plate painted at Canton in *famille rose* enamels (*yang ts'ai*, "foreign colouring"). Yung Chêng period. Diameter 21½ inches. *S. E. Kennedy Collection.*

Fig. 2.—Arrow Stand, painted in late *famille verte* enamels. About 1720. Height 19¼ inches. *V. & A. Museum.*

Fig. 1

Fig. 2

Fig. 3

Fig. 4

Plate 119.—Yung Chêng Porcelain, painted at Canton with *famille rose* enamels. *British Museum.*

Fig. 1.—"Seven border" Plate. Diameter 8¼ inches.

Fig. 2.—Eggshell Cup and Saucer with painter's marks (see p. <u>212</u>). Diameter of saucer, 4½ inches.

Fig. 3.—Eggshell Plate with vine border. Diameter 8¼ inches.

Fig. 4.—Armorial Plate with arms of Leake Okeover. Transition enamels, about 1723. Diameter 8⅞ inches.

Thirdly, there are the reproductions of the enamelled porcelain of the Chêng Tê and Wan Li periods[385] (q.v.), characterised, no doubt, by the combination of underglaze blue and overglaze enamels. We have already seen[386] from the note on Nien yao in the *T'ao lu* that this combination was conspicuous at this period, and it is probable that much of the "five colour" porcelain in late

Ming style should be dated no further back than the Yung Chêng revival. Other types of Ming coloured wares reproduced at this time were "porcelain with ornament in Hsüan Tê style in a yellow ground,"[387] which seems to mean underglaze blue designs with the ground filled in with yellow enamel—a not unfamiliar type—and porcelain with designs painted in iron red (*ts'ai hung*) "reproduced from old pieces."[388] But the most prominent feature of the enamelled porcelains of this time is the rapid development of the *famille rose* colours. We have already noted the first signs of their coming in the thick rose pink and opaque white, which made their appearance in the latter years of K'ang Hsi. The group derives its name from its most conspicuous members, a series of rose pinks graduating from pale rose to deep crimson, all derived from gold, the use of which as a colouring agent for vitreous enamel was only at this period mastered by the Chinese potters. It includes besides a number of other colours distinguished from those of the *famille verte* palette by their relative opacity. They display, moreover, a far wider range of tints, owing to scientific blending of the various enamels and to the judicious use of the opaque white to modify the positive colours. Most of the opaque colours have considerable body, and stand out on the porcelain like a rich incrustation, and they are laid on not in broad washes, but with careful brush strokes and miniature-like touches.

The *famille rose* colours are known to the Chinese as *juan ts'ai* ("soft colours," as opposed to the *ying ts'ai*, or hard colours of the *famille verte*), *fên ts'ai* (pale colours), or *yang ts'ai* (foreign colours). Their foreign origin is generally admitted, and T'ang Ying in the seventeenth of his descriptions of the processes of manufacture alludes to them under the heading, "Decorating the round ware and vases with foreign colouring."[389] Painting the white porcelain in polychrome (*wu ts'ai*) after the manner of the Europeans (*hsi yang*), he tells us, is called foreign colouring, and he adds that the colours employed are the same as those used for enamels on metal (*fo lang*). Taking this statement with the note on "foreign coloured wares" in the Imperial list,[390] where reference is made to painting on enamels (*fa lang*) "landscapes and figure scenes, flowering plants and birds," it is evident that *fa lang* is used here not in the usual sense of cloisonné enamel, but for the painted enamels on copper which we distinguish as Canton enamels. These, we are told elsewhere,[391] were first made in the kingdom of Ku-li, which is washed by the Western sea. Ku-li is identified as Calicut, but it does not necessarily follow that the Chinese associated the origin of the painted enamels with India. The expression was probably used quite vaguely in reference to European goods which came by way of India, and does not really conflict with the other phrase, *hsi yang* (Western foreigners), which is always rendered "Europeans."

There is quite a number of references to the foreign or European colours in the Imperial list,[392] e.g. "porcelain in yellow after the European style," which Bushell considers to be the lemon yellow which originated in this reign; "porcelain in purple brown (*tzŭ*) after the European style"; "European red-coloured wares," i.e. rose pink; "European green-coloured wares," which Bushell explains as pale bluish green or *eau de nil* enamel; and "European black (*wu chin*) wares." In fact the words, "foreign or European," seem to be practically synonymous with "opaque enamel."[393]

The most complete display of the foreign colouring is given by a special group of porcelain which is painted in a characteristic and mannered style. It is best known as "eggshell" or "ruby-back" porcelain, from the fact that it is usually very thin and translucent and beautifully potted, and that the exterior of the dishes and plates is often coated with a gold pink enamel varying from pale ruby pink to deep crimson. It usually consists of saucer-shaped dishes, plates, and tea and coffee wares, obviously intended for European use. Occasionally there are vases and lanterns of exquisite lightness and translucency, but the vase forms usually required a more substantial construction, and such specimens as Plate 120, are strongly built, though decorated in the same style as the eggshell wares.

The decoration of these porcelains is scarcely less distinctive than their colouring. The central design usually consists of one of the following: a Chinese interior with figures of ladies and children, groups of vases and furniture, baskets of flowers and dishes of fruit, a pheasant on a rock, two quails and growing flowers, a cock and peonies, etc.; and these designs are enclosed by rich borders, sometimes totalling as many as seven in number, composed of hexagon and square, lozenge, trellis or matting diapers, in varying colours, and broken by small irregular panels of flowers or archaic dragons. There are, of course, many other kinds of decoration on these wares. Sometimes the whole design is executed in opaque blue enamel, sometimes it is black and gold. On some the borders are simpler, merely delicately gilt patterns; on others they are ruby pink, plain or broken by enamelled sprays. On the vase forms the ruby either covers the entire ground or is broken, as in Plate 121, Fig. 3, by fan-shaped or picture-shaped panels with polychrome designs. The painting is, as a rule, very finely and carefully executed, but almost always in a distinctive style which is closely paralleled by the Canton enamels.

Indeed, it is impossible to resist the conclusion that much of this ware was actually decorated in the enamelling establishments at Canton, the porcelain itself being sent in the white from Ching-tê Chên. The same designs are found on both the porcelain and the enamels, and there is one instance at least of an artist whose paintings were used on both materials, as is testified by his signature. This is the painter whose art-name is *Pai shih shan jên* (hermit of the white rock), or in a shortened form, Pai-shih (see vol. i., p. 223). He was evidently a Cantonese, for one of his designs on a saucer in the British Museum is inscribed *Ling nan hui chê* (a Canton picture), the subject being a vase of flowers and a basket of fruit. His signature is also attached to a dish with cock and peonies in the Victoria and Albert Museum,[394] and to a similar design figured by Jacquemart,[395] which also bears the date corresponding to 1724. It occurs, besides, fairly frequently on Canton enamels, though in this case usually attached to landscape designs. In all these instances, however, it is placed in the field of the design appended, as a rule, to a stanza of verse or a descriptive sentence. This is a usual position for the signature of a painter on silk or paper, and we can hardly be wrong in inferring that Pai-shih was the artist whose designs were copied on the wares, perhaps one who was specially employed to design for the enamellers, rather than an actual pot-painter or enameller. The proper place for the signature of the latter is underneath the ware, on the base; and here we find on a cup and saucer in the British Museum the name apparently of the real decorator whose painting is not to be distinguished from that on the piece with the Pai-shih signature, just mentioned as in the same collection. Under the saucer (Plate 119, Fig. 2) is the seal *Yü fêng yang lin*, i.e. Yang Lin of Yü-fêng, an old name for the town of K'un-shan; and under the cup is the seal *Yu chai* (quiet pavilion), which is no doubt the studio name of Yang-lin.[396] K'un-shan Hsien is situated between Su-chou and Shanghai, in the province of Kiangsu, and we are to understand that Yang-lin was either a native of K'un-shan or that he resided there—more probably the former, for his work is typical of the Canton enamellers. It is, however, probable enough that there were decorating establishments working for the European markets in the neighbourhood of Shanghai as well as at Canton, just as there are still decorating kilns not only at Ching-tê Chên but "at the other towns on the river."[397]

It is highly probable that the brushwork of the Canton enamellers, like the enamels themselves, was copied at Ching-tê Chên, and even that some of the enamellers migrated thither. A tankard among the armorial porcelain in the British Museum, bearing the arms of Yorke and Cocks, combines a few touches of underglaze blue with passages of *famille rose* decoration in the Canton style. The blue can only have been applied at the place of manufacture, and as no porcelain of this kind was actually made at Canton, it is evident that the piece was made and decorated elsewhere (which can only mean at Ching-tê Chên), unless we assume the improbable alternative that the tankard travelled from the factory, bare save for a faintly outlined shield with a saltire in blue, to be finished off at Canton.

Needless to say there is much *famille rose* porcelain in which the Cantonese style is not apparent, and this we assume without hesitation to have been decorated at Ching-tê Chên.

It only remains to say a few words on the dating of the *famille rose* wares and for this we must return to the ruby-back porcelains. Dated pieces are rare, but the British Museum is fortunate in possessing a few documentary specimens. The most interesting of these is a bowl with pale ruby enamel covering the exterior, and a dainty spray of flowers in *famille rose* enamels inside. It is marked in blue under the glaze with the cyclical date "made in the *hsin chou* year recurring" (see p. 213). The only year to which this can be referred is 1721, when the *hsin chou* year came round for the second time in the long reign of K'ang Hsi.[398] It is of course possible that this bowl was not enamelled in the year of its manufacture, but there are two other pieces in the same case, an octagonal plate with ruby border and a dish, both with the mark of the Dresden collection, and therefore not later than the early years of Yung Chêng. A fourth document is a ruby-back saucer dish delicately painted with a lady and boys, vases and furniture in typical style, which has the mark of the Yung Chêng period.

Unfortunately it is no longer possible to regard the year 1724, to which the signature Pai-shih is attached on the plate mentioned above, as conclusive evidence of the date of decoration.[399] It is certainly the date of the design, and it is probable enough that the porcelain was painted within a few years of the original picture, but beyond that no further inferences can be drawn.[400] The Yorke-Cocks tankard, however, to which we have also alluded, must for heraldic reasons have been painted between the years 1720 and 1733; and there is an eggshell cup and saucer in the British Museum painted in rose pink and other enamels of this type, with the arms of the Dutch East India Company and the date 1728.

From this cumulative evidence it is clear that the manufacture of eggshell dishes and services with *famille rose* enamels in the Canton style and with "ruby backs" was in full swing in the Yung Chêng period, and the general tendency to label them all Ch'ien Lung errs on the side of excessive caution.

Passing from this particular group, which was affected by special influences, the general character of the Yung Chêng enamelled decoration is one of great refinement in design and execution. The over-elaboration and the overcrowding which are observable on the later Ch'ien Lung *famille rose* are absent at this period. The tendency was on the contrary towards elegant and restrained effects, such as a flowering spray thrown artistically across the field, birds on a bough and other graceful designs which left plenty of scope for the fine quality of the white background. It is this nicely balanced decoration coupled with the delicacy of the painting and the beautiful finish of the porcelain itself, which gives the Yung Chêng enamelled wares their singular distinction and charm.

There are still a few special types of painted wares to be noticed before passing to the monochromes. One of these is named in the Imperial list,[401] under the heading "Porcelain painted in ink (ts'ai shui mo)," a figurative expression, for Indian ink could not stand the heat even of the enamelling kiln, and could never have served as a true ceramic pigment. The material used was a dry black or brown black pigment derived from manganese, and closely allied to the pigment which had long served in a subordinate position for tracing outlines. Evidently this material was now greatly improved, and could be used for complete designs which resembled drawings in Indian ink or in sepia. It is certain, however, that the Chinese, whose methods were necessarily empirical, had first experimented with actual ink, for Père d'Entrecolles wrote in 1722[402]—"an attempt made to paint in black some vases with the finest Chinese ink met with no success. When the porcelain had been fired, it turned out white. The particles of this black had not sufficient body, and were dissipated by the action of the fire; or rather they had not the strength to penetrate the layer of glaze or to produce a colour differing from the plain glaze." Between that date and about 1730 when the Imperial list was drawn up, the secret of the proper pigment seems to have been mastered, and we find the black designs effectively used on Yung Chêng eggshell and other wares, alone or brightened by a little gilding. Among other uses it was found to be admirably suited for copying the effect of European prints and line engravings, a *tour de force* in which the proverbial patience and imitative skill of the Chinese are well exemplified. Another effect sometimes mistaken for black painting is produced by silvered designs which become rapidly discoloured; but it is generally possible to see a slight metallic sheen even on the blackened silver if the porcelain is held obliquely to the light.

Another refined and unobtrusive decoration was effected by pencilling in pale iron red supplemented with gilding. There is a large series of this red and gold porcelain in the Dresden collection, and it seems to belong to the late K'ang Hsi or the Yung Chêng period. Another telling combination, including black, red and gold, dates from this time. The black and gold variety is well illustrated by an interesting plate in the British Museum which represents European figures in early eighteenth-century costume in a Chinese interior (Plate 131, Fig. 1). The Imperial list[403] alludes to the use of silver and gold both to cover the entire surface like a monochrome (*mo yin* and *mo chin*), and in painted designs (*miao yin* and *miao chin*).[404] Three of these decorations are said to have been in Japanese style, but the precise significance of this is not clear. Gilding was freely used in combination with red and blue, and especially over the blue, on Arita porcelain, but the application of it does not seem to differ from the ordinary Chinese gilding. The one feature common to the Chinese and Japanese gilding is its lightness and restraint as compared with the heavy gilding of European porcelains.

Plate 125 illustrates a peculiar ware which belongs in part to the reign of Yung Chêng and in part to that of Ch'ien Lung. It attempts to reproduce the soft colouring on the enamelled glass made by Hu,[405] whose studio-name was Ku-yüeh-hsüan ("ancient moon pavilion"). A small brush holder[406] of this glass is shown on Fig. 125, an opaque white material, not unlike our old Bristol glass, delicately painted in *famille rose* colours with groups of the Seven Worthies of the Bamboo Grove. It is said that[407] the Emperor admired the soft colouring on this ware, and expressed a wish to see the same effect produced in porcelain. T'ang Ying thereupon set out to solve the problem by making a highly vitreous body with glassy glaze on which the enamels assumed the soft tints of the original model. This type of porcelain, known as *fang ku yüeh hsüan* ("imitation of Ku-yüeh-hsüan"), is greatly prized. Mr. A. E. Hippisley has described a small group in the catalogue of his collection from which I have been permitted to illustrate an example (Plate 125). Mr. Hippisley states that the earlier specimens of the glass are marked with the four characters *ta ch'ing nien chih* (made in the great Ch'ing period), the reign name Yung Chêng being omitted; the later pieces, of which the brush pot in our illustration is one, have the Ch'ien Lung mark in four characters. Bushell[408] has figured a yellow glazed snuff bottle with the actual mark *Ku yüeh hsüan chih* (see vol. i. p. 219).

The reigns of Yung Chêng and Ch'ien Lung were prolific in monochromes. Never since the Sung dynasty had these wares been produced in such quantity, and the tale of the glazes was swollen to an unprecedented extent by the accumulated traditions of the past centuries, and by the inventive genius of T'ang Ying. It is scarcely practicable to attempt to distinguish very closely between the Yung Chêng monochromes and those of the early years of Ch'ien Lung. The activities of T'ang-ying extended from 1728–1749, and we are expressly told that many of the types enumerated in the Imperial list were his inventions, besides which there was nothing made by the potters of the past which he could not reproduce. To enumerate all the colours now used would be merely to repeat what has been said under the heading of monochrome porcelain in the previous chapters. Moreover, the Imperial list given on page 223 serves to draw attention to the principal types, and it is only necessary here to supplement it with a few comments.

A special feature of the time was the reproduction of the glazes made in the classical periods of the Sung and Ming dynasties, and in many cases these copies were based on originals lent to the factory from the Imperial collections. Thus the Ju, Kuan, Ko, Lung-chüan, Tung-ch'ing, Chün and Ting wares, all the specialities of the Sung dynasty, are included in the list, and though one type of Kuan glaze is specifically stated to have been laid on a white porcelain body, many of the others, we read, were provided with special bodies imitating the copper-and-iron-coloured wares of antiquity. But experience shows that in the majority of cases the potters were content to simulate the "brown mouth and iron foot" of the dark-bodied Sung wares by dressing the mouth and the exposed part of the base with ferruginous clay. This is observable on the lavender crackles which imitate the Kuan, and the stone grey crackles of the Ko type, by which the Sung originals were until recent years represented in most Western collections.

In other cases coarse clays of impure colour, and even earthenware bodies were used in the reproductions. The admirable imitations of the mottled and *flambé* Chün glazes which were apparently a special triumph of T'ang-ying appear both on a white porcelain which had to be carefully concealed by the coloured glazes, and on a soft earthenware body. Both these kinds are found with the Yung Chêng mark stamped in the paste, and so correct are the glaze effects that even collectors of considerable experience have been deceived by specimens from which the mark in question has been ground away.

In addition to the copies of the high-fired Chün glazes, there was the "Chün glaze of the muffle kiln" (*lu chün yu*) which is described as something between the glaze applied to the Yi-hsing stoneware and the Kuangtung glazes. The items immediately following this information in the Imperial list[409] make it clear that the writer refers to the glazes of Ou on the Yi-hsing pottery, and to the blue mottled glazes of the Canton stoneware. The enamel which most closely answers to the description of this Chün glaze of the muffle kiln[410] is that illustrated in Fig. 4 of Plate 128, a vase with dark-coloured foot rim, and an opaque greenish blue enamel flecked with dark ruby pink. This enamel varies considerably in appearance according to the preponderance of the red or the blue in the combination; but it is an enamel of the muffle kiln and its markings recall the dappled Chün glazes. I have, moreover, seen this glaze actually applied to a teapot of Yi-hsing red stoneware. This glaze seems to belong to a type, which was largely developed in the Ch'ien Lung period, of glazes resembling if not actually imitating the mottled surface of certain birds' eggs, e.g. the robin, the lark, the sparrow, etc. In these instances one colour seems to have been powdered or blown on to another, the commonest kind having a powdering of ruby pink on pale blue or green. This glaze differs from the Chün glaze, described above, only in the size of the pink specks. It was probably in experimenting for the effect of the *flambé* Chün glazes that T'ang Ying acquired the mastery of the furnace transmutations (*yao pien*) which made it possible for him and his successors to produce at will the variegated glazes. These had been described by Père d'Entrecolles a few years earlier as accidental effects in his time, but the French father already foresaw the day when they would be brought under control.

Of the celebrated Ting Chou wares only the fine ivory white Ting (*fên ting*) was copied at the Imperial factory; but this does not preclude the reproduction of the other kind, the creamy crackled *t'u-ting*, in the other potteries. There are, at any rate, many lovely porcelains in both styles which appear to belong to the Yung Chêng and early Ch'ien Lung periods. Coloured glazes with crackle and crackled grey-white of the Ko type were made in great quantity, and most of the choicer crackles in our collections, especially those of antique appearance but on a white and neatly finished porcelain body, date from this time.

The reproductions of Ming monochromes include the underglaze red and the purplish blue as in the previous reign, and the eggshell and pure white of the Yung Lo and Hsüan Tê periods. The purplish blue or *chi ch'ing* of this time is illustrated by a large dish in the British Museum which is further enriched with gilding. It is covered with a splendid deep blue of slightly reddish tinge, varying depth and rather stippled appearance, and it was found in Turkey, where this colour has been much prized. Turquoise green, aubergine purple and yellow of the *demi-grand feu*, and the lustrous brown (*tzŭ chin*) in two shades, brown and yellow, are all mentioned in the Imperial list as used with or without engraved and carved designs under the glaze.

As for the K'ang Hsi porcelains it may be assumed that practically all their glaze colours were now reproduced. A few only are specified in the list, eel yellow, snake-skin green, spotted yellow, *soufflé* red, *soufflé* blue (powder blue) and mirror black (*wu chin*). The term *soufflé* red may refer to the underglaze red from copper or the overglaze iron red. The latter is further subdivided into *mo hung* or *ta hung*, the deep red of Ming origin, and the *tsao'rh hung* or jujube red, a softer and more vitreous[411] variety of the same colour which Dr. Bushell considered to have originated in the Yung Chêng period. On the *soufflé* red under the glaze we may quote Bushell's remarks[412]: "Two of the colours especially characteristic of the Nien yao or 'Nien porcelain' of this epoch are the *clair de lune* or *yüeh pai*, and the bright *soufflé* copper red." The latter is further described on a vase in the Walters collection "exhibiting the characteristic monochrome glaze of bright ruby red tint, and stippled surface. The *soufflé* glaze is applied over the whole surface with the exception of a panel of irregular outline reserved on one side, where it is shaded off so that the red fades gradually into a nearly white ground." This panel was afterwards filled in with a design in overglaze enamels. A tazza in the British Museum has this same red covering three-quarters of the exterior, and fading into the white ground. This red also occurs in its beautiful translucent ruby tints on a pair of small wine cups in the same collection, and on a set of larger cups belonging to Mr. Eumorfopoulos. One would say it was the "liquid dawn" tint of the celebrated wine cups of the late Ming potter, Hao Shih-chiu.

The *clair de lune* or moon white (*yüeh pai*), an exquisite glaze of palest blue, is illustrated on Plate 130. It is often faintly tinged with lavender which bears out its description in the Imperial list[413]: "This colour somewhat resembles the Ta Kuan glaze, but the body of the ware is white. The glaze is without crackle, and there are two shades—pale and dark." The Kuan glaze, it should be explained, was characterised by a reddish tinge.

In addition to the foreign colours which were capable of being used as monochromes as well as in painted designs, there are a few other new glazes named in the Imperial list. The *fa ch'ing* (cloisonné blue) which "resulted from recent experiments to match" the deep blue of the enamellers on copper, is identified by Bushell with the dark sapphire blue known as *pao shih lan* (precious stone blue). It was, we are told, darker and bluer than the purplish *chi ch'ing*, and it had not the orange peel and palm eye markings of the latter. It has, however, a faint crackle, and is apparently a glaze of the *demi-grand feu*. We learn elsewhere that this cloisonné blue was one of T'ang-ying's inventions.

Among the yellows are "porcelain with yellow after the European style" which is identified by Bushell with the opaque lemon yellow enamel introduced at this time, and there are two kinds of *mi sê* (millet colour) glazes,[414] pale and dark, which we are told "differed from the Sung *mi sê*." Bushell's explanation of the term *mi sê* given in Monkhouse's *Chinese Porcelain*,[415] traverses his rendering of the terms as rice colour in other books: "The Chinese term used here is *mi sê*, which Julien first translated *couleur du riz*, and thereby misled us all. It really refers to the colour (*sê*) of the yellow millet (*huang mi*), not of rice (*pai mi*). *Mi sê* in Chinese silks is a full primrose yellow; in Chinese ceramic glazes it often deepens from that tint to a dull mustard colour when the materials are less pure. It has often been wondered why the old "mustard crackle" of collectors is apparently never alluded to in "L'Histoire des Porcelaines de King-tê-chin." It is necessary to substitute yellow for "rice coloured" in the text generally, remembering always that a paler tone is indicated than that of the Imperial yellow, which Mr. Monkhouse justly likens to the yolk of an egg."

In Giles's Dictionary *mi sê* is rendered "straw colour, the colour of yellow millet," and all my inquiries among Chinese collectors as to the tint of the *mi sê* glaze have led to the same conclusion. One of the Chinese experts indicated a bowl with pale straw yellow glaze of the K'ang Hsi period as an example of *mi sê*, and this I take to be the *mi sê* which "differed from the Sung colour," being, in fact, an ordinary yellow glaze, following the type made in the Ming dynasty, and entirely different in technique from the Sung glazes.

PLATE 120

Covered Jar or *potiche* painted in *famille rose* or "foreign colours" (*yang ts'ai*) with baskets of flowers: deep borders of ruby red enamel broken by small panels and floral designs. On the cover is a lion coloured with enamels on the biscuit. From a set of five vases and beakers in the collection of Lady Wantage. Late Yung Chêng period (1723–1735)

Height 34 inches.

The precise nature of the Sung *mi sê* which is included among the Ko yao, Chün yao and Hsiang-hu wares reproduced by the Yung Chêng potters according to the Imperial list is a little doubtful. Possibly one type was illustrated by the "shallow bowl with spout: grey stoneware with opaque glaze of pale sulphur yellow," which Mr. Alexander exhibited at the Burlington Fine Arts Club in 1910.[416] Another is indicated in the Pierpont Morgan collection[417] in a "shallow bowl with greenish yellow crackled glaze," apparently of the type found occasionally in Borneo, where such wares are still treasured by the Dyaks. The vase in the Victoria and Albert Museum which is figured by Monkhouse (op. cit., Fig. 22) as a specimen of old *mi sê*, appears for reasons already given[418] to be a Yung Chêng reproduction of this type. The "mustard yellow" which Bushell included under the description *mi sê* is an opaque crackled enamel which can hardly have originated before the Yung Chêng period, and it is possible that it resulted from an attempt to reproduce the old Sung *mi sê* crackle.

The following list of the decorations used at the Imperial factory was compiled by Hsieh Min, the governor of the province of Kiangsi from 1729 to 1734.[419] It was translated by Bushell in his *Oriental Ceramic Art*; but reference has been made to it so often in these pages, and its importance is so obvious, that no apology is necessary for giving it in full. The following version is taken from the *Chiang hsi t'ung chih*, bk. 93, fols. 11 to 13, and in most cases Bushell's rendering has been followed:—

1. Glazes of the Ta Kuan period (i.e. Sung Kuan yao) on an "iron" body, including moon white (*yüeh pai*), pale blue or green (*fên ch'ing*) and deep green (*ta lü*).**

2. Ko glaze on an "iron" body, including millet colour (*mi sê*) and *fên ch'ing*.**

3. Ju glaze without crackle on a "copper" body: the glaze colours copied from a cat's food basin of the Sung dynasty, and a dish for washing brushes moulded with a human face.

4. Ju glaze with fish-roe crackle on a "copper" body.**

5. White Ting glaze. Only the *fên Ting* was copied, and not the *t'u Ting*.

6. Chün glazes. Nine varieties are given, of which five were copied from old palace pieces and four from newly acquired specimens; see p. 000.

7. Reproductions of the *chi hung* red of the Hsüan Tê period: including fresh red (*hsien hung*) and ruby red (*pao shih hung*).

8. Reproductions of the deep violet blue (*chi ch'ing*) of the Hsüan Tê period. This glaze is deep and reddish (*nêng hung*), and has orange peel markings and palm eyes.

9. Reproductions of the glazes of the Imperial factory: including eel yellow (*shan yü huang*), snake-skin green (*shê p'i lü*), and spotted yellow (*huang pan tien*).

10. Lung-ch'üan glazes: including pale and dark shades.

11. Tung-ch'ing glazes: including pale and dark, shades.

12. Reproductions of the Sung millet-coloured (*mi sê*) glaze: copied in form and colour from the fragmentary wares dug up at Hsiang Hu (q.v.).

13. Sung pale green (*fên ch'ing*) glaze: copied from wares found at the same time as the last.

14. Reproduction of "oil green" (*yu lü*) glaze: "copied from an old transmutation (*yao pien*) ware like green jade (*pi yü*), with brilliant colour broken by variegated passages and of antique elegance."

15. The Chün glaze of the muffle stove (*lu chün*). "The colour is between that of the Kuangtung wares and the Yi-hsing applied glaze[420]; and in the ornamental markings (*hua wên*) and the transmutation tints of the flowing glaze it surpasses them."

16. Ou's glazes, with red and blue markings.

17. Blue mottled (*ch'ing tien*) glazes: copied from old Kuang yao.

18. Moon white (*yüeh pai*) glazes. "The colour somewhat resembles the Ta Kuan glaze, but the body of the ware is white. The glaze is without crackle, and there are two shades—pale and dark."

19. Reproductions of the ruby red (*pao shao*) of Hsüan Té: in decoration consisting of (1) three fishes, (2) three fruits, (3) three funguses, or (4) the five Happinesses (symbolised by five bats).

20. Reproductions of the Lung-ch'üan glaze with ruby red decoration of the types just enumerated. "This is a new style of the reigning dynasty."

21. Turquoise (*fei ts'ui*) glazes. Copying three sorts, (1) pure turquoise, (2) blue flecked, and (3) gold flecked (*chin tien*).[421]

22. *Soufflé* red (*ch'ui hung*) glaze.

23. *Soufflé* blue (*ch'ui ch'ing*) glaze.

24. Reproductions of Yung Lo porcelain: eggshell (*t'o t'ai*), pure white with engraved (*chui*) or embossed (*kung*) designs.

25. Copies of Wan Li and Chêng Té enamelled (*wu ts'ai*) porcelain.

26. Copies of Ch'êng Hua enamelled (*wu ts'ai*) porcelain.

27. Porcelain with ornament in Hsüan Té style in a yellow ground.

28. Cloisonné blue (*fa ch'ing*) glaze.[422] "This glaze is the result of recent attempts to match this colour (i.e. the deep blue of the cloisonné enamels). As compared with the deep and reddish *chi ch'ing*, it is darker and more vividly blue (*ts'ui*), and it has no orange peel or palm eye markings."

29. Reproductions of European wares with lifelike designs carved and engraved. "Sets of the five sacrificial utensils, dishes, plates, vases, and boxes and the like are also decorated with coloured pictures in European style."

Fig. 1   Fig. 3

Fig. 2

Plate 121.—Two Beakers and a Jar from sets of five, *famille rose* enamels. Late Yung Chêng Porcelain.

Fig. 1.—Beaker with "harlequin" ground. Height 15¾ inches. *S. E. Kennedy Collection.*

Fig. 2.—Jar with dark blue glaze gilt and leaf-shaped reserves. Height 21½ inches. *Burdett-Coutts Collection.*

Fig. 3.—Beaker with fan and picture-scroll panels, etc., in a deep ruby pink ground. Height 14½ inches. *Wantage Collection.*

30. Reproductions of wares with incised green decoration in a yellow glaze (*chiao huang*).

31. Reproductions of yellow-glazed wares: including plain and with incised ornament.

32. Reproductions of purple brown (*tzŭ*) glazed wares: including plain and with incised ornament.

33. Porcelain with engraved ornament: including all kinds of glazes.

34. Porcelain with embossed (*tui*) ornament: including all kinds of glazes.

35. Painted red (*mo*[423] *hung*): copying old specimens.

36. Red decoration (*ts'ai hung*): copying old specimens.

37. Porcelain in yellow after the European style.[424]

38. Porcelain in purple brown (*tzŭ*) after the European style.

39. Silvered (*mo yin*) porcelain.

40. Porcelain painted in ink (*shui mo*): see p. 214.

41. Reproductions of the pure white (*t'ien pai*)[425] porcelain of the Hsüan Tê period: including a variety of wares thick and thin, large and small.

42. Reproductions of Chia Ching wares with blue designs.

43. Reproductions of Ch'êng Hua pale painted (*tan miao*) blue designs.

44. Millet colour (*mi sê*) glazes. "Differing from the Sung millet colour." In two shades, dark and light.

45. Porcelain with red in the glaze (*yu li hung*): including (1) painted designs exclusively in red, (2) the combination of blue foliage and red flowers.[426]

46. Reproductions of lustrous brown (*tzŭ chin*) glaze: including two varieties, brown and yellow.

47. Porcelains with yellow glaze (*chiao huang*) decorated in enamels (*wu ts'ai*). "This is the result of recent experiments."

48. Reproductions of green-glazed porcelain: including that with plain ground and with engraved ornament.

49. Wares with foreign colours (*yang ts'ai*). "In the new copies of the Western style of painting in enamels (*fa-lang*) the landscapes and figure scenes, the flowering plants and birds are without exception of supernatural beauty and finish."[427]

50. Porcelain with embossed ornament (*kung hua*): including all kinds of glazes.

51. Porcelain with European (*hsi yang*) red colour.

52. Reproductions of *wu chin* (mirror black) glazes: including those with black ground and white designs and those with black ground and gilding.

53. Porcelain with European green colour.

54. European *wu chin* (mirror black) wares.

55. Gilt (*mo chin*) porcelain: copying the Japanese.

56. Gilt (*miao chin*)[428] porcelain: copying the Japanese.

57. Silvered (*miao yin*) porcelain: copying the Japanese.

58. Large jars (*ta kang*) with Imperial factory (*ch'ang kuan*) glazes. "Dimensions: diameter, at the mouth, 3 ft. 4 or 5 in. to 4 ft.; height, 1 ft. 7 or 8 in. to 2 ft. Glaze colours, (1) eel yellow, (2) cucumber (*kua p'i*) green, and (3) yellow and green mottled (*huang lü tien*)."

This last item, which is not included in Bushell's list, appears to be almost a repetition of No. 9, with slightly different phrasing. *Huang lü tien*, which is used instead of the difficult phrase *huang pan tien*, may perhaps be taken as a gloss on the latter, indicating that the spots in the mottled yellow were green. In this case it would appear that the "spotted yellow" was a sort of tiger skin glaze, consisting of dabs of green and yellow (and perhaps aubergine as well). Bushell interpreted it in this sense.

CHAPTER XIII

CH'IEN LUNG 乾隆(1736–1795)

The brief reign of Yung Chêng was followed by that of his son, who ruled under the title of Ch'ien Lung for a full cycle of sixty years, at the end of which he abdicated in accordance with his vow that he would not outreign his grandfather, K'ang Hsi. Ch'ien Lung was a devotee of the arts, and they flourished greatly under his long and peaceful sway. He was himself a collector, and the catalogue of the Imperial bronzes compiled under his orders is a classic work; but more than that, he was personally skilful in the art of calligraphy, which ranks in China as high as painting; and he was a voluminous poet. It is no uncommon thing to find his compositions engraved or painted on porcelain and other artistic materials. Bushell[429] quotes an example from a snuff bottle in the Walters Collection; there is a bowl for washing wine cups in the Eumorfopoulos Collection with a descriptive verse engraved underneath, and entitled, "Imperial Poem of Ch'ien Lung"; and a beautiful coral red bowl in the British Museum has a similar effusion pencilled in gold in the interior.

His interest in the ceramic art is further proved by the command given in 1743 to T'ang Ying to compose a description of the various processes of manufacture as a commentary on twenty pictures of the industry which belonged to the palace collections; and one of the earliest acts of his reign was to appoint the same celebrated ceramist in 1736 to succeed Nien Hsi-yao in the control of the customs at Huai-an Fu, a post which involved the supreme control of the Imperial porcelain manufacture.

There is little doubt that T'ang Ying[430] was the most distinguished of all the men who held this post. He is, at any rate, the one whose achievements have been most fully recorded. He was himself a prolific writer, and a volume of his collected works has been published with a preface by Li Chü-lai. His autobiography is incorporated in the *Chiang hsi t'ung chih*; his twenty descriptions of the processes of porcelain manufacture are quoted in the *T'ao shuo* and the *T'ao lu*, and in themselves form a valuable treatise on Chinese porcelain; and before taking up his post at Huai-an Fu in 1736 he collected together, for the benefit of his successors at Ching-tê Chên, the accumulated notes and memoranda of eight years. This last work is known as the *T'ao ch'êng shih yu kao* ("Draughts of Instructions on the Manufacture of Porcelain"), and the preface[431] quoted in the Annals of Fou-liang furnishes some interesting details concerning Tang's labours. We learn, for instance, that when he was appointed to the factory at Ching-tê Chên in 1728, he was "unacquainted with the finer details of the porcelain manufacture in the province of Kiangsi," having never been there before. He worked with heart and strength, however, sleeping and eating with the workmen during a voluntary apprenticeship of three years, until in 1731 "he had conquered his ignorance of the materials and processes of firing, and although he could not claim familiarity with all the laws of transformation, his knowledge was much increased."

The commissionership of the customs was transferred in 1739 from Huai-an Fu to Kiu-kiang, which is close to the point of junction between the Po-yang Lake and the Yangtze, and considerably nearer to the Imperial factory at Ching-tê Chên, the control of which remained in T'ang's hands until 1749.

The *Ching-tê Chên T'ao lu*[432] is almost verbose on the subject of T'ang's achievements. He had a profound knowledge, it tells us, of the properties of the different kinds of clay and of the action of the fire upon them, and he took every care in the selection of proper materials, so that his wares were all exquisite, lustrous, and of perfect purity. In imitating the celebrated wares of antiquity he never failed to make an exact copy, and in the imitation of all sorts of famous glazes there were none which he could not cleverly reproduce. There was, in fact, nothing that he could not successfully accomplish. Furthermore, his novelties[433] included porcelains with the following glazes and colours: foreign purple (*yang tzŭ*), cloisonné blue (*fa ch'ing*), silvering (*mo yin*), painting in ink black (*ts'ai shui mo*), foreign black (*yang wu chin*), painting in the style of the enamels on copper (*fa lang*), foreign colouring in a black ground (*yang ts'ai wu chin*), white designs in a black ground (*hei ti pai hua*), gilding on a black ground (*hei ti miao chin*), sky blue (*t'ien lan*), and transmutation glazes (*yao pien*). The clay used was white, rich (*jang*) and refined, and the body of the porcelain, whether thick or thin, was always unctuous (*ni*). The Imperial wares attained their greatest perfection at this time.

The preface to T'ang's collected works, which is quoted in the same passage, singles out as special triumphs of his genius the revival of the manufacture of the old dragon fish bowls (*lung kang*) and of the Chün yao, and the production of the turquoise and rose (*mei kuei*) colours in "new tints and rare beauty." It is obvious from these passages that T'ang was responsible for many of the types enumerated in Hsieh Min's list in the preceding chapter, not only among the reproductions of antiques but among the new inventions of the period, such as the cloisonné blue, foreign purple, silvering, painting in ink black, and foreign black. It follows, then, that these novelties could not have been made much before 1730, for T'ang was still at that time occupied chiefly with learning the potter's art. It is equally certain that he continued to make a specialty of imitating the older wares during the reign of Ch'ien Lung, so that we may regard the best period of these reproductions as extending from 1730–1750.

In reading the list of T'ang's innovations the reader will perhaps be puzzled by the varieties of black decoration which are included. Before attempting to explain them it will be best to review the different kinds of black found on Chinese porcelain of the Ch'ing dynasty. There is the high-fired black glaze, with hard shining surface likened to that of a mirror and usually enriched with gilt traceries. This is the original *wu chin* described by Père d'Entrecolles.[434] The other blacks are all low-fired colours of the muffle kiln applied over the glaze and ranking with the enamel colours. They include at least five varieties: (1) The dry black pigment, derived from cobaltiferous ore of manganese, applied like the iron red without any glassy flux. (2) The same pigment washed over with a transparent green enamel. This is the iridescent greenish black of the *famille verte*, and it continued in use along with the *famille rose* colours in the Yung Chêng and Ch'ien Lung periods and onwards to modern times. (3) A black enamel in which the same elements—manganese black and copper green—are compounded together. This is the modern *wu chin*, of which a sample in the Sèvres Museum (from the collection of M. Itier) was described by Julien[435] as "noir mat; minerai de manganese cobaltifère et oxyde de cuivre avec céruse." It appears on modern Chinese porcelain as a sticky greenish black enamel, inferior in depth and softness to the old composite black of the *famille verte*; but for all that, this is the *yang wu chin* (foreign black) of the Yung Chêng and Ch'ien Lung periods. In the days of T'ang Ying it was a far superior colour. (4) A mottled greenish black occurs as a monochrome and as a ground colour with reserved discs enamelled with *famille rose* colours on the exterior of two bowls in the British Museum, both of which have the cyclical date, *wu ch'ên*, under the base, indicating the year 1748 or 1808, probably the latter. (5) An enamel of similar texture but of a purplish black colour is used on a snuff bottle in the same collection to surround a figure design in underglaze blue. This piece has the Yung Chêng mark in red, but from its general character appears to be of later date.

In the list of T'ang's innovations there is *yang wu chin* (foreign black), which is doubtless the same as the *hsi yang wu chin* (European black) of Hsieh Min's list. It is clear that this is something different from the old green black of the *famille verte* porcelain, and we can hardly be wrong in identifying it with the *wu chin* enamel described above in No. 3. Compared with the original mirror black *wu chin* glaze this enamel has a dull surface, and we can only infer that the term *wu chin* had already lost its special sense of metallic black, and was now used merely as a general term for black.

Assuming this inference to be correct, the term yang *ts'ai wu chin* (foreign painting in a black ground) should mean simply *famille rose* colours surrounded by a black enamel ground of the type of either No. 2 or No. 3. It is, of course, possible that the *wu chin* here is the old mirror black glaze on which enamelling in *famille rose* colours would be perfectly feasible; but I do not know of any example, whereas there is no lack of choice porcelains answering to the alternative description.

The two remaining types, *hei ti pai hua* (white decoration in a black ground) and *hei ti miao chin* (black ground gilt), apparently leave the nature of the black undefined, but as the expressions appear verbatim in the note attached to No. 52 of Hsieh Min's list, which is "reproductions of *wu chin* glaze," we must regard the black in this case, too, as of the *wu chin* type. The black ground with gilding can hardly refer to anything but the well-known mirror black glaze with gilt designs; and the white designs in black ground is equally clearly identified with a somewhat rarer type of porcelain in which the pattern is reserved in white in a ground of black enamel of the type of No. 3. There are two snuff bottles in the British Museum respectively decorated with "rat and vine," and figure subjects white with slight black shading and reserved in a sticky black enamel ground. Both these are of the Tao Kuang period, but there are earlier and larger examples elsewhere with a black ground of finer quality. Such a decoration is scarcely possible with anything but an enamel black, and though there is some inconsistency in the grouping of an enamel and a glaze together in Hsieh Min's list, they were apparently both regarded as "reproductions" of the old mirror black *wu chin*.

Out of the remaining innovations ascribed to T'ang's directorate, the *fa ch'ing* (cloisonné or enamel blue) and the *fa long hua fa* (painting in the style of the enamels on copper) have already been described in connection with Hsieh Min's list. The latter expression occurs verbatim in the note attached in the Annals of Fou-liang[436] to No. 49 of the list, which is "porcelain with foreign colouring," and it clearly refers to the free painting on the Canton enamels for reasons already given.[437] It is true that *fa lang* (like *fo lang*, *fu lang*, and *fa lan*, all phrases suggestive of foreign and Western origin) is commonly used in reference to cloisonné enamel, but the idea of copying on porcelain "landscapes, figure subjects, flowering plants, and birds" from cloisonné enamels is preposterous to anyone who is familiar with the cramped and restricted nature of work bounded by cloisons. It is a pity that Bushell has confused the issue by rendering this particular passage "painting in the style of cloisonné enamel" in his *Oriental Ceramic Art*.[438]

But, it will be objected, the painting in foreign colours has been already shown to have been in full swing some years before T'ang's appointment at Ching-tê Chên. The inconsistency is only apparent, however, for it is only claimed that T'ang introduced this style of painting on the Imperial porcelain, and it may—and indeed must—have been practised in the enamelling establishments at Canton and elsewhere for some time before. Indeed, when one comes to consider the list of T'ang innovations which we have discussed so far, they are mainly concerned with the adaptation of various foreign colours and of processes already in use in the previous reign.

Of those which remain, the *t'ien lan* or sky blue may perhaps be identified with a light blue verging on the tint of turquoise, a high-fired glaze found occasionally in the Ch'ien Lung monochromes. But probably the greatest of T'ang's achievements was the mastery of the *yao pien* or furnace transmutation glazes, which were a matter of chance as late as the end of the K'ang Hsi period. These are the variegated or *flambé* glazes in which a deep red of *sang de bœuf* tint is transformed into a mass of streaks and mottlings in which blue, grey, crimson, brown and green seem to be struggling together for pre-eminence. All these tints spring from one colouring agent—copper oxide— and they are called into being by a sudden change of the atmosphere of the kiln, caused by the admission of wood smoke at the critical moment and the consequent consumption of the oxygen. Without the transformation the glaze would be a *sang de bœuf* red, and in many cases the change is only partial, and large areas of the deep red remain. Fig. 1 of Plate 123 illustrates a small but characteristic specimen of the Ch'ien Lung *flambé*. It will be found that in contrast with the K'ang Hsi *sang de bœuf* these later glazes are more fluescent, and the excess of glaze overrunning the base has been removed by grinding.

Fig. 1   Fig. 2   Fig. 3

Plate 122.—White Porcelain with designs in low relief.

Fig. 1.—Vase, peony scroll, *ju-i* border, etc. Ch'ien Lung period. Height 7 inches. *O. Raphael Collection.*

Fig. 2.—Bottle with "garlic mouth," Imperial dragons in clouds. Creamy crackled glaze imitating Ting ware. Early eighteenth century. Height 9½ inches. *Salting Collection.*

Fig. 3.—Vase with design of three rams, symbolising Spring. Ch'ien Lung period. Height 3½ inches. *W. Burton Collection.*

Another development of the *yao pien* at this time is the use of a separate "transmutation" glaze which could be added in large or small patches over another glaze, and which assumed, when fired, the usual *flambé* appearance. When judiciously applied the effect of this superadded *flambé* was very effective, but it is often used in a capricious fashion, with results rather curious than beautiful. There are, for instance, examples of blue and white vases being wholly or partially coated with *flambé*, which have little interest except as evidence that the potters could now produce the variegated effect at will and in more ways than one.

The use of double glazes to produce new and curious effects is characteristic of the period. The second glaze was applied in various ways by blowing, flecking, or painting it over the first. The Chün glaze of the muffle kiln belongs to this type if it has, as I think, been correctly identified with the blue green dappled with crimson on Fig. 4 of Plate 128; and the bird's egg glazes mentioned on p. 217 belong to the same class.[439] Others of a similar appearance, though not necessarily of the same technique, are the tea dust (*ch'a yeh mo*) and iron rust (*t'ieh hsiu*).

The tea dust glaze has a scum of dull tea green specks over an ochreous brown or bronze green glaze, applied either to the biscuit or over an ordinary white glazed porcelain; and it seems to have been a speciality of the Ch'ien Lung period, though there are known specimens with the Yung Chêng mark and many fine examples were made in later reigns. But neither this glaze nor double glazes in general are inventions of this time. It would be more correct to speak of them as revivals, for the early Japanese tea jars, which are based on Chinese originals, illustrate the principle of the double glaze, and there are specimens of stoneware as old as the Sung if not the T'ang dynasty, with dark olive glaze flecked with tea green, and scarcely distinguishable from the Ch'ien Lung tea dust. It is stated on the authority of M. Billequin (see Bushell, *O. C. A.*, p. 518) that a "sumptuary law was made restricting the use of the tea dust glaze to the Emperor, to evade which collectors used to paint their specimens with imaginary cracks,[440] and even to put in actual rivets to make them appear broken."

The iron rust is a dark lustrous brown glaze strewn with metallic specks (due to excess of iron), and in the best examples clouded with passages of deep red. But these are only two examples of skill displayed by the Ch'ien Lung potters in imitating artistic effects in other materials. Special success was attained in reproducing the many tints of old bronze and its metallic surface. Bright-coloured patina was suggested by touches of *flambé*, and the effects of gilding or gold and silver inlay were rendered by the gilder's brush. The appearance of inlaid enamels was skilfully copied. "In fact," to quote from the *T'ao shuo*,[441] "among all the works of art in carved gold, embossed silver, chiselled stone, lacquer, mother-of-pearl, bamboo and wood, gourd and shell, there is not one that is not now[442] produced in porcelain, a perfect copy of the original piece." Nor is this statement much exaggerated, for I have seen numerous examples in which grained wood, red lacquer, green jade, bronze, and even *mille fiori* glass have been so closely copied that their real nature was not detected without close inspection.

Reverting to T'ang's achievements, we find special mention made of the reproductions of Chün yao which have been already discussed in detail,[443] and of the revived manufacture of the large dragon fish bowls. The latter are the great bowls which caused such distress among the potters in the Wan Li period. They are described in the *T'ao lu*[444] as being fired in specially constructed kilns, and requiring no less than nineteen days to complete their baking. The largest size is said to have measured 6 ft.[445] in height, with a thickness of 5 in. in the wall, one of them occupying an entire kiln. The old Ming dragon bowl found by T'ang Ying[446] at the factory was one of the smaller sizes, and measured 3 ft. in diameter and 2 ft. in height. They were intended for the palace gardens for keeping gold-fish or growing water-lilies, and the usual decoration consisted of Imperial dragons. They are variously described as *lung kang* (dragon bowls), *yü kang* (fish bowls), and *ta kang* (great bowls).

PLATE 123

Eighteenth Century Glazes

Fig. 1.—Square Vase with tubular handles, and apricot-shaped medallions on front and back. *Flambé* red glaze. Ch'ien Lung period (1736–1795). Height 6¾ inches.

British Museum.

Fig. 2.—Bottle-shaped Vase with deep blue (*ta ch'ing*) glaze: unglazed base. Early eighteenth century. Height 15¾ inches.

British Museum.

Fig. 3.—Vase with fine iron red enamel (*mo hung*) on the exterior. Ch'ien Lung period (1736–1795). Height 5 inches.

Salting Collection (V. & A. Museum).

Owing to the tremendous difficulty of firing these huge vessels the order for their supply in the reign of Shun Chih was eventually cancelled, and no attempt was made to resume their manufacture until T'ang's directorate. The usual fish bowl of the K'ang Hsi period is a much smaller object, measuring about 20 in. (English) in diameter by 1 ft. in height; but from the note appended to Hsieh Min's list in the *Chiang hsi t'ung chih* on the Imperial *ta kang*, it appears that already (about 1730) the manufacture had been resumed on the old scale,[447] for the dimensions of those described are given as from 3 ft. 4 or 5 in. to 4 ft. in diameter at the mouth, and from 1 ft. 7 or 8 in. to 2 ft. in height. An example of intermediate size is given on Plate 133, one of a pair in the Burdett-Coutts Collection measuring 26½ in. in diameter by 20 in. in height.

It remains to notice two glaze colours to which T'ang Ying appears to have paid special attention: the *fei ts'ui* (turquoise) and the *mei kuei* (rose colour). The former has already been dealt with in connection with Ming, K'ang Hsi, and Yung Chêng porcelain, and it is only necessary to add that it occurs in singularly beautiful quality on the Ch'ien Lung porcelains, often on vases of antique bronze form, but fashioned with the unmistakable "slickness" of the Ch'ien Lung imitations. Occasionally this glaze covers a body of reddish colour due to admixture of some coarser clay, which seems to have assisted the development of the colour, and it is worthy of note that there are modern imitations on an earthen body made at the tile works near Peking which, thanks to the fine quality of their colour, are liable to be passed off as old. I have noticed that Ch'ien Lung monochrome vases—especially those which have colours of the *demi-grand feu* like the turquoise—are often unglazed under the base. The foot is very deeply cut, and the biscuit is bare or skinned over with a mere film of vitreous matter, which seems to be an accidental deposit.

The *mei kuei* is the colour of the red rose (*mei kuei hua*), and it is obviously to be identified with the rose carmines derived from gold which were discussed in the last chapter. These tints are found in considerable variety in the early Ch'ien Lung porcelains, from deep crimson and scarlet or rouge red to pale pink, and they are used as monochromes, ground colours, and in painted decoration. A superb example of their use as ground colour was illustrated on the border of Plate 120, which is probably a Yung Chêng piece. Among the gold red monochromes of the the Ch'ien Lung period one of the most striking is a dark ruby pink with uneven surface of the "orange peel" type. Mr. S. E. Kennedy has a remarkable series of these monochromes in his collection.

Speaking generally, the Ch'ien Lung monochromes repeat the types in vogue in the previous reigns of the dynasty with greater or less success. Among the greens, the opaque, crackled glazes of pea, apple, sage, emerald, and camellia leaf tints described on p. 187 were a speciality of the time, and the snake-skin and cucumber tints were also made with success. There were, besides, beautiful celadon glazes of the *grand feu*, and an opaque enamel of pale bluish green *eau de nil* tint. Underglaze copper red was used both for monochromes and painted wares, but with the exception of the liver or maroon colour the former had not the distinction of the K'ang Hsi *sang de bœuf* or the Yung Chêng *soufflé* red. There is a jug-shaped ewer with pointed spout in the British Museum which has a fluescent glaze of light liver red deepening into crimson, and known in Japan as *toko*. It has the Hsüan Tê mark, but I have seen exactly similar specimens with the mark of Ch'ien Lung, to which period this colour evidently belongs. On the other hand, great improvement is observable in the overglaze coral red monochrome derived from iron, whether it be the thin lustrous film of the *mo hung* or the richly fluxed "jujube" red which attains the depth and fullness of glaze. Fig. 3, Plate 123, is a worthy example of the iron red monochrome of the period. As a thick, even and opaque colour this enamel was used in small pieces which wonderfully simulate the appearance of red cinnabar lacquer.

An endless variety of blue glazes were used, the pure blue in dark and light shades, *soufflé* or plain, the purplish blues and violets, the lavenders and *clair de lunes*. These are mainly high-fired glazes, but a favourite blue of this period is a deep purplish blue of soft, fluescent appearance and minutely crackled texture which is evidently a glaze of the *demi-grand feu*. The "temple of heaven" blue is of this nature, though of a purer and more sapphire tint. It is the colour of the ritual vessels used in the worship of heaven and of the tiles with which the temple was roofed. Another variety of this glaze has the same tint, but is harder and of a bubbly, pinholed texture, apparently a high-fired colour. The *t'ien ch'ing* (sky blue) has already been mentioned—a lighter colour between lavender and turquoise. And among the blue enamels which were sometimes used as monochromes at this time is an opaque deep blue of intense lapis lazuli tone.

Among the yellows, in addition to the transparent glazes of the older type, there are opaque enamels, including the lemon yellow with rough granular texture, the waxen[448] sulphur yellow which often displays lustrous patches, and the crackled mustard yellow.

Among the purples and browns there are few changes to note, though much of the greenish brown crackle probably belongs to this time; and there is little to be said about the white wares except that both the true porcelain, whether eggshell or otherwise, and the opaque crackled wares of the Ting yao type were still made with exquisite refinement and finish. The uneven glaze surface, happily compared to "orange peel," was much affected on the Ch'ien Lung whites in common with many other wares of the time. But there were many new enamel monochromes formed by blending the *famille rose* colours, shades of opaque pink, lavender, French grey, and green, which are sometimes delicately engraved with close scroll patterns all over the surface, a type which is known by the clumsy name of *graviata*. These enamel grounds are often interrupted by medallions with underglaze blue or enamelled designs, as on the vase illustrated in Plate 125, Fig. 4, and on the so-called Peking bowls; or, again, they are broken by reserved floral designs which are daintily coloured in *famille rose* enamels. But we are already drifting from the monochromes into the painted porcelains of the period, and we shall return to the Peking bowls presently.

With regard to the Ch'ien Lung blue and white, little need be added to what was said of this kind of ware in the last chapter. It was still made in considerable quantity, and T'ang Ying, in his twenty descriptions of the manufacture of porcelain, supplies a commentary to three pictures[449] dealing with the "collection of the blue material," "the selection of the mineral," and "the painting of the round ware in blue." From these we learn that large services were made in blue and white, and the decoration was still rigidly subdivided, one set of painters being reserved for the outlining of the designs and another for filling them in, while the plain blue rings were put on by the workman who finished the ware on the polishing wheel, and the inscriptions, marks and seals were added by skilful calligraphers. The blue material was now obtained in the province of Chêkiang, and close attention was paid to the selection of the best mineral. There was one kind of blue "called onion sprouts, which makes very clearly defined strokes, and does not run in the fire, and this must be used for the most delicate pieces." This latter colour is to be looked for on the small steatitic porcelains and the fine eggshell cups.

In common with the other Ch'ien Lung types, the blue and white vases are often of archaic bronze form, and decorated with bronze patterns such as borders of stiff leaves, dragon feet and ogre heads. Another favourite ornament is a close pattern of floral scrolls studded with lotus or peony flowers, often finely drawn but inclined to be small and fussy. These scrolls are commonly executed in the blotchy blue described on p. 13, and the darker shades are often thickly heaped up in palpable relief with a marked tendency to run into drops. On the other hand, one sometimes finds the individual brush strokes, as it were, bitten into the porcelain body, and almost suggesting scratched lines. Both peculiarities, the thick fluescent blue and the deep brush strokes, are observable on a small vase of unusually glassy porcelain in the Franks Collection. Two other pieces in the same collection may be quoted. One is a tazza or high-footed bowl with a band of Sanskrit characters and deep borders of close lotus scrolls, very delicately drawn in a soft pure blue, to which a heavily bubbled glaze has given a hazy appearance. This piece (Plate 93, Fig. 1) has the six characters of the Ch'ien Lung seal-mark in a single line inside the foot. The other is a jar which bears the cyclical date corresponding to 1784. Like the last, it has a decoration of Buddhistic import, viz. the four characters 天竺恩波 t'ien chu ên po (propitious waves from India), each enclosed by formal cloud devices. It is painted in a soft but rather opaque blue, and the glaze is again of bubbly texture.

Fig. 1   Fig. 2

Fig. 3

Plate 124.—Miscellaneous Porcelain.

Fig. 1.—Magnolia Vase with *flambé* glaze of crackled lavender with red and blue streaks. Ch'ien Lung period. Height 7 inches. *Alexander Collection.*

Fig. 2.—Bottle with elephant handles, yellow, purple, green and white glazes on the biscuit. Ch'ien Lung period. Height 8¼ inches. *British Museum.*

Fig. 3.—Dish with fruit design in lustrous transparent glazes on the biscuit, covering a faintly etched dragon pattern. K'ang Hsi mark. Diameter 9⅞ inches. *British Museum.*

Fig. 1 Fig. 3

Fig. 2 Fig. 4

Plate 125.—Ch'ien Lung Wares. *Hippisley Collection.*

Fig. 1.—Brush Pot of enamelled Ku-yüeh-hsüan glass. Ch'ien Lung mark. Height 2⅜ inches.

Fig. 2.—Bottle, porcelain painted in Ku-yüeh style, after a picture by the Ch'ing artist Wang Shih-mei. Height 7 inches.

Fig. 3.—Imperial Presentation Cup marked *hsü hua t'ang chih tsêng.* Height 2 inches.

Fig. 4.—Medallion Vase, brocade ground with bats in clouds, etc. Ch'ien Lung mark. Height 7¼ inches.

Plate 126.—Vase with "Hundred Flower" design in *famille rose* enamels.

Ch'ien Lung period (1736–1795). Height 19¼ inches. *Grandidier Collection* (*The Louvre*).

Plate 127.—Vase painted in mixed enamels. The Hundred Deer. *Grandidier Collection* (*Louvre*).

Late Ch'ien Lung period. Height 18 inches.

In the commoner types of Ch'ien Lung blue and white, the blue is usually of a dullish indigo tint, wanting in life and fire. There is, in fact, none of the character of the K'ang Hsi ware; the broad washes, the clear trembling sapphire, and the subtle harmony existing between the glaze and blue, are all missing. Moreover, the decoration, with its careful brushwork and neat finish, has none of the freedom and breadth of the older types. On the whole, it is small wonder that the collector finds little to arouse enthusiasm in the blue and white of this period, if we except the steatitic[450] or "soft pastes," which are eagerly acquired.

Underglaze red painting, and the same in combination with blue or with high-fired glazes and coloured slips, celadon, white, golden brown, olive brown and coffee brown, were perpetuated from the previous reigns; and underglaze blue designs are found accompanied by yellow or coral red enamel grounds in old Ming style, and even by *famille rose* painting.

Decoration in transparent glazes of three colours—green, yellow and aubergine—applied direct to the biscuit is not common on Ch'ien Lung porcelain, but when used it displays the characteristic neatness and finish of the period. I suspect that many of the trim rice bowls with neatly everted mouth rim and dragon designs etched in outline and filled in with aubergine in a green ground, yellow in an aubergine, or the other combinations of the three colours, belong to this reign, in spite of the K'ang Hsi mark under the base. At any rate, the body, glaze and form can be exactly paralleled in other bowls which have a Ch'ien Lung mark.

This criticism applies equally to a striking group of porcelain of which Fig. 3 of Plate 124 is an example. It consists of bowls and dishes, so much alike in decoration that one might suppose all existing examples to be parts of some large service. The body is delicately engraved with five-clawed dragons pursuing pearls, and somewhat inconsequently over these are painted large and boldly designed flowering sprays (rose, peony, etc.) or fruiting pomegranate branches with black outlines filled in with fine, transparent aubergine, full yellow and green in light and dark shades. The remaining ground space is coated with the thin greenish wash which does duty for white in this colour scheme, but in these particular pieces it is unusually lustrous and iridescent. In fact, on the back of a dish in the British Museum it has developed patches of golden lustre of quite a metallic appearance and similar to those noted on the sulphur yellow monochrome described on p. 239. This lustrous appearance, however, is probably no more than an exaggerated iridescence, for there is no reason to suppose that the Chinese ever used metallic lustre of the Persian or European kind.[451] This group of porcelain always bears the K'ang Hsi mark, but a comparison with the bowls of later date, both in material and in the general finish of the ware and the style of the colouring, irresistibly argues a later period of manufacture, unless, indeed, we admit that the Imperial bowls of the late K'ang Hsi and the Ch'ien Lung periods are not to be differentiated. The finish of these wares, in fact, compares more closely with that of the finer Tao Kuang bowls than with the recognised types of K'ang Hsi porcelain.

Another kind of on-biscuit decoration of the Ch'ien Lung—and perhaps the Yung Chêng—period is best described from a concrete example, viz., Fig. 2 of Plate 124, a pear-shaped bottle in the British Museum with sides moulded in shallow lobes, an overlapping frill or collar with scalloped outline on the neck, and above this two handles in shape of elephants' heads. The ground colour is a deep brownish yellow relieved by borders of stiff leaves with incised outline filled in with smooth emerald green; and the collar and handles are white with cloud scroll borders of pale aubergine edged with blue. The general colouring, as well as the form of this vase, is closely paralleled in fine pottery of the same period.

It may be added that *famille rose* enamels are sometimes used in on-biscuit polychrome decoration, but the effect is not specially pleasing. Some of the opaque colours serving as monochromes are also applied in this way, but here the absence of a white glaze beneath is scarcely noticeable, owing to the thickness and opacity of the enamels.

But all the other forms of polychrome decoration at this period must yield (numerically, at any rate) to the on-glaze painting in *famille rose* enamels, or, as the Chinese have named them, "foreign colours." The nature of these has been fully discussed, but there is no doubt that their application was widely extended in the Ch'ien Lung period, and one point of difference, at least, is observable in their technique, viz. the mixing of the tints in the actual design so as to produce the European effect of shading. By this means the graded tints in the petals of a flower, and the stratified surface of rocks and mountains, are suggestively rendered.

It would be impossible to enumerate the endless varieties of design employed in this large group. Contrasting the decoration of his own time with that of the Ming porcelain, the author of the *T'ao shuo*,[452] which was published in 1774, says: "Porcelain painted in colours excelled in the Ming dynasty, the majority of the patterns being derived from embroidery and brocaded satins, three or four only out of each ten being from nature and copies of antiques. In modern porcelain, out of ten designs you will get four of foreign colouring, three taken from nature, two copies of antiques, one from embroidery or satin brocade."

In their ordinary acceptation the terms are not mutually exclusive, and the last three types might be, and indeed are, all expressed in foreign colouring; but presumably the writer refers especially to that kind of "foreign colouring" which was directly based on the Canton enamels and is illustrated in the ruby-back eggshell dishes.

The designs taken from nature would include figure subjects representing personages and interiors, landscapes, growing flowers and fruit, and the like, good examples of which are shown on Plates 126 and 127. The one represents the "Hundred Flowers," the vase being, as it were, one great bouquet and the flowers being drawn naturalistically enough to be individually recognised. The other recalls the celebrated picture of the "Hundred Deer" by the late Ming artist, Wên Chêng-ming.[453]

The copies of antiques would comprise bronze patterns and designs borrowed from old porcelain, examples of which are not uncommon. And the brocade patterns, in spite of the low proportion assigned to them in the *T'ao shuo*, occur in relatively large numbers in Western collections. They mostly consist of flowers or close floral scrolls in colour, and reserved in a monochrome ground of yellow, blue, pink, etc. This is the characteristic Ch'ien Lung scroll work which is used both in borders and over large areas such as the exterior of a bowl or the body of a vase. The reserved pattern, highly coloured and winding through a ground of solid opaque enamel, suggests analogy with the scroll grounds of the contemporary cloisonné enamel; but this incidental likeness has nothing to do with the question of "painting in *fa lang* style," which was discussed among T'ang's innovations. The finer Ch'ien Lung porcelains, and especially those enamelled with brocade designs, are frequently finished off with a coating of opaque bluish green enamel inside the mouth and under the base, a square panel being reserved for the mark. Needless to say, with all this weight of enamelling little or nothing is seen of the porcelain itself, the fine quality of which is only indicated by the neatness of the form and the elegance of the finish.

The green black which was discussed earlier in the chapter is used with striking effect, both in company with *famille rose* colours (as on Fig. 2 of Plate 131) and without them. An effective decoration of the latter kind is shown on a beautiful bottle-shaped vase with wide, spreading mouth in the Salting Collection, which is covered with close floral scrolls reserved in a ground of black pigment, the whole surface being washed over with transparent green. The result is a peculiarly soft and rich decoration of green scrolls in a green black ground.

Nor was the iron red—a colour much employed in monochromes at this time—neglected in the painted wares. Indeed, it occurs as the sole pigment on many pieces, and on others it forms a solid brick red or stippled *soufflé* ground for floral reserves, medallions and panels of *famille rose* enamelling.

Among the opaque enamels a few shades of blue are similarly used, while the others, as already mentioned, form plain or engraved backgrounds for floral reserves and panel decoration as on Fig. 2 of Plate 125, and on the Peking bowls. The latter are so named not because they were made at Peking, but because the specimens acquired by Western collectors have been chiefly obtained from that source. Many of them have the Ch'ien Lung mark, and their ground colours comprise a variety of pinks, yellow, green, French grey, dark blue, slaty blue, amaranth, lavender, bluish green,[454] delicate greenish white and coral red. The medallions on the bowls—usually four in number— are commonly decorated with growing flowers, such as the flowers of the four seasons in polychrome enamels, while others have figure subjects, frequently European figures in landscape setting and with Chinese attributes, such as a *ju-i* or *ling-chih* fungus. The finish of these bowls is extremely fine, and they are well worthy of the Imperial use to which they were mostly destined.

The mention of a delicate greenish white enamel on these medallion bowls reminds us that this colour is used with exquisite effect for borders of floral design, or even for the main decoration of tea and coffee wares; and there is a little plate in the British Museum with Ch'ien Lung mark on which it appears with a peculiar chilled or shrivelled surface as a background for painted designs in iron red.

There is a large class of enamelled porcelain, doubtless made chiefly for export, which found its way into our country houses in the last half of the eighteenth century. It is painted with panels of figure subjects in which rose pink and iron red are uncompromisingly blended, and the space surrounding the panels is filled with composite designs of blue and white with passages of pink scale diaper or feathery gilt scrolls broken by small vignettes in which a bird on a bough, insects, growing plants or fragments of landscape are painted in *camaieu* pink, red or sepia. In some cases the panels are framed with low, moulded reliefs, which extend into the border spaces, and the groundwork in these parts is powdered with tiny raised dots. The wares include large punch bowls, bottle-shaped ewers with their basins, and sets of five vases, two of which are beakers and three covered jars with lion knobs, ovoid or square, and sometimes of eggshell thinness. Others again have their panels enclosed by wreaths of flowers and foliage or "rat and vine pattern" in full relief, and many of them have a glaze of lumpy, "orange peel" texture. The name "Mandarin" has been given to these wares because the central figure subjects usually contain personages in official dress; and the large punch bowls brought back by the tea-merchants are included in this group, though the mandarin figures in the panels are in this case often replaced by European subjects.

Elaborately moulded and pierced ornament coloured in *famille rose* enamels often appears on the table ware of this period, a familiar example being the lotus services in which the motive of the pink lotus flower is expressed partly by moulding and partly by painting, the tendrils and buds being utilised for feet and handles; and there are elegant *famille rose* teapots which have outer casings with panels of prunus, bamboo and pine carved in openwork in the style of the Yi-hsing pottery.

Gilding was, of course, freely employed, and, to a lesser extent, silvering. Elaborate gilt patterns are found covering dark blue, powder blue, lustrous black, bronze green, pale celadon, and iron red monochrome grounds; and the finer enamelled vases and bowls are often finished off with gilt edging, which does not seem to have been much used before this period, though traces of gilding are sometimes seen on the lustrous brown edges of the older plates and bowls.

The manual dexterity of the Ch'ien Lung potters is shown in openwork carving and pierced designs on lanterns, perfume boxes, insect cages, spill vases, etc., but more especially on the amazing vases with free-working belts, revolving necks, or decorated inner linings which can be turned round behind a pierced outer casing, chains with movable links, and similar *tours de force.*

There are, beside, two types of ornament dating from this period which demand no little manual skill. These are the lacework and rice grain. In the former the design is deeply incised in the body and the whole covered with a pale celadon green glaze, and it is usually applied to small vases and tazza-shaped cups, the pattern consisting of close and intricate Ch'ien Lung scrollwork. The resultant effect is of a very delicate green lace pattern, which appears as a partial transparency when held to the light (Plate 128, Fig. 2). The rice-grain ornament carries the same idea a step farther, for the incised pattern is cut right through the body, leaving small perforations to be filled up by the transparent glaze. Only small incisions could be made, and these generally took the lenticular form which the French have likened to grains of rice (Plate 128, Fig. 1). The patterns made in this fashion are naturally limited. Star-shaped designs or flowers with radiating petals are the commonest, though occasionally the transparencies are made to conform to the lines of painted decoration and even of dragon patterns.

Both ordinary and steatitic porcelain are used for this treatment; and the ware is either plain white or embellished with underglaze blue borders and designs, and occasionally with enamels. The effect is light and graceful, especially when transmitted light gives proper play to the transparencies.

As to the antiquity of this decoration in China, I can find no evidence of its existence before the eighteenth century, and I am inclined to think it was even then a late development. There are two cups in the Hippisley Collection with apocryphal Hsüan Tê dates, but the majority of marked examples are Ch'ien Lung or later. Out of fourteen pieces in the Franks Collection five have the Ch'ien Lung mark, two have palace marks of the Tao Kuang period,[455] and one has a long inscription stating that it was made by Wang Shêng-Kao in the fourth month of 1798.[456] The rest are unmarked. The manufacture continues to the present day, and the same process has been freely used in Japan, where it is called *hotaru-de*, or firefly decoration. In this type of ornament the Chinese were long forestalled by the potters of Western Asia, for the rice-grain transparencies were used with exquisite effect in Persia and Syria in the twelfth century if not considerably earlier.

It remains to mention a species of decoration which is not strictly ceramic. It consists of coating the porcelain biscuit with black lacquer in which are inlaid designs in mother-of-pearl, the *lac burgauté* of the French (Plate 128, Fig. 3). This porcelain is known by the French name of *porcelaine laquée burgautée*, and it seems to have been originally a product of the Ch'ien Lung period; at any rate, I can find no evidence of its existence before the eighteenth century.

In the Ch'ien Lung period Chinese porcelain reaches the high-water mark of technical perfection. The mastery of the material is complete. But for all that the art is already in its decline. By the middle of the reign it is already overripe, and towards the end it shows sure signs of decay. At its best the decoration is more ingenious than original, and more pretty than artistic. At its worst it is cloying and tiresome. The ware itself is perfectly refined and pure, but colder than the K'ang Hsi porcelain. The *famille rose* painting is unequalled at its best for daintiness and finish, but the broken tints and miniature touches cannot compare in decorative value with the stronger and broader effects of the Ming and K'ang Hsi brushwork. The potting is almost perfect, but the forms are wanting in spontaneity; and the endless imitation of bronze shapes becomes wearisome, partly because the intricate forms of cast metal are not naturally suited to the ceramic material, and partly because the elaborate finish of the Ch'ien Lung wares makes the imitation of the antique unconvincing. In detail the wares are marvels of neatness and finish, but the general impression is of an artificial elegance from which the eye gladly turns to the vigorous beauty of the earlier and less sophisticated types.

Fig. 1

Fig. 2

Plate 128.—Ch'ien Lung Porcelain. *British Museum.*

Fig. 1.—Vase with "rice grain" ground and blue and white design. Height 7¾ inches.

Fig. 2.—Vase with "lacework" designs. Ch'ien Lung mark. Height 7¾ inches.

Fig. 3.—Vase with the Seven Worthies of the Bamboo Grove in *lac burgauté.* Height 14½ inches.

Fig. 4.—Vase with "robin's egg" glaze. Height 4⅛ inches.

Plate 129.—Octagonal Vase and Cover, painted in *famille rose* enamels. Ch'ien Lung period (1736–1795).

Height 35 inches. *One of a pair in the Collection of Dr. A. E. Cumberbatch.*

As already mentioned, T'ang Ying was commanded by the Emperor in 1743 to arrange and explain twenty pictures of the manufacture of porcelain which were sent to him from the palace. In twelve days he completed the descriptions which have since been incorporated in various books on porcelain, including the *T'ao shuo* and the *T'ao lu*. They have been translated by Julien[457] and by Bushell,[458] and as most of their facts have been embodied in the previous pages, it would be superfluous to give a verbatim translation of them. The following summary, however, will give the drift of them, and Bushell's translation of the *T'ao shuo* can be consulted for a full rendering.

Illustration

I.—   Collection of the Stones and Fabrication of the Paste.

The porcelain stone (*petuntse*) was obtained at this time
from *Ch'i-mên*, in the province of Kiangnan. "That of pure
colour and fine texture is used in the manufacture of
bowls and vases of eggshell (*t'o-t'ai*), pure white (*t'ien pai*),
and blue and white porcelain." Other earths, including
kaolin, were mined within the limits of Jao-chou Fu.

II.—   Washing and Purification of the Paste.

III.—   Burning the Ashes and Preparing the Glaze.

The ashes of burnt lime and ferns were mixed with *petuntse*
in varying proportions to form the glazing material.

IV.—   Manufacture of Seggars.

The seggars, or fireclay cases, by which the porcelain was
protected in the kiln were made of a coarse clay from Li-
ch'un, near Ching-tê Chên, and we are told that the
seggar-makers also manufactured rough bowls for the use
of the workmen from the same material.

V.—   Preparing the Moulds for the Round Ware.

VI.—   Fashioning the Round Ware on the Wheel.

VII.—   FABRICATION OF THE VASES (*cho ch'i*).

VIII.—   Collection of the Blue Colour.

The mineral was obtained at this time from Shao-hsing
and Chin-hua in Chêkiang.

IX.—   Selection of the Blue Material.

X.—   Moulding the Paste and Grinding the Colours.

XI.—   Painting the Round Ware in Blue.

XII.—   Fabrication and Decoration of Vases.

XIII.—   Dipping the Ware into the Glaze or Blowing the Glaze
on to it.

Three methods of glazing are described: the old method of
painting the glaze on with goat's-hair brush; dipping the

ware into a large jar of glaze; and blowing on the glaze with a bamboo tube covered at the end with gauze.

XIV.— Turning the Unbaked Ware and Hollowing out the Foot.

This turning or polishing was done on a wheel. For convenience of handling the foot of the vessel was left with a lump of clay adhering until all the processes, except firing, were complete; the foot was then trimmed and hollowed out, and the mark painted underneath.

XV.— Putting the Finished Ware into the Kiln.

XVI.— Opening the Kiln when the Ware is Baked.

XVII.— DECORATING THE ROUND WARE AND VASES IN FOREIGN COLOURING. See p. 242.

XVIII.— The Open Stove and the Closed Stove.

Two types of small kiln used to fire the on-glaze enamels.

XIX.— Wrapping in Straw and Packing in Casks.

XX.— Worshipping the God and Offering Sacrifice.

There are a few illustrations appended to the *T'ao lu* which cover much the same field, but they are roughly drawn. A much better set of coloured pictures is exhibited in frames in the Franks Collection in the British Museum, showing most of the processes described by T'ang.

CHAPTER XIV

EUROPEAN INFLUENCES IN THE CH'ING DYNASTY

Hitherto the references to European influence on Chinese porcelain have been of an incidental nature. But the use of Western designs on the porcelains of the Ch'ing dynasty, and especially in the eighteenth century, attained such large proportions that it is necessary to treat the wares so decorated as a class apart. A highly instructive collection of this type of porcelain is exhibited in the British Museum, where it has been subdivided in groups illustrating porcelain painted in China with European armorial designs, porcelain painted in China after pictures, engravings and other patterns of European origin, European forms in Chinese porcelain, and, lastly, Chinese porcelain decorated in Europe.

The un-Chinese nature of these decorations, which is apparent at the first glance, justifies their segregation. Indeed, the foreign features are in many cases so conspicuous that it is small wonder if in days when little was known of Chinese ceramic history these wares were often attributed to European manufacture. We now know so much of the intercourse between China and Europe in the past, and of the enormous trade carried on by the various East India companies, that no surprise is felt at the idea of orders for table services sent out to China with armorial and other designs for their decoration. Not that anyone whose eye was really trained to appreciate the peculiarities of Chinese porcelain could ever mistake the nature of these wares. The paste and glaze are, with few exceptions, uncompromisingly Chinese, no matter how closely the decorator with his proverbial genius for imitation may have rendered the European design. And even here, if the Oriental touch is not betrayed in some detail, the Chinese colours and gilding will disclose themselves to the initiate.

It is hardly necessary here to allude to the absurd notion that any of this group was made at the little English factory of Lowestoft. If an error which has once had currency is ever completely dissipated, Chaffers's great blunder on the subject of Chinese armorial porcelain should be forgotten by now. But it is high time that those who are fully aware of the facts of the case should abandon the equally stupid and wholly illogical expression, "Oriental Lowestoft," not for Lowestoft porcelain decorated in Chinese style, which would be reasonable enough, but (save the mark!) for Chinese porcelain decorated with European designs. As if, indeed, an insignificant Suffolk pottery, which made no enamelled porcelain[459] until about 1770, had any influence on the decoration of a Chinese ware which was distributed all over Europe during the whole of the century.

The European style of flower painting and the European border patterns were used by the Chinese decorators on this class of ware in the last half of the century, but they were the patterns which originated at Meissen and Sèvres, and which were adopted and developed at Chelsea, Derby and Worcester. Any of these wares might have found their way to China and served as models to the Canton decorators, but the likelihood of Lowestoft porcelain exerting any appreciable influence in the Far East is simply laughable.

But to return to the subject of this chapter, the actual European shapes found in Chinese porcelain can be dismissed in a few words. There are a few figures, such as the well known pair reputed to represent Louis XIV. and his queen. These are of K'ang Hsi type, and decorated with enamels on the biscuit. And there are numerous groups or single figures of the same period in the white Fukien porcelain, discussed on p. 111. A few vase forms, copied apparently from Italian wares and belonging to a slightly later date, and a curious pedestal in the British Museum, modelled in the form of a tree trunk with two Cupids in full relief near the top, are purely Western.[460] Needless to say, the bulk of the useful ware, being intended for European consumption, was made after European models, which speak for themselves.

Much might be written on the painted designs of this class if space permitted, but we must be content with citing a few typical instances, most of which may be seen in the Franks Collection. To the K'ang Hsi period belong some curious imitations of Dutch Delft, in which even the potter's marks are copied, the designs having been, oddly enough, borrowed in the first instance from Oriental wares by the Dutch potters. There are the so-called "Keyser cups," tall, covered cups with saucers, painted in blue with kneeling figures surrounding a king and queen, who probably represent St. Louis of France and his consort; and in the border is the inscription, L'EMPIRE DE LA VERTU EST ESTABI JUSQ'AU BOUT DE L'UNERS. Another cup has a design of a ship and a syren, with legend, GARDES VOUS DE LA SYRENE; and there are small plates with the siege of Rotterdam[461] copied in blue from a Dutch engraving.

PLATE 130

Vase with pear-shaped body and wide mouth; tubular handles. Porcelain with delicate *clair de lune* glaze recalling the pale blue tint of some of the finer Sung celadons. About 1800

Height 7¾ inches.

British Museum.

But the group which probably commands the greatest interest is that known as "Jesuit china," decorated with subjects bearing on the Christian religion. The earliest examples are painted in underglaze blue, the Christian designs being accompanied by ordinary Chinese ornaments. An early (to judge from the general style of the piece, late Ming) example is a pear-shaped ewer, with elongated spout and handle, in the Kunstgewerbe Museum, Berlin. On the side is the sacred monogram IHS, surrounded by formal ornament, and it has been plausibly suggested that the little vessel had been used for Communion purposes. A bowl with fungus mark in the Franks Collection has a Crucifixion on the exterior, framed in a pattern of cloud-scrolls, and inside with truly Chinese tolerance is painted a Buddhist pearl symbol in flames and clouds. A cup in the same series with the "jade" mark[462] has a Crucifixion half lost among the surrounding arabesque scrolls. These two are of the K'ang Hsi period, and were probably made with the pieces to which Père d'Entrecolles[463] alludes, in his letter dated 1712, as follows: "From the debris at a large emporium they brought me a little plate which I treasure more than the finest porcelain made during the last thousand years. In the centre of the plate is painted a crucifix between the Virgin and St. John, and I am told that this kind of porcelain was shipped sometimes to Japan, but that this commerce came to an end sixteen or seventeen years ago. Apparently the Japanese Christians took advantage of this manufacture at the time of the persecution to obtain pictures of our mysteries, and these wares, mingled with others in the crates, eluded the vigilance of the enemies of our religion. This pious artifice was no doubt eventually discovered and rendered useless by more stringent investigation, and that is why the manufacture of this kind of ware has ceased at Ching-tê Chên."

These early types, which are rare to-day, have a special interest because they were decorated at Ching-tê Chên, and their general style indicates that they were made for Oriental use.

After an interval of some years the Jesuit china reappeared in a more sophisticated form, probably the work of Canton decorators. The designs, various Biblical scenes, are copied in black and gold from European engravings, and they occur on plates with rims, tea and coffee services, and other articles of European use. The earliest may date from the Yung Chêng period, but they are mostly Ch'ien Lung, and the same designs are occasionally executed in enamel colours. In addition to the Christian china there are plates and dishes decorated with rings of Koranic inscriptions in Arabic, surrounding magic squares, and destined for the Mussulman markets.

The Franks Collection includes, besides, numerous examples of profane subjects[464] copied in black or in colours from European engravings and designs. A striking instance of the patient skill of the Chinese copyist is given by two large plates completely covered with the designs—the Triumph of Mordecai and Achilles dipped in the Styx—copied line for line, apparently, from Le Sueur's engravings. The effect of the fine lines and cross-hatching is perfectly rendered, and one would say at first that they had been transfer-printed if this process had ever been used by the Chinese. It is amusing, too, to find English topical and political subjects rendered on Chinese porcelain, mugs and punch bowls, with busts of the Duke of Cumberland, Prince Charles Edward, and John Wilkes with appropriate inscriptions. There are, too, satirical pictures in the style of Hogarth, and a few popular but not overrefined subjects which gain an additional drollery from the obviously Chinese rendering of the figures. Many large punch bowls still survive decorated to suit their owner's tastes, with a full-rigged ship for the sea captain, a hunting scene for the master of hounds, and agricultural designs for the farmer, often proudly inscribed with the name of the destined possessor and the date of the order. The Chinese touch is usually betrayed in these inscriptions, which are obviously reproduced mechanically, and with no compunction felt for a letter here and there inverted or misplaced.

These porcelains with European pictorial designs are, as a rule, more curious than beautiful, but it cannot be denied that the next group with European coats of arms emblazoned in the centre is often highly decorative. This is particularly true of the earlier examples in which the shields of arms are not disproportionately large, and are surrounded with tasteful Chinese designs. The heraldry is carefully copied and, as a rule, the tinctures are correct. In the older specimens the blue is usually under the glaze, and from this, and from the nature of the surrounding decoration in *famille verte* or transition colours, one may assume that the pieces in question were decorated at Ching-tê Chên. From the middle of the Yung Chêng period onwards a large and constantly increasing proportion of the ware was decorated at Canton, in the enamelling establishments which were in close touch with the European merchants, and from this time European designs begin to encroach on the field of the decoration. Finally, in the last decades of the century the Chinese armorial porcelain is decorated in purely European style. An important though belated witness to the Canton origin of this decoration is a plate in the Franks Collection with the arms of Chadwick in the centre, a band of Derby blue, and a trefoil border on the rim, and on the reverse in black the legend, *Canton in China, 24th Jan", 1791.*

Side by side with this armorial porcelain, and apparently also decorated at Canton, there was painted a large quantity of table ware for Western use with half-European designs in which small pink rose-sprays are conspicuous. These are the cheaper kinds of useful ware which are found everywhere in Europe, and must have formed a large percentage of the export trade in the last half of the eighteenth century. The decoration, though usually slight and perfunctory, is quite inoffensive and suitable to the purpose of the ware.

But to return to the armorial porcelain: apart from its heraldic and decorative value, it is often important to the student of Chinese ceramics, because there are specimens which can be dated very precisely from the armorial bearings and other internal evidence. In the British Museum series there are some twenty pieces belonging to the K'ang Hsi period, including an early underglaze blue painted dish with arms of Talbot, and one or two specimens of pure *famille verte*, including the plate dated 1702, which has already been mentioned as being of a peculiar white and glassy-looking ware. There are examples with underglaze blue and enamel decoration in the Chinese Imari style, and there is a very distinctive group which can be dated armorially[465] to the late K'ang Hsi and early Yung Chêng period. These latter pieces are usually decorated with a shield of arms in the centre in enamel colours, with or without underglaze blue; the sides are filled with a band of close floral scrolls or brocade diaper in red and gold, broken by small reserves containing flowers and symbols; on the rim are similar groups of flowers and symbols and a narrow border of red and gold scrolls; and on the reverse are a few floral sprays in red. The enamels are of the transition kind, *famille verte* with occasional touches of rose pink and opaque yellow. The porcelain is the crisp, sonorous, well potted ware with shining oily glaze of K'ang Hsi type, and the accessory ornament is of purely Chinese character. A border of trefoil cusps, not unlike the strawberry leaves of the heraldic crown, but traceable to a Chinese origin, makes its first appearance on this group. It is a common feature of subsequent armorial wares, like the narrow border of chain pattern which seems to have come into use about 1730.

Dated specimens of Yung Chêng armorial, with painting in the "foreign colours," have been already described.[466] Other examples of this period have the decoration in underglaze blue outlines washed with thin transparent colours, in black pencilling and in black and gold. The border patterns of lacework, vine scrolls, bamboos wreathed with foliage and flowers, and fine floral scrolls, are often beautifully executed in delicate gilding or in brown and gold.

In the Ch'ien Lung period there was an ever-increasing tendency to displace the Chinese patterns in favour of European ornament. About the middle of the century small bouquets and scattered floral sprays in the well-known Meissen style of painting made their appearance, and the gradual invasion of the border patterns by European motives is apparent. It may be of interest to note a few of the latter as they occur on dated specimens:

1. Light feathery scrolls, gilt or in colours: first half of Ch'ien Lung period.

2. Rococo ornaments combined with floral patterns: first half of Ch'ien Lung period.

3. Large shell-like ornaments and scroll edged frames of lattice work, loosely strung together: early Ch'ien Lung period.

4. Similar motives with more elaborate framework, enclosing diapers, and interrupted by four peacocks at regular intervals and generally black and gold: about 1740 to 1760.

5. Black and brown hexagon diaper, edged with dragon arabesques in gold: an early type of border, but lasting as late as 1780.

6. Composite borders with diapers, symbols, flowers, etc., and sometimes including butterflies, half Chinese and half European: on specimens ranging from 1765 to 1820.

This last border pattern was adopted at Coalport and in other English factories to surround the willow pattern.[467]

In the last decades of the century, such purely European borders as the swags of flowers used at Bow and Bristol, floral and laurel wreaths and husk festoons; the pink scale patterns of Meissen; ribbons and dotted lines winding through a floral band, feather scrolls, etc., of Sèvres origin, and afterwards adopted at Worcester, Bristol, Lowestoft and elsewhere in England; blue with gilt edges and gilt stars, as on the Derby borders, which also derive from Sèvres; and the corn-flower sprigs of the French hard-paste porcelains.

A conspicuous feature of the Ch'ien Lung export porcelain in general is the use of a thin, washy pink in place of the thick carmine of the early *famille rose*. This is a colour common to European porcelain of the period, and it may have been suggested to the Chinese by specimens of Western wares. We may, perhaps, note here a design of Oriental figures (as on the Mandarin porcelain) in pink and red surrounded by borders of pink scale diaper, broken by small panels of ornament. It has no connection with the armorial group, but it has apparently been bandied back and forward from East to West. Based on a Chinese original, it was largely copied on English porcelain, such as Worcester, Lowestoft, etc., and apparently services of the English make found their way east and were copied again at some coast factory, or even in Japan, for the export trade. Much of this hybrid ware is found in Australia and on the east coast of Africa, and though the material and the colours are obviously Oriental, the drawing of the faces reflects a European touch. The porcelain is coarse and greyish, and the decoration roughly executed, probably in the first decades of the nineteenth century.

The trade in Chinese armorial porcelain seems to have gradually died out in the nineteenth century, for reasons which are not far to seek. As far as England was concerned, the improvements in the manufacture both of porcelain and fine earthenware changed her position from that of a consumer to that of a producer. In addition to which, a high protective duty must have adversely affected the import trade, for we read[468] in the notes of Enoch Wood, the Staffordshire potter, that alarm was felt in 1803 in the potteries at the "proposed reduction of £59 8s. 6d. per cent. from the duty on the importation of Oriental porcelain, leaving it at 50 per cent."

Not the least interesting part of the Franks Collection is the section devoted to Chinese porcelain decorated in Europe. In the early years of the eighteenth century a number of enamelling establishments appeared in Holland and in other countries where glass and pottery were decorated in the enamel colours which were then coming into play. As the supply of home-made porcelain was as yet practically non-existent, the enamellers had to look for this material in the Oriental market. Chinese porcelains with slight decoration, plain white wares, or those mainly decorated with incised and carved design under the glaze, and white Fukien porcelain offered the most suitable surface; and these we find treated by Dutch enamellers with the decoration then in vogue among the Delft potters. In the British Museum there are plates with portraits of Dutch celebrities, with designs satirising John Law's bubble, and even with Japanese and Chinese patterns, especially those which the Delft potters were in the habit of copying from the "old Imari." Thus we find the curious phenomenon of Chinese porcelain decorated in Europe with Oriental patterns, and, as may be imagined, these pieces have caused much perplexity to collectors. They are, however, to be recognised by the inferior quality of the enamels and the stiff drawing of the copyists. In the case of the Fukien porcelain with relief ornament, the decorators often confined themselves to touching the raised pattern with colour.

As a rule, these added decorations are crude and unsightly, but there were artists of great skill among the German *chambrelans* (as these unattached enamellers were called), such men as Ignatius Bottengruber and Preussler of Breslau,[469] who flourished about 1720 to 1730. Their designs of figures, mythical subjects, etc., enclosed by baroque scrollwork, were skilfully executed in *camaieu* red or black, heightened with gilding, and their work, which is very mannered and distinctive, is highly prized at the present day. Occasionally we find the handiwork of the Dutch lapidary on Chinese porcelains, a design of birds and floral scrolls being cut through a dark blue or brown glaze into the white biscuit.

About the middle of the eighteenth century a more legitimate material was found for the European decorator in small quantities of Chinese porcelain sent over "in the white." Regular supplies in this state must have been forwarded from Ching-tê Chên to Canton for the enamellers there, and, no doubt, the European merchants were able to secure a small amount of this. Thus it was that Chinese porcelain is occasionally found with decoration by artists whose touch is recognised on Chelsea and other wares. It is not necessary to assume that such pieces were painted in the Chelsea factory. That may have been the case, but we know of important enamelling establishments, such as Duesbury's in London, where Chelsea, Bow and Worcester porcelains obtained in the white were decorated to order. It is probable that the painters trained in this work afterwards passed into the porcelain factories. There are rare examples of Chinese porcelain with transfer prints executed at Battersea or even at Worcester, and apparently one or two pieces have had inscriptions added at Lowestoft; but, after all, this group of decorated Oriental is a very small one, and the specimens painted in the style of any particular English factory except Chelsea could be counted on one's fingers. No doubt the same proceedings were repeated in various parts of the Continent, and there are certainly specimens decorated in the Meissen style, and in one piece in the Franks Collection the Meissen mark has been added.

But besides this more or less legitimate treatment of Chinese porcelain, there is a large group of hideously disfigured wares known by the expressive name of "clobbered china." On these pieces Chinese underglaze decoration has been "improved" by the addition of green, yellow, red, and other enamels and gilding, which fill up the white spaces between the Chinese painting and even encroach on the blue designs themselves. This malpractice dates from the early years of the eighteenth century, and we find even choice specimens of K'ang Hsi blue and white among the victims. Possibly there was a reaction at this time against the Chinese blue and white with which the Dutch traders had flooded the country, but it is pitiful to find nowadays a fine vase or bottle of this ware plastered with meaningless daubs of inferior colour.

Strange to say, the clobberer became an established institution, and he was at work in London in the last century, and maybe he is not yet extinct; and, stranger still, his wretched handiwork has been actually taken as a model for decoration in English potteries, even to the ridiculous travesties of Oriental marks which he often added as the last insult to the porcelain he had defaced. As a rule, the clobbered decoration occurs on blue and white and follows more or less the lines of the original, though it is at once betrayed by its clumsiness and the wretched quality of the enamels used. Occasionally the clobberer was more ambitious, as on a bottle in the British Museum decorated with three spirited monsters in underglaze red. Into this admirably spaced design the clobberer has inserted graceless trees and three ridiculous figures in classical dress standing in Jack-the-giant-killer attitudes with brandished swords over the Chinese creatures. The effect is laughable, but it was vandal's work to deal in this way with choice K'ang Hsi porcelain.

CHAPTER XV

NINETEENTH CENTURY PORCELAINS
Chia Ch'ing 嘉慶(1796–1820)

There is little to distinguish the porcelain of this reign from that of Ch'ien Lung. The old traditions were followed and the high standard of technical skill was maintained to a great extent, though in the absence of original ideas the natural tendency was towards a gradual decline. The blue and white is a mere echo of the Ch'ien Lung blue and white, as is shown by a square jar in the Franks Collection, which bears the date corresponding to 1819. Another dated specimen in the same collection is a little bowl with design of the "Eight Ambassadors of the Tribes of Man" mounted on strange beasts, painted in thin garish blue under a bubbly glaze. There are well-finished monochromes of the Ch'ien Lung type, conspicuous among which is an intense brick red (derived from iron), which has all the depth and solidity of a glaze. The enamelled wares are in no way inferior to their late Ch'ien Lung models, and the medallion bowls with engraved enamel grounds are particularly choice. Plate 132, a richly decorated vase belonging to the Lady Wantage, illustrates a type common to both periods. The design of ladies of the harem in an Imperial pleasure ground is carefully painted in mixed colours and enclosed by rich borders of dark ruby pink enamel, brocaded with polychrome floral scrolls. Another vase in the same collection (marked Chia Ch'ing) has a movable inner lining and pierced outer shell richly enamelled in the same style. The blue green enamel of the Ch'ien Lung porcelain was freely used to finish off the base and mouth of the vases of this time.

Bushell[470] describes as a speciality of the Chia Ch'ing period, vases with elaborate scrollwork of various kinds in underglaze blue enhanced by a richly gilded background; and the mark of this reign will be found on many of the choicer snuff bottles, including those sumptuous little vessels with richly carved and pierced outer casing as finely tooled as Su Chou or Peking lacquer.

We have already seen that rice-grain decoration was effectively used at this time, and no doubt many specimens of the kindred "lacework" were also made. In fact in a general classification of Chinese porcelain it would be almost superfluous to separate the Chia Ch'ing from the Ch'ien Lung groups.

Tao Kuang 道光(1821–1850)

The reign of Tao Kuang is the last period of which collectors of Chinese ceramics take any account. It is true that the general deterioration which was already remarked in the previous reign became more and more conspicuous towards the middle of the nineteenth century. It seemed as though the wells of inspiration in China had dried up and the bankrupt arts continued to exist only by virtue of their past. Curiously enough the same wave of decadence was felt all the world over at this period, and if we compare the porcelain of Tao Kuang with the contemporary English and Continental productions we must confess that the decadence of China was Augustan beside the early Victorian art. The Tao Kuang porcelain in the main is saved from utter banality by the high traditions on which it was grounded and by the innate skill of the Chinese potters. Indeed there are not a few out of the numerous specimens of this period in our collections which have a certain individuality and distinction entitling them to a place beside the eighteenth-century wares.

But, speaking generally, the porcelain is a weak edition of the Yung Chêng types. The forms are correct but mechanical, the monochromes are mere understudies of the fine old colours, and the enamels are of exaggerated softness and weak in general effect.

There are numerous marked specimens of all varieties in the Franks Collection. These include a blue and white vase with bronze designs of ogre heads, etc., in the K'ang Hsi style, but painted in pale, lifeless grey blue, and a bowl with lotus designs and symbols surrounding four medallions with the characters *shan kao shui ch'ang*[471] neatly painted in the same weak blue and signed by Wen Lang-shan in the year 1847. Among the monochromes is a dignified vase of bronze form with deep turquoise glaze dated 1844, besides coffee brown bowls, full yellow bowls, vases with curiously bubbled glaze of dark liver red, and a coral red jar and cover. There is also a large bowl with "tiger skin" glaze patched with yellow, green, aubergine and white. All of these pieces are lacking in quality and distinction, though I have seen far superior specimens of lemon yellow monochrome and tea dust glaze.

The enamelled wares are much more attractive, and many of the rice bowls are prettily decorated in soft colours. The Peking or medallion bowls, for instance, are little if anything below the standard of previous reigns, and in addition to the medallions in engraved enamel grounds of pink, green, grey, etc., outside, the interior is often painted in underglaze blue. There are tasteful bowls with white bamboo designs reserved in a ground of coral red, and there are dishes with blackthorn boughs with pink blossom in a white ground. The Yung Chêng style of underglaze blue outlines with washes of thin-transparent enamels was also affected, but the most characteristic enamelling of the period is executed in a mixture of transparent and opaque enamels, a blend of *famille verte* and *famille rose*. This colouring, soft and subdued, but often rather sickly in tone, is frequently seen on bowls and tea wares with Taoist subjects, such as the Eight Immortals, the fairy attendants of Hsi Wang Mu in boats, or the goddess herself on a phœnix passing over the sea to the *t'ien t'ang* or cloud-wrapt pavilions of Paradise, preceded by a stork with a peach of longevity in its beak. The sea is usually rendered by a conventional wave pattern delicately engraved in greenish white, and sometimes the ground of the design is washed with the same thin, lustrous, greenish white, which was remarked on a group of porcelains described on page 151. The porcelain of these bowls has a white, if rather chalky, body and a greenish white glaze of exaggerated oily sheen, and of the minutely bubbled, "muslin-like" texture which is common to Japanese porcelains. But the ordinary Tao Kuang wares are of poor material, greyish in tone and coarser in grain, with the same peculiarities in the texture of the glaze in an exaggerated degree.

Fig. 1

Plate 131.—Eighteenth Century Painted Porcelain.

Fig. 1.—Plate painted in black and gold, European figures in a Chinese interior. Yung Chêng period. Diameter 9 inches. *British Museum.*

Fig. 2.—Dish with floral scrolls in *famille rose* enamels in a ground of black enamel diapered with green foliage scrolls. Ch'ien Lung period. Diameter 23¼ inches. *Wantage Collection.*

Plate 132.—Vase painted in mixed enamels, an Imperial park and a bevy of ladies. *Wantage Collection.*

Deep ruby pink borders with coloured floral scrolls and symbols. Ch'ien Lung mark. About 1790. Height 30 inches.

A typical example of the fine Tao Kuang rice bowl with Taoist design in the Franks Collection, delicately painted in mixed colours, which recall the Ku-yüeh-hsüan ware of the early Ch'ien Lung period, has the palace mark, *Shên tê t'ang*,[472] in red under the base. A specimen with this mark in the Hippisley Collection[473] is inscribed with a poem by the Emperor Tao Kuang, definitely fixing the date of this hall mark, which is found on choice porcelains made for Imperial use. It occurs on a vase of fine workmanship in the British Museum, decorated with polychrome five-clawed dragons in a lavender enamel ground, of which the base and interior are coated with blue green enamel; and we have already[474] commented on an interesting dish with archaic designs in Ming red and green, which is explained in the mark as an "imitation of the antique made for the *Shên-tê* Hall."

It is worthy of note that most of the porcelain with hall and studio marks in red belong to the nineteenth century, chiefly to the Tao Kuang period. Several of these marks are figured and explained on p. <u>220</u> (vol. i.), but it may be useful if we describe here a few of the specimens on which they occur. The hall mark, *Ch'êng tê t'ang*, appears on a shallow bowl in the Franks Collection painted inside with a coiled dragon in green and a border of bats in red, while outside is a landscape carefully painted in mixed colours in a style similar to Plate 125, Fig. 3. The latter has the Imperial hall mark, *Hsü hua t'ang*, with addition of the word *tsêng* (for presentation), and it has besides an inscription proclaiming that it is the "cup of him who departed as General and returned as Grand Secretary" (*ch'u chiang ju hsiang chih pei*). It is painted with a scene in the palace grounds with the Emperor receiving a military officer.[475] A pretty bowl in the Franks Collection with rockery, flowering plants, fungus, etc., in colours has the palace mark, *ssŭ pu t'ang*; and there are two saucer dishes with Buddhist decoration of palmettes in cruciform arrangement, and a border of Sanskrit characters painted in underglaze blue with washes of transparent enamels marked respectively *Ts'ai jun t'ang*, and *Ts'ai hua t'ang* (hall of brilliant colours and hall of brilliant decoration), which are probably synonymous.

A distinctive group of porcelain, which seems to belong to the Tao Kuang period, consists of small boxes and of vases with landscapes and similar elaborate ornament deeply carved in the manner of red lacquer. The surface is usually covered with an opaque green or yellow monochrome enamel, but occasionally it is left in white biscuit. These pieces have almost always a maker's mark, such as Wang Ping-jung, Wang Tso-t'ing (see vol. i., p. 223), and probably come from one factory. Bushell[476] also alludes to white unglazed porcelain made at this time, and recalling the English Parian ware. It is chiefly seen on small objects for the writing table.

The collector will always be glad to secure specimens of the palace porcelains of the Tao Kuang period, and of the smaller objects on which the weakness of the colouring is not noticeable. There are, for instance, many exquisite snuff bottles with the mark of this reign, with carved, monochrome and enamelled ornament. On the other hand quantities of these little objects coarsely manufactured and sketchily decorated were made at this time, and among them the crude specimens with a floral spray on one side, a line of verse in grass characters on the other, and a granulated border coated with opaque yellowish or bluish green enamel, whose supposed discovery in ancient Egyptian tombs made a sensation some sixty years ago. It is not difficult to guess how these objects traded among the Arabs found their way into the tombs which were in course of excavation, but for a time they were believed to prove the existence of Chinese porcelain in the second millennium before Christ.[477]

Three other types of indifferent ware may be mentioned here in passing. They belong to the middle of the nineteenth century, and in part at least to the Tao Kuang period. One is painted with a large pink peony and foliage in a bright green enamel ground; the second has cut flowers, butterflies and insects in strong rose colours on a celadon green glaze; and the third has rectangular panels with crowded figure subjects in red and pink enclosed by a brocade pattern of flowers, fruit and insects as in the second type. This third class is often represented by large and rather clumsily shaped vases with two handles of conventionalised dragon form, and the border patterns are sometimes backed with gilding; but it also occurs in quite recent manufacture in tea and toilet services made for the export trade. The porcelain in all these cases is of a rough, coarse-grained make, and the reader might have been spared a description of them were it not that in spite of their inferior quality they are the subject of frequent inquiries.

Hsien Fêng 咸豐 (1851–1861)

In the third year of Hsien Fêng the T'ai p'ing rebels captured Ching-tê Chên and burnt down the Imperial factory, which was not rebuilt till 1864. The potters themselves were killed or scattered; and, naturally, marked examples of this reign are scarce. Such, however, as do exist are of little account, and may be regarded as continuations of the Tao Kuang manufacture. Bushell[478] mentions vases of good form painted in soft colours with nine five-clawed dragons on a white background, which is etched in the paste with scrolled waves, and a dinner service of bowls, cups and saucer dishes painted in colours with processional figures of the eighteen Lohan. And in the British Museum there is a large globular bowl on a high foot painted with green dragon designs and a bowl with medallions of lanterns and vases separated by lotus ornament, neither of which are in any way different from the Tao Kuang wares. No doubt a good deal of porcelain was made at the private factories even during this troubled period, but the specimens which I have seen are not worthy of description.

T'ung Chih 同治 (1862–1873)

When the T'ai p'ing rebels had been expelled from the province of Kiangsi by the celebrated viceroy, Li Hung-chang, in 1864, the Imperial factory was rebuilt on the old lines by the new director, Ts'ai Chin-ch'ing. In the same year a list of the porcelain forwarded to the Emperor was drawn up, and it is published in the *Chiang hsi t'ung chih*[479] immediately after Hsieh Min's list. It consists mainly of bowls, wine and tea cups, saucer dishes and plates classified as *yüan ch'i* (round ware), and a few vases under the general heading, *cho ch'i*; and though there is little originality in the designs, lists of this kind are so rare and so instructive that I have no hesitation in giving it in full below, following Bushell's[480] renderings in most cases.

Actual examples of T'ung Chih porcelain are not inspiring. Those in the British Museum include a covered bowl with coloured sprays in a ground of red diaper; a bowl with enamelled sprays on a pale brown (*tzŭ chin*) glaze; a saucer with dragons etched under a transparent green glaze, the exterior in unglazed biscuit painted in black; a cup with red dragons in a ground of black enamel and the cyclical date 1868; a low, octagonal bowl with the Eight Trigrams in relief outside, the interior of this and of the preceding specimen as well being coated with blue green enamel; and a basin enamelled with the Eight Ambassadors of the Tribes of Man. The most favourable specimen of the ware in the same collection is a carefully painted wedding bowl with canary yellow ground and medallions of appropriate symbols, the peach-and dragon-headed staff of longevity, the double fish symbol of conjugal felicity, and the group of pencil brush, cake of ink and *ju-i* sceptre forming the rebus *pi ting ju i*, "may things be as you wish."

LIST OF IMPERIAL PORCELAINS SUPPLIED IN THE THIRD YEAR OF T'UNG CHIH (1864)

VASES (*cho ch'i*)

1.   Quadrangular vases with apricot medallions and two tubular handles with Chün glaze. [For the shape see Plate 123, and for the glaze see p. 1.]

2.   Vases of the same form with Ko glaze.

3.   Quadrangular vases with the Eight Trigrams (*pa kua*), and Ko glaze. [The form is quadrangular body with round neck and foot, moulded in relief with the trigrams; for the Ko glaze see vol. i., p. 71.]

4.   Vases in form of jade ewers (*yü hu ch'un*) with *chi hung* (or copper red) glaze.

5.   Vases of the same form, with blue and white decoration and raised threads. [Bushell explains that the surface is divided into patterns or sections by raised rings.]

6.   Vases of the same form, with blue and white decoration with balcony (*lan kan*). [Bushell explains, "garden scenes enclosed by railings."]

7.   Paper-beater (*chih ch'ui*) vases with the *t'ai chi* symbol and the glaze of the Imperial factory decorated in colours. [The form is the club-shape or *rouleau*; and the symbol is apparently the *yin-yang*, the Confucian symbol for the Absolute.]

8.   Quadrangular vase with elephant symbol of great peace (*t'ai ping yu hsiang*, a rebus meaning "augury of great peace"). [These are apparently square vases with two handles in form of elephant (*hsiang*) heads.]

ROUND WARES (*yüan ch'i*)

1.   Medium-sized bowls with dragons in purple brown (*tzŭ*).

2.   Medium-sized bowls with *chi hung* glaze.

3.   Large bowls (*wan*) with Indian lotus (*hsi lien*) in blue.

4.   Five-inch dishes (*p'an*), similarly decorated.

5.   Medium-sized bowls with storks and Eight Trigrams (*pa kua*).

6.   Wine cups with narcissus flowers (*shui hsien hua*) in enamels.

7.   Wine cups with spreading rim painted with dragons in red.

8.   Dishes (*p'an*) a foot in diameter decorated in blue with a pair of dragons filling the surface.

9.   Soup bowls (*t'ang wan*) with incised dragons under a dark yellow monochrome glaze. [These, according to Bushell, are smaller and shallower than rice bowls.

10.   Medium-sized bowls, barrel shaped, with dragons engraved under a yellow monochrome glaze.

11.   Yellow monochrome tea cups.

12.   Medium-sized bowls with dragons engraved under a yellow monochrome glaze.

13.   Medium-sized bowls with the three fruits in groups (*pan tzŭ*[481]) painted in blue. [The fruits are peach, pomegranate and finger citron.]

14.   Soup bowls with expanding rim and dragons incised under yellow monochrome glaze.

15.   Six-inch bowls with a pair of dragons in blue.

16.   One-foot dishes painted in blue with silkworm scrolls (*ts'an wên*) and longevity characters.

17.   Tea cups decorated in blue with *mu hsi* flowers (a small variety of the *olea fragrans*).

18.   Medium-sized bowls with precious lotus in enamel colours.

19.   Tea cups with white bamboo on a painted red ground.

20.   Six-inch dishes painted in blue with the "three friends" (*san yu*) and figure subjects. [The three friends in floral language are the pine, bamboo and prunus. It is also a name given to the group of Confucius, Buddha, and

Lao-tzŭ, who are often represented examining a picture scroll or standing in conversation.]

21.   Tea dishes (*ch'a p'an*) with a pair of dragons in blue. [Bushell describes these as "little trays with upright borders, of oblong, four-lobed, and fluted outline." They must in fact have closely resembled the old teapot stands of European services.]

22.   Six-inch dishes with green dragons on a ground of engraved water-pattern painted in colour.

23.   One-foot dishes painted in blue with archaic phœnixes (*k'uei fêng*). [These designs are ornaments of bird form, terminating in scrolls such as appear on ancient bronzes.]

24.   Nine-inch dishes with blue ground and dragons in clouds painted in yellow.

25.   Medium-sized bowls with pure white glaze and ruby red (*pao shao*) phœnix medallions.

26.   Tea cups with dragons and clouds painted in yellow in a blue ground.

27.   Six-inch dishes with *chi hung* (copper red) glaze.

28.   Medium-sized bowls with *chi ch'ing* (deep violet blue) glaze.

29.   Nine-inch dishes with *chi hung* glaze.

30.   Soup bowls, barrel shaped, with lustrous brown glaze.

31.   Medium-sized bowls with red phœnix medallions in a celadon (*tung ch'ing*) glaze.

32.   Nine-inch dishes with silkworm scrolls and *ju-i*[482] ornament in enamel colours.

33.   Tea cups enamelled in colours with mandarin ducks and lotus flowers.

34.   Tea bowls (*ch'a wan*) with *chi ch'ing* glaze.

35.   Tea bowls decorated in colours with the *pa pao* (eight attributes of the Taoist Immortals; see p. 287).

36.   Large bowls with the Eight Immortals in blue on red enamelled waves.

37.   Medium-sized bowls, blue and white inside, and with coloured lotus flowers outside.

38. Bowls with the Eight Buddhist symbols of happy augury (*pa chi hsiang*).

39. Porcelain bowls with green designs and peach yellow ground.

40. Five-inch dishes with purple and green dragons in a yellow monochrome ground.

41. Three-inch platters with similar ornament.

42. Soup bowls of the fourth size (*ssǔ hao*) with green monochrome glaze.

43. Five-inch dishes with phœnixes in clouds.

44. Medium-sized bowls with dragons and phœnixes among flowers in coloured enamels.

45. Four-inch platters (*tieh*) with purple and green dragons in yellow monochrome ground.

46. Nine-inch dishes painted in colours with the eight Buddhist symbols among flowers.

47. Large bowls painted in colours with archaic phœnixes (*k'uei fêng*) among flowers.

Kuang Hsü 光緒 (1875–1909)

Marked examples of this modern ware in the Franks Collection include a saucer with coloured sprays in a cloudy pink enamel ground; a covered cup with spout decorated in red with cartouches of seal characters accompanied by translations in the ordinary script, and a dish with blackthorn bough and pink blossoms in Tao Kuang style. In every case the ware is coarse-grained and rough to the touch, while the glaze is of the lustrous surface and "musliny" texture, which is characteristic of the nineteenth century porcelains; and the painting is mechanical and devoid of any distinction. There are two little saucers of better quality both in material and painting, with stork and lotus designs in mixed enamels and marks[483] which show that they are palace pieces made for the Empress Dowager.

But the collector's interest in Kuang Hsü porcelain is of a negative kind. When it is frankly marked he sees and avoids it. But the Chinese potters towards the close of the century evidently recovered some part of the skill which the ravages of the T'ai p'ing rebels seemed to have effectually dissipated; for they succeeded in making many excellent *sang de bœuf* reds and crackled emerald green monochromes which have deceived collectors of experience. Even the best, however, of these wares should be recognised by inferiority of form and material, and in the case of red the fluescent glaze will be found in the modern pieces to have overrun the foot rim, necessitating grinding of the base rim. There are also fair imitations of the K'ang Hsi blue and white and the enamelled vases of *famille verte* or on-biscuit colours, and even of the fine black and green grounds. But here again the inferior biscuit, the lack of grace in the form and the stiffness of the designs will be at once observed by the trained eye. When marked most of these imitations have the *nien hao* of K'ang Hsi, and this is almost invariable on the modern blue and white.

There is, of course, a great quantity of modern porcelain, chiefly enamelled and blue and white, made for the export trade and sold at prices which compete successfully with those of the European wares. It is chiefly in the style of the K'ang Hsi and Ch'ien Lung wares, and is marked accordingly; but the ware is coarse-grained, and the decorations summary, and there is no excuse for mistaking these obvious reproductions for anything but what they are and, in fact, what they pretend to be.

The brief reign of Hsüan T'ung 宣統 (1909–1911) is a blank so far as ceramic history is concerned; and with the fall of the Ch'ing dynasty in 1912 the Imperial works ceased its activity, and it remains to be seen whether Ching-tê Chên will again have the advantage of a state factory to set a standard for the industry in general.

CHAPTER XVI

PORCELAIN SHAPES IN THE CH'ING DYNASTY

A considerable number of the forms which Chinese porcelain assumes have been described in the chapters dealing with the Ming wares; but these may be usefully supplemented by a rapid survey of those employed by the potters of the Ch'ing dynasty. The latter will, of course, include many of the former because the Chinese delight in reproducing the older types.

The brief summary of the eighteenth-century porcelain forms given in the opening pages of the *T'ao shuo*[484] begins in the correct style with the reproductions of the ancient ritual vessels *tsun*, *lei*, *yi*, *ting*, *yu* and *chüo*. These are all bronze forms, *tsun* being applied to wine vessels, *lei* to vases ornamented with the meander pattern known as "cloud and thunder" scrolls,[485] *yi* to bowl-shaped vessels without feet, *ting* to cauldrons with three or four legs and two handles, *yu* to wine jars with covers, and large loop handles for suspension, and *chüo* to libation cups of helmet and other shapes. The bronze forms are commonly decorated with bronze patterns such as the key-fret, archaic dragon and phœnix scrolls, cicada pattern, ogre heads and bands of stiff (banana) leaves, either painted, moulded, engraved, or carved in relief; and the complicated bronze shapes are usually fashioned in moulds, and in many cases furnished with ring handles attached to monster heads. Another ritual type manufactured in porcelain as well as bronze is the altar set of five pieces (*wu kung*), which consists of a *ting* or tripod incense vase, two flower vases, and two pricket candlesticks. A humbler altar set was composed of a single censer or a tazza-shaped cup (Plate 93, Fig. 1) for flowers, and a pair of lions on stands fitted with tubes for holding sticks of incense. The bronze forms have always been used by the Chinese potters, but they were specially affected in the archaising period of Ch'ien Lung.

In the Western judgment, however, which is unbiased by the associations of these antique forms, the true pottery shapes, made on the wheel, will appear far more attractive; for nothing can surpass the simple rounded forms which sprang to life beneath the deft fingers of the Chinese thrower. Their simplicity, grace, and perfect suitability for their intended uses have commended them as models to the Western potter far more congenial than the cold perfection of the Greek vases. Naturally they vary in quality with the skill and taste of the individual, but a high level of manual skill ruled among the Chinese potters, and their wheel-work rarely fails to please.

It would be useless to attempt to exhaust all the varieties of wheel-made forms. Many of them are due to slight alterations of line according to the caprice of the thrower. It will be enough to enumerate the principal types and to note a few of the more significant changes which came in at ascertained periods. By comparing the illustrations in different parts of this book, and better still, by comparing the specimens in some well classified collection, the reader will soon learn to notice the periodical changes of shape. To take the familiar bottle-shaped vases as an instance, there is probably no shape on which more numerous changes have been rung, nor one which is more susceptible to the individual touch; and yet the trained eye will generally distinguish the K'ang Hsi bottle from the later forms, though the distinction is often more subtle than that which separates the typical K'ang Hsi form (Plate 123, Fig. 2) from that with depressed body and straight wide neck (Plate 128, Fig. 3), which is characteristic of the Ch'ien Lung period.

The K'ang Hsi bottles vary in themselves in length and slenderness of neck, and in the form of the body, which may be globular, ovoid, barrel shaped or pear shaped. Again they are often of double or even triple gourd shape, or plain with a bulbous swelling on the upper part of the neck or actually at the mouth. The last variety are called "garlic-shaped" bottles by the Chinese. The normal types are used to hold a single spray or a flowering branch, but there are others with slender necks tapering to a point which are designed for sprinkling perfumes and are generally known as sprinklers.

Of flower vases there are numerous varieties: egg-shaped vases; baluster-shaped vases with spreading mouth; high-shouldered vases with small mouth, the *mei p'ing* of the Ming period; beakers (*ku*) with slender body, swelling belt in the middle and flaring mouth; the so-called *yen yen* vase with ovoid body and high neck with trumpet mouth,[486] which is used for some of the choicest K'ang Hsi decorations (Plate 101); the *Kuan yin*[487] vase of ovoid form with short neck and spreading mouth; the cylindrical vase with short straight neck and spreading mouth (Plate 103), called by the French *rouleau* and by the Chinese "paper-beater" (*chih ch'ui p'ing*), whence our name "club-shaped." A smaller form of the same is known to the Chinese as *yu ch'ui p'ing* (oil-beater vase). . There is besides the wide oval jar or *potiche* with dome-shaped cover (*tsun*), and the more slender form known as *t'an*, which often has a lion or *ch'i-lin* on the cover serving as a knob; the tall cylinder to hold arrows and the low cylinder for brushes, and numerous pots and jars for various uses.

Most of these rounded forms have counterparts among the square and polygonal vases which are made in moulds or built up by the difficult process of joining together flat bats of clay. The square vases made by the latter method were a source of much trouble to the potters owing to the danger of imperfect jointing or of warping in the kiln. Fig. 1 of Plate 104 illustrates an effective type of the square vase with gracefully tapering body, the four sides of which are so often appropriately decorated with the flowers of the four seasons. Occasionally the angles are flattened, giving an irregular octagonal form. Another form selected for sumptuous decoration is the square vase with pendulous body and two dragon handles figured on Plate 97; and another is the arrow stand and square tube with deeply socketed stand and railed border (Plate 118).

The pilgrim bottle supplies an effective model with a flattened circular body, small neck and foot, and loops on the periphery to carry a cord. These loops tended to disappear when the form had lost its first significance and was only regarded as a vase.

The list of Imperial wares made in the reign of T'ung Chih includes vases for divining rods of square form with low round neck and base, ornamented with *pa kua* designs in relief; vases with apricot medallions and tubular handles like Fig. 1 of Plate 123. Other familiar types are the bag-shaped vases with the mouth tied with silk, melon and gourd forms, and the vase shaped like a double fish erect on its tail or a single fish rising from waves.

To quote a few of the types named in the *T'ao shuo*[488]:—"For holding flowers there are vases from two or three inches to five or six feet high, round like a *hu*, round and swelling below like a gallbladder (*tan*), round and with spreading mouth and contracted below like a *tsun*, with flat sides and full angles like a ku, upright like bamboo joints, square like a corn measure (*tou*), with contracted mouth and flattened sides, with square and round flutings, and cut in halves with flat backs for hanging on walls."

For pot-pourri and for fragrant flowers to perfume the rooms various covered jars were provided, hanging vases with reticulated sides (Plate 114), and boxes with perforated covers. For growing plants there were deep flower pots and shallow bulb bowls, and the large and small fish bowls were used for growing water-lilies as well as for keeping gold-fish; and shallow bowls were apparently used as arenas for fighting crickets.[489] As for the vessels in which the crickets were kept, various suggestions have been made in reference to the "cricket pots" mentioned in Chinese books, and the name is sometimes given to reticulated vases and boxes; but we are told that the cricket prefers a damp dwelling, and that their pots were consequently made as a rule of absorbent earthenware. There is a snuff bottle decorated with crickets in the British Museum, and one is represented perched on an overturned pot from which he has apparently escaped, the lid having fallen off. This pot is of ordinary ovoid jar form apparently ornamented with incised fret pattern.

The apparatus of the library table is peculiarly Chinese; and as calligraphy and painting were regarded as among the highest accomplishments, so the potter lavished on the implements of the writer his most ingenious fancies and his most beautiful workmanship. There were porcelain handles for the pencil brush called *pi kuan*; a brush rest (*pi ko*) of many fanciful forms (see Fig. 3 of Plate 60) of which a miniature range of hills was the commonest; a bed (*pi ch'uang*) for it to lie down on, and a cylindrical jar (*pi t'ung*) for it to stand up in; vessels called *hsi* to wash it in, usually of shallow bowl form or shaped like crinkled lotus leaves or in some such dainty design. There were rests for the writer's wrist and paper weights of fantastic form. For the ink (*mo*), there is the pallet (*mo yen*) for rubbing (Plate 94, Fig. 2), and a bed for the ink-cake (*mo ch'uang*), a screen (*yen p'ing*) behind which it was rubbed, small water pots (*shui ch'êng*) in innumerable shapes and served by a tiny ladle, and water droppers (*shui ti*) of quaint and ingenious designs.[490] There were rollers for picture scrolls (*hua chou*) with porcelain ends, and stands for books in the form of small elegantly shaped tables with three or four legs often beautifully painted in enamels on the biscuit.

With these is the incense-burning apparatus which consists of incense box (*hsiang ho*), the vase to hold the tiny tongs and shovel used for the charcoal and incense, and the urn or burner (*shao hsiang lu*). The last appears in very varied shapes, of which the most usual is the tripod cauldron (*ting*) with upright ear-handles. Others take the purely fantastic form of figures of animals, birds and even human beings with open mouth or nostrils to emit the smoke. Tiny vases for a single flower are usually placed upon the writing table, the furniture of which is completed by seals (*yin*), which are commonly modelled after Han dynasty jades with handles in form of camels, tortoises, dragons, tigers, etc., and small boxes to contain the seal vermilion (*yin sê ch'ih*).

Other porcelain objects which combined use and ornament were plaques (*pan*) for screens and slabs for inlaying in pillows, beds, couches and verandah partitions; actual pillows of oblong or semicircular shape with concave surface, the inside hollow and capable of being filled with fragrant herbs; bowls, shaped like the Buddhist alms bowl, for holding black and white chess pieces, and the other requisites for chess (*wei-ch'i*) or *gô*.

With regard to the plaques, we learn that the Emperor Shun Chih gave an order in 1659 for oblong plaques 3 feet by 2½ feet and 3 inches in thickness, but these like the large fish bowls were beyond the powers of the potters at that time. Indeed Père d'Entrecolles tells us that in 1712, the date of his first letter,[491] the potters had much difficulty in executing the orders given by the European merchants for plaques for table tops, etc., and that the largest practicable size was only about a foot square. No advantage was obtained by giving them additional thickness to prevent the fatal warping in the kiln, and it was found better to make the two faces in separate slabs united by cross pieces. Bushell points out that these double plaques were frequently sawn apart and mounted in screens, etc., as separate panels. The complete plaque is usually decorated on one side with a figure subject and on the other with flowers.

We should mention also among miscellaneous objects the beautiful hanging lanterns of eggshell thinness or perforated in openwork patterns; the barrel-shaped garden seats; the curious hat stands, a sphere on top of a tall stem or a little box mounted on long curved legs, the top in either case being hollow and perforated to hold perfumes or ice or charcoal according to the season; boxes of all kinds; small personal ornaments such as hair-pins, ear-rings, girdle-clasps, rosary beads, thumb rings, fingernail covers, tubes for mandarin feathers, buttons and pendants; the little bottles or flasks originally intended for drugs but afterwards consecrated to snuff when the Spaniards or Portuguese had introduced the tobacco plant into China at the end of the sixteenth century; and finally the ornamental heads of opium pipes made chiefly in pottery.

For household use the *T'ao shuo* enumerates rice spoons, tea spoons (*ch'a shih*), sets of chop sticks, vessels for holding candle snuffs, wax pots, vinegar droppers, washing basins (*tsao p'ên*), pricket candle sticks (*têng ting*), pillows (*chên*), square and round, tubs (*p'ên ang*), jars (*wêng*) with small mouth, alms bowls (*po*) with globular body and contracted mouth, plates (*tieh*), and bowls (*wan*); and for tea and wine parties and dinner services, tea pots, wine vessels, bowls, and dishes of every sort.

Bowls (wan) are found in many sizes and shapes, the commonest being the small rice bowl; the shallower type was used for soup (*t'ang wan*). There are deep bowls with covers which might almost be described as jars, and there are tea bowls with covers used for infusing tea in the absence of a tea pot. In drinking from these it was usual to tilt the cover very slightly so as to leave only a narrow egress for the tea and to prevent the leaves accompanying it.

When a tea pot was used, the liquid was served in a tea cup (*ch'a chung*) of tall upright form without handle[492] or cover. The Chinese cup is not furnished with a saucer in European style, but there are straight-edged trays which serve a similar purpose, holding one or more cups, and the old tea bowls and wine cups used to be provided with a circular stand with hollow ring in which the base of the cup could be inserted. The tea pot itself does not seem to be older than the Ming dynasty, and before that time tea bowls only had been used, the vessels with spouts and handles being reserved for wine and other liquids.

A tiny bowl is the usual form of wine cup, but beside these there are goblets with deep bowl, and the shallow-bowled *tazze* with high stems, like the early Ming "stem cups." For ceremonial purposes, the wedding cups and libation cups were shaped after bronze ritual vessels or rhinoceros horn cups; and wine cups for ordinary use sometimes take the ornamental form of a lotus leaf or a flower. The commonest form of wine ewer is the Persian type with pear-shaped body, long graceful handle and spout. Others take fanciful forms like that of a peach or aubergine fruit, a gourd or melon. The peach-shaped ewer with opening under the base is the original of our Cadogan tea pot, and we need be surprised at nothing in Chinese art when we find this same principle and practically the same form in a ewer of T'ang date in the Eumorfopoulos collection. The tall cylindrical ewers with body jointed like a bamboo, and the front shaped at the top like a tiara, are used for sweet syrups.

The Chinese dish is for the most part saucer-shaped. When over half a foot in diameter it is called *p'an*, the smaller dishes or platters being named *tieh*. There are large dishes for fragrant fruits to perfume the room, and lotus-leaf shaped dishes for sweetmeats and various small trays of fanciful form for the dinner table; and there are the "supper sets" consisting of a varying number of ornamental trays which can be used separately, or joined together to form a pattern suggesting a lotus or some other many-petalled flower.

In addition to the native Chinese forms there is a host of specialised objects made for export and designed in foreign taste; such as the deep bowls with pagoda covers for Siam; weights to hold down the corners of a mat for India, in form like a door knob mounted on a circular base; narghili bowls and ewers for Persia, besides the bottle-shaped pipes with mammiform mouthpieces, which sometimes take animal or bird forms such as those of the elephant or phœnix; round covered dishes for Turkey; and all the familiar objects to meet European requirements. The sets of five vases (three covered jars and two beakers) are a purely European garniture intended for the mantelpiece or the sideboard.

There are, besides, all manner of figures—human, animal, or mythical—but they belong rather to the chapter on ornamental motives.

CHAPTER XVII

MOTIVES OF THE DECORATION

Chinese decoration, its motives and its meaning, might form the subject for a substantial and very interesting volume. But it can only be treated here in a summary fashion by enumerating a few of the motives which occur most frequently in porcelain. The designs on the earlier wares have already been discussed in the chapters dealing with the Ming and the preceding periods, but in view of the conservatism of the Chinese artists a certain amount of repetition will be inevitable in discussing the ornament of the Ch'ing dynasty porcelain.

If we except some of the hybrid designs on the export wares which were made for people unfamiliar with Chinese thought, we may assume that there is a meaning in all Chinese decoration apart from its ornamental intention; and this applies not only to the central motives but also as a rule to the subsidiary ornament such as borders and formal patterns. Consequently it is clear that a study of this inner meaning is a necessary condition for the full appreciation of the decorated porcelain.

Figure subjects and symbolical ornaments probably require the most explanation for the Western student; but unfortunately the former are often so difficult to identify that we have to be content with general headings such as court scenes, military scenes, dramatic subjects, illustrations of romance, etc. Possibly to the unusually well-read native most of these scenes would recall some known story, but the European can only hope to identify one here and there by a lucky chance. He can, of course, take a book of Chinese legends and by the exercise of a little imagination find a story for every scene; but such methods are not to be recommended, and it is infinitely preferable to give the design no label at all unless the identification is fully established. That at least leaves the question open.

Fig. 1

Plate 133.—Late *famille rose* Enamels.

Fig. 1.—Bowl painted in soft enamels, attendants of Hsi Wang Mu in boats. Mark, *Shên tè t'ang chih*. Tao Kuang period. Diameter 6⅞ inches. *British Museum.*

Fig. 2.—Imperial Fish Bowl with five dragons ascending and descending, borders of wave pattern, *ju-i* pattern, etc., *famille rose* enamels. Late eighteenth century. Height 20 inches. *Burdett-Coutts Collection.*

Plate 134.—Porcelain Snuff Bottles. Eighteenth Century. *British Museum.*

Fig. 1.—Subject from the drama, black ground. Yung Chêng mark. Height 2¾ inches.

Fig. 2.—Battle of demons, underglaze blue and red. Mark, *Yung-lo t'ang.* Height 3¾ inches.

Fig. 3.—Blue and white "steatitic" ware. Height 2½ inches.

Fig. 4.—Crackled cream white *ting* glaze, pierced casing with pine, bamboo and prunus. Height 3¼ inches.

Fig. 5.—"Steatitic" ware with Hundred Antiques design in coloured relief. Chia Ch'ing mark. Height 2½ inches.

These scenes from history and romance were favourite subjects with the K'ang Hsi decorators of blue and white and *famille verte* porcelains. To instance a few types: the scene of the half-legendary Yao with his cavalcade coming to greet the Emperor Shun who is engaged, like the Roman Cincinnatus, in ploughing; the episodes of the three heroes of the Han dynasty, Chang Liang, Ch'ên P'ing and Han Hsin[493]; the heroes of the romantic period of the Three Kingdoms (221–265 A.D.) whose stories may be compared with those of our knights of the Round Table; the stories of brigands in the reign of Hui Tsung of the Sung dynasty.[494] The story of Su Wu, the faithful minister of Han Wu Ti, tending cattle in captivity among the Hiung-nu, is depicted on a bowl in the British Museum, and a dish in the same collection shows an emperor (perhaps Kao Tsu, the first of the T'ang dynasty) surrounded by his captains.

Processional scenes and subjects illustrating the life and customs of the times, peaceful domestic scenes with interiors of house or garden peopled by women and children, are more common in the *famille rose* period when the warlike tastes of the Manchus had already been softened by a long period of peace. A civil procession and a military procession sometimes balance each other on two vases, the one being the *wên p'ing* (civil vase), and the other the *wu p'ing* (military vase). A mock dragon-procession formed by children at play is a not uncommon motive. Indeed playing children (*wa wa*) have been from the earliest times a subject frequently and most sympathetically depicted on Chinese porcelain. A historical child-scene is that in which the boy Ssŭ-ma Kuang broke the huge fish bowl with a stone to let out the water and save his drowning companion.

There are many motives intended to appeal to the Chinese literatus, and specially suited to ornament the furniture of the writing table. Symposia of literary personages, for instance, make an appropriate design for a brush pot, or again, the meeting of the celebrated coteries, the Seven Worthies of the Bamboo Grove who lived in the third century, and the worthies of the Orchid Pavilion, including the famous calligrapher, Wang Hsi-chih, who met in the fourth century to drink wine, cap verses, and set their cups floating down the "nine-bend river" (see Plate 104, Fig. 1). The Horace of China, Li T'ai-po, the great T'ang poet, is represented in drunken slumber leaning against an overturned wine jar or receiving the ministrations of the Emperor and his court. He also figures among the Eight Immortals of the Wine Cup, a suitable subject for an octagonal bowl. Poets, painters, and sages are often seen in mountain landscapes contemplating the beauties of Nature; two sages meeting on a mountain side is a frequent subject and is known as the "happy meeting," or again, it is a single sage, with attendant carrying a bowl, book, and fan, or sometimes bringing an offering of a goose. In rare instances these figures can be identified with Chinese worthies such as Chiang Tzŭ-ya, who sits fishing on a river bank, or Chu Mai-ch'ên, the wood-cutter, reading as he walks with his faggots on his back.

The stories of the *Twenty-four Paragons of Filial Piety* provide a complete series of popular subjects, which may be seen in the panels of Plate 91, Fig. 3. Women are represented by the Virtuous Heroines; by celebrated beauties such as Yang Kuei-fei, consort of the T'ang ruler Ming Huang,[495] and Hsi Shih, the Chinese Delilah who was the undoing of Fu Ch'ai, prince of Wu, in the fifth century B.C.; by the poetess Tan Hui-pan, and by a hundred nameless figures which occur in genre designs, and by the idealised beauties, *mei jên* (graceful ladies), which the Dutch ungallantly dubbed with the name of *lange lijsen* or long Elizas. The domestic occupations of a lady form another series of subjects for polygonal vessels; and women are sometimes seen engaged in the Four Subjects of Study—Poetry, Rites, History, and Music— or in the Four Liberal Accomplishments—Writing, Painting, Music, and Checkers—but the groups who make up these scenes are more often composed of men. The game of checkers or *gô*, which is so often loosely rendered chess,[496] is *wei ch'i* the "surrounding game," a favourite Chinese amusement, which figures in two well-known subjects of porcelain decoration. One of these is the legend of Wang Chih, the Taoist patriarch, watching the game played by two old men, the spirits of the Pole Stars, in a mountain retreat; the other is the story of the general Hsieh An, who refused to allow the news of an important victory to disturb his game.

Ladies of the court picking lotus flowers from boats on an ornamental lake in the presence of the Emperor and Empress represent the annual Lotus Fête at Peking, and there are numerous scenes in the Imperial pleasure grounds in which bevies of ladies from the harem are depicted.

The Eight Ambassadors of the Tribes of Man, the barbarian nations from the eight points of the compass, form a processional subject suitable for the exterior of bowls and cups. The ambassadors are grotesquely drawn figures, sometimes mounted on strange beasts, and carrying gifts as tribute to the Emperor. Dreams and visions are depicted in the usual Oriental manner by a cloud issuing from the dreamer's head and expanding into a scene which represents the subject of the dream. Thus the youthful scholar is seen asleep with a vision of his future dignity floating above his head. Divine apparitions are differentiated by the presence of clouds around or below the main figures.

Deities and deified mortals are favourite subjects for porcelain decoration as well as for figures and groups modelled in the round. The three principal Chinese religions—Confucianism, Buddhism, and Taoism—exist side by side with perfect mutual toleration. Indeed the principles of the one are in many cases incorporated in the others. Buddhist and Taoist emblems are freely mingled in decorative art, and the three founders—Confucius, Buddha, and Lao-tzŭ—are grouped together in friendly conversation or examining a scroll on which is drawn the Yin-yang symbol of the duality of Nature.[497]

Confucianism is the religious or rather philosophical system officially recognised in China, but its adherents are chiefly among the literati. Though it inculcates ancestor-worship, it is not in itself concerned with an after life, and it contains few romantic superstitions calculated to fire the popular imagination or to suggest motives for decorative art. Confucius himself is frequently represented both in painting and sculpture, and his meeting with Lao-tzŭ is familiar in pictorial art. Confucianism recognises certain canonised mortals, the logical outcome of ancestor-worship, and among these the best known in art is Kuan Yü, a warrior famous at the end of the Han dynasty, who was not, however, canonised until the Sung period, and only in 1594 raised to the rank of a god (of War) under the title of Kuan Ti. It is reasonable to suppose that most of the numerous statuettes of this popular deity were made after the latter date. He is usually represented as a dignified personage with flowing beard seated in full armour with right hand raised in a speaking attitude; but he figures also on horseback or beside his charger, and with his faithful squires—Chou Ts'ang, who carries a halberd, and Kuan P'ing, his own son. Occasionally he is seen seated with a book in his hand, in which case he is regarded as a literary rather than a military power.

The gods of Literature have a very large following in China, where scholarship has been the key to office for upwards of two thousand years, the chief deity of the cult being Wên Ch'ang, or in full, Wên Ch'ang ti chün. He is the star god who resides in one of the groups of the Great Bear, a dignified bearded figure in mandarin dress seated with folded hands or mounted on a mule. A lesser but more popular divinity is the demon-faced K'uei Hsing, who was canonised in the fourteenth century. Originally a scholar, who though successful in the examinations was refused office on the ground of his preternatural ugliness, he threw himself in despair into the Yangtze and was carried up to heaven on a fish-dragon. He is easily recognised as a demon-like person, poised with one foot on the head of a fish-dragon (yü lung) which is emerging from waves. He brandishes triumphantly in his hands a pencil brush and a cake of ink.[498] The fish-dragon is itself a symbol of literary aspiration, from the legend that when the salmon come every year up the river to the famous falls of Lung-mên (the dragon gate), those which succeed in leaping up the falls are transformed into fish-dragons. This metamorphosis of the fish as it emerges from the water into the dragon is a favourite motive for porcelain decoration.

Buddhism, which was officially recognised in China by the Emperor Ming Ti in 67 A.D., had a far-reaching influence over the arts of sculpture and painting, and the revolution which it worked in the greater arts was naturally reflected in the lesser handicrafts. Buddhistic motives appear early in the Chinese pottery, and in the period with which we are at present concerned, the Buddhist religion supplied a great number of motives for the porcelain painter and the figure modeller. Sakyamuni himself is depicted or sculptured in various poses: (1) As an infant standing on the lotus and proclaiming his birth; (2) as an ascetic returning from his fast in the mountains; (3) seated cross-legged on a lotus throne with right hand raised in teaching attitude, the most frequent representation; (4) recumbent on a lotus pillow, in Nirvana; (5) in the Buddhist Trinity holding the alms bowl or patra between the Bodhisattvas Manjusri and Samantabhadra. These two last when represented singly are usually mounted, Manjusri on a lion, and Samantabhadra on an elephant.

But by far the most popular figure of the Buddhist theogony in China is Kuan-yin, the Compassionate, and Kuan-yin, the Maternal; in the latter capacity she holds a child in her arms and displays a wonderful likeness to our images of the Virgin. But a full account of her has been given on p. 110, and need not be repeated. Next in popularity perhaps is the jolly monk with the hempen bag, Pu-tai Ho-shang, a semi-nude, corpulent person, with smiling face, and a large bag full of the "precious things." He is also a great favourite in Japan, where he is known as Hotei, and worshipped as the god of Contentment. By the Chinese he is also regarded as Mi-lo Fo, the Maitreya or coming Buddha, and he has been added by them to the list of Arhats or apostles of Buddha. He is often represented surrounded by playful children to whom he is devoted.

The Arhats, or Lohan, are all known by their several attributes, but in porcelain decoration they usually appear in groups consisting of the whole or a large part of their number, which, originally sixteen, was increased in China to eighteen by the inclusion of Ho-shang and Dharmatrata. The latter is a long-haired individual who carries a vase and a fly whisk in his hands and a bundle of books on his back while he sits gazing at a small image of Buddha.

He is not to be confused with Tamo, the Indian Bodhidharma, the first Chinese patriarch, who came to Lo-yang and remained there in contemplation for nine years. The legend is that after his death (about 530 A.D.) he was seen returning to India wrapped in his shroud and carrying one shoe in his hand, the other having been left behind in his tomb. This is the guise in which he frequently appears in art (Plate 86), and he is often depicted crossing the Yangtze on a reed.

Many of the symbolical ornaments on porcelain have a Buddhistic significance, such as the eight emblems (see p. 298), the crossed dorjes or thunderbolts of Vajrapani,[499] the Buddhist jewel in a leaf-shaped halo of flames; and Sanskrit characters of sacred import are used as decoration for bowls and dishes, made no doubt for the use of the faithful. The principal animals associated with Buddhist designs are the elephant, who carries the jewel vase on his back, the white horse (*pai ma*), who brought the Buddhist scriptures across the desert from India, the hare, who offered himself as food to Buddha, and the Chinese lion who, under the name of the "dog of Fo" (Buddha), acts as guardian of Buddhist temples and images.

But the religion which has taken the greatest hold on Chinese imagination and which consequently has supplied the largest number of motives for their decorative art is undoubtedly Taoism. As originally taught by Lao-tzǔ, a contemporary of Confucius, in the sixth century B.C., the doctrine of Tao (the Way) pointed to abstraction from worldly cares and freedom from mental perturbation as the highest good. But just as the later but closely analogous doctrine of Epicurus degenerated into the cult of pleasure, so the true teaching of Lao-tzǔ was afterwards lost among the adventitious beliefs and superstitions which were grafted on to it by his followers. The secret of transmuting metals into gold and of compounding the elixir of life became the chief preoccupations of the Taoist sages, the latter quest appealing particularly to the Chinese with their proverbial worship of longevity; and a host of legends grew up concerning mortals who won immortality by discovering the elixir, about fairies and the denizens of the Shou Shan or Hills of Longevity, about the Isles of the Blessed and the palace of Hsi Wang Mu in the K'un-lun mountains. It is this later and more popular phase of Taoism which figures so largely in porcelain decoration.

Lao-tzǔ is represented as a venerable old man with bald, protuberant forehead, who rides upon an ox, the same in features as the god of Longevity, Shou Lao, who is in fact regarded as his disembodied spirit. Shou Lao, however, is more commonly shown enthroned upon a rocky platform in the Hills of Longevity, holding in one hand a curious knotted staff, to which are attached rolls of writing, and in the other a peach, and surrounded by his special attributes, the spotted deer, the stork, and the *ling chih* fungus. Thus seated he receives homage from the Eight Immortals and the other Taoist genii or *hsien*, who are as numerous as the fairies of our countryside. Other designs represent Shou Lao riding on a deer or flying on the back of a stork, or simply standing with his staff and peach, his robes embroidered with seal forms of the character *shou* (longevity). In this last posture he is often grouped with two other popular deities, one in mandarin robes and official hat holding a *ju-i* sceptre, which fulfils every wish, and the other also in official robes but holding a babe who reaches out for a peach in his other hand. Together they form the Taoist triad, Shou-hsing, Lu-hsing, and Fu-hsing, star-gods (*hsing*) of Longevity, Preferment, and Happiness. Fu-hsing in addition has sometimes two boy attendants carrying respectively a lotus and a hand-organ.

The Eight Taoist Immortals (*pa hsien*) are:—

1. Chung-li Ch'üan, also known as Han Chung-li, represented as a fat man, half-draped, who holds a *ling chih* fungus in one hand and a fly-whisk or fan in the other.

2. Lü Tung-pin, a figure of martial aspect armed with a sword to slay dragons and evil spirits. He is the patron of barbers.

3. Li T'ieh-kuai, Li with the iron crutch, a lame beggar with a crutch and pilgrim's gourd from which issue clouds and apparitions. He is patron of astrologers and magicians.

4. Ts'ao Kuo-ch'iu, in official robes, wearing a winged hat, and carrying a pair of castanets. He is patron of mummers and actors.

5. Lan Ts'ai-ho, of uncertain sex, carrying a hoe and a basket of flowers. Patron of gardeners and florists.

6. Chang Kuo Lao, the necromancer with the magic mule, of which he kept a picture folded up in his wallet. He would make the beast materialise from the picture by spurting water on to it; and at other times he would conjure it out of a gourd. His attribute is a musical instrument consisting of a drum and a pair of rods. He is patron of artists and calligraphers, and ranks as one of the gods of Literature.

7. Han Hsiang Tzŭ, who gained admission to the Taoist paradise and climbed the peach-tree of Immortality. He is shown as a young man playing on a flute, and is specially worshipped by musicians.

8. Ho Hsien Ku, a maiden who wears a cloak of mug-wort leaves and carries a lotus. She is patroness of housewives.

The Immortals are commonly represented in a group paying court to Shou Lao, or crossing the sea on the backs of various strange creatures or other supernatural conveyances on their way to the Islands of Paradise. Grouped in pairs they lend themselves to the decoration of quadrangular objects.

Other frequenters of the Shou Shan are the twin genii[500] of Union and Harmony (*ho ho êrh hsien*), an inseparable pair, depicted as ragged mendicants with staff and broom, or as smiling boyish figures, the one with a lotus and the other holding a Pandora box of blessings, from which a cloud is seen to rise; Tung-fang So, who stole the peaches of Hsi Wang Mu and acquired thereby a longevity of nine thousand years, is represented as a smiling bearded old man, not unlike Shou Lao himself, carrying an enormous peach, or as a boy with a peach to recall his youthful exploit. Liu Han, with his familiar three-legged toad, a wild-looking person, who waves a string of cash in the air, and very closely resembles the Japanese Gama Sennin (the Hou Hsien Shêng of China); Wang Tzǔ-ch'iao, who rides on a crane playing a flute, and Huang An, the hermit, whose steed is a tortoise. The god of Alchemy is figured, according to the identification of a statuette in the Musée Guimet, as a tall, draped person with beard and moustaches flowing down in five long wisps, a leaf-shaped fan in his left hand, and beside him a small figure of a devotee who holds up a book with questioning gesture.

The Queen of the Genii is Hsi Wang Mu (Queen Mother of the West). Her home is in the K'un-lun mountains, and the peach tree of Longevity grows in her gardens. In the tenth century B.C., the Emperor Mu Wang is reputed to have visited her palace, and the reception forms a pleasing subject for the artist, as does also her return visit paid to the Emperor Wu Ti of the Han dynasty. She also figures frequently on porcelain with her fair attendants crossing the sea on a raft, flying on the back of a phœnix or standing with a female attendant who carries a dish of peaches. Her messengers are blue-winged birds like the doves of Venus, who carry the fruit of longevity to favoured beings. With her attendant phœnix she presents a strong analogy with Juno and her peacock; and her Western habitat has favoured the theories which would connect her with Græco-Roman mythology, though her consort Hsi Wang Fu (King Father of the West and a personage obviously invented *ad hoc*) is quite insignificant and has nothing in common with the cloud-compelling Jove.

There is a female figure which is scarcely distinguishable from one of the attendants of Hsi Wang Mu on the one hand and from Lan Ts'ai-ho on the other. This is the Flower Fairy (*Hua hsien*) who carries a basket of flowers suspended from a hoe. And there are besides numerous magicians of more or less repute, such as Chang Chiu-ko, who is seen transforming pieces cut from his scanty garments into butterflies; and a host of nameless *hsien* of local fame who figure in mountain retreats, such as the *Ssǔ hao* or four hoary hermits.[501]

The animals connected with Taoist lore include the eight fabulous horses of Mu Wang which brought him to the palace of Hsi Wang Mu. They are usually seen at pasture frisking about in wild gambols. The deer, the familiar of Shou Lao, is depicted usually with a *ling chih* fungus in his mouth; the toad and hare live in the moon where they pound the elixir of immortality; and the tortoise develops a long bushy tail after a thousand years of existence. All these are suggestive of longevity, as is also the crane and a number of flowers, fruits and trees such as the pine, bamboo and prunus (the three friends), the chrysanthemum, the willow, the peach, the gourd, and more especially the *ling chih* fungus, the *polyporus lucidus*, which was originally an emblem of good luck, but afterwards of longevity.

The head of the *ling chih* closely resembles[502] that of the familiar *ju-i* sceptre which grants every wish, an auspicious object commonly seen in the hands of Taoist genii; and the same form occurs in a decorative border (see Plate 77, Fig. 2) which is variously known as the *ju-i* head border, the *ju-i* cloud border, or the cloud-scroll border, the conventional cloud being commonly rolled up in this form. It will also be found that formal ornaments, pendants and lambrequins often take the form of the *ju-i* head in Chinese decoration.

The attributes of the Eight Immortals occur among the many symbols used in porcelain ornament; and among the landscapes will be found the gardens of Hsi Wang Mu and Mount P'êng-lai,[503] one of the three islands of the blessed, situated in the ocean east of China. Here the fountain of life flows in a perpetual stream: "the pine, the bamboo, the plum, the peach, and the fungus of longevity grow for ever on its shores; and the long-haired tortoise disports in its rocky inlets, and the white crane builds her nest on the limbs of its everlasting pines."[504] Presumably, too, the Shou Shan is situated on this delectable island; and perhaps also the heavenly pavilion (*t'ien t'ang*), which appears among clouds as the goal to which a crane is often seen guiding some of the Taoist genii. Possibly, too, the conventional border of swirling waves punctuated by conical rocks carries a suggestion of the rocky islands of paradise rising from the sea.

Fig. 1.—The Yin-yang and Pa-kua

There are besides many primitive beliefs traceable for the most part to Nature-worship, which prevailed in China long before the days of Confucius, Lao-tzŭ or Buddha. Some of these have been incorporated in the later religious systems, especially in that of Taoism, which was ready to adopt any form of demonology. The oldest system is that expounded by the legendary Fu Hsi, in which the phenomena of Nature were explained by reference to the mystic diagrams revealed to him on the back of a dragon horse (*lung ma*) which rose from the Yellow River. These are the *pa-kua* or eight trigrams formed by the permutations of three lines, broken and unbroken, as in Fig. 1. A more common arrangement of them is according to the points of the compass, and enclosing another ancient device, the Yin-yang, a circle bisected by a wavy line, which symbolises the duality of Nature, *yin* being the female and *yang* the male element.

Demons abound in Chinese superstitions, and the demon face appears early in art on the ancient bronzes, from which it was sometimes borrowed by the porcelain decorator. This is the face of the *t'ao t'ieh* (the gluttonous ogre) supposed originally to have represented the demon of the storm, and as such appropriately appearing against a background of "cloud and thunder" pattern, as the key-fret is called by the Chinese. Afterwards the *t'ao t'ieh* seems to have been regarded, on homœopathic principles, as a warning against greed. Demons also appear in complete form in certain battle scenes and conflicts, such as the combat of the demons of the water and of air which proceeds in front of a group of Chinese dignitaries seated in the Kin-shan temple on the Yangtze river (see Plate 134, Fig. 2).

The sky and the stars of course contribute their quota of divinities. Beside the Taoist star-gods of Longevity, Honours and Happiness, there is the Jade Emperor or supreme lord of the universe, Yü wang shang ti, who is represented in mandarin dress holding a *ju-i* sceptre and closely resembling Lu Hsing, the star-god of Honours. There is, too, the goddess of the Moon with a butterfly ornamenting the front of her robes, and a mirror in her right hand, besides the other denizens of the moon—Liu Han, the moon-hare and the moon-toad. A cassia tree also grows in the moon, and the "cassia of the moon" is a symbol of literary success.

The Sun is represented as a disc on which is a three-legged bird; and it is probable that the sun-disc is represented also in the so-called "pearl"[505] which is pursued or grasped by dragons; but this idea of the power of the storm threatening the sun was lost sight of in later art, and "a dragon pursuing a pearl" was considered a sufficient description of the motive. A curious scene depicting a mandarin shooting arrows at a dog in the sky alludes to the dog who devours the sun and so causes the eclipse.

The zodiacal animals are named on p. 211 (vol. i), and the four points of the compass are symbolised by the azure dragon for the East, the white tiger for the West, the black tortoise for the North, and the red bird for the South. The romance of two stars is embodied in the story of the Spinning Maiden (*Chih Nü*) and her lover, the Cowherd (*Ch'ien Niu*), who are separated for all the year save on one night when the "magpies fill up the Milky Way and enable the Spinning Damsel to cross over."

Chang Ch'ien, the celebrated minister of Han Wu-ti, was one of the first great travellers of China, and among the legends which grew around his exploits is one which makes him ascend the Milky Way and meet the Spinning Damsel herself. This story arose because he was reputed to have discovered the source of the Yellow River, which had hitherto been supposed to rise in heaven, being in fact a continuation of the Milky Way. Chang Ch'ien is sometimes represented in Chinese art as floating on a log-raft on the Yellow River, and carrying in his hand a shuttle given to him by the Spinning Maiden.[506] The poet Li T'ai-po is also figured in the same kind of craft, but he is distinguished by a book in place of the shuttle.

Motives borrowed from the animal world are frequent on porcelain, though they represent to a large extent mythical creatures, first and foremost of which is the dragon. We need not enter into the conflicting theories as to the origin of the Chinese dragon. Whether he sprang from some prehistoric monster whose remains had come to light, or was evolved from the crocodile, he appears in any case to have belonged to Nature-worship as the power of the storm and the bringer of fertilising rain. There, are, however, various kinds of dragons—those of the air, the sea, the earth—and the monster takes many different forms in Chinese art. The archaic types borrowed by the porcelain decorators from ancient bronzes and jades are the *k'uei lung* 夔龍 or one-legged dragon, and the *ch'ih lung* 螭龍, the former a tapir-like creature which is said to have been, like the *t'ao t'ieh*, a warning against greed,[507] the latter a smooth, hornless reptile of lizard-like form with divided tail, who is also described as a *mang*.

But the dragon (*lung*) *par excellence* is a formidable monster with "bearded, scowling head, straight horns, a scaly, serpentine body, with four feet armed with claws, a line of bristling dorsal spines, and flames proceeding from the hips and shoulders." Such is the creature painted by the great master of dragon painting, Chang Sêng-yu, of the sixth century, and as such he is the emblem of Imperial power and the device of the Emperor. The Imperial dragon in the art of the last two dynasties has been distinguished by five claws on each of his four feet[508]; the four-clawed dragon was painted on wares destined for personages of lesser rank. The dragons are usually depicted flying in clouds, and pursuing the disc or pearl, which was discussed above, or rising from waves. Nine dragons form a decoration specially reserved for the Emperor; and on the palace porcelain the dragon and the phœnix (*fĕng*) frequently appear together as emblems of the Emperor and Empress.

The *fĕng-huang*,[509] a phœnix-like bird, is usually shown with the "head of a pheasant and the beak of a swallow, a long flexible neck, plumage of many gorgeous colours, a flowing tail between that of an argus pheasant and a peacock, and long claws pointed backward as it flies." It is the special emblem of the Empress. In archaic designs there is a *k'uei fĕng* or one-legged phœnix, a bird-like creature terminating in scrolls, which, like the corresponding *k'uei lung*, occasionally appears in porcelain designs. Another bird-like creature scarcely distinguishable from the *fĕng* is the *luan*; the former being based, as it is said, on the peacock of India, and the latter on the argus pheasant. Another creature of dual nature is the *ch'i lin*, commonly called the kylin, which consists of the male (*ch'i*) and the female (*lin*). It is in itself a composite animal with the "body of a deer, with the slender legs and divided hoofs; the head resembles that of a dragon, the tail is curled and bushy, like that of the conventional lion, and the shoulders are adorned with the flame-like attributes of its divine nature. It is said to attain the age of a thousand years, to be the noblest form of animal creation, and the emblem of perfect good; and to tread so lightly as to leave no footprints, and so carefully as to crush no living creature." Its appearance was the sign of the coming of a virtuous ruler. It is important to note that the *ch'i lin* is quite distinct from the Chinese lion, and is also to be carefully separated from the other chimera-like creatures known in Chinese art under the general title *hai shou* or sea monsters.

The lion in Chinese art (*shih* or *shih tzŭ*, the Japanese *shishi*), though of qualified ferocity in appearance, is in reality a peaceful, docile creature who expends his energy on a ball of silk brocade, the streamers from which he holds in his massive jaws. In general aspect (Plate 25), in his tufts of hair and his bushy tail, he closely resembles the Peking spaniel, who is in fact called after him the lion dog (*shih tzŭ kou*). He is usually represented in pairs, the one with one foot on a ball of brocade, and the other, presumably the lioness, with a cub. The larger lion figures are placed as guardians by the gates of Buddhist temples, from which function the lion has earned the name of "dog of Fo" (i.e. Buddha); the smaller sizes, usually mounted on an oblong base with a tube attached to hold an incense-stick, have a place on the domestic altar. Another mythical creature not unlike the lion is the *pi hsieh* of archaic art which is supposed to ward off evil spirits.[510]

The king of beasts in China is the tiger (*hu*), whose forehead is marked by Nature with the character *wang* 王 (prince). He is the solar animal, the lord of the mountains, and the chief of all quadrupeds. The white tiger represents the western quadrant and the autumn; and images of tigers in ancient times served many purposes, such as guarding the graves of the dead and summoning the living to battle.

In addition to the sea monsters there are sea horses, who speed at a flying gallop over waves; and there are the *pai ma* and *lung ma* and the eight horses of Mu Wang, already described, to represent the horse in art. The deer is a Taoist emblem of longevity, and also in its name *lu* suggests the auspicious word *lu* (preferment); and there is a fabulous one-horned creature distinct from the *ch'i lin*, and known as the *t'ien lu* or deer of heaven. Rams are sometimes represented as personifying the revivifying powers of spring; and the monkey occasionally figures in decoration, his name *hou* suggesting another word *hou*, which means to expect (office), and providing an appropriate design for presentation to a candidate in the State examinations. Another motive suitable for the same purpose is the fish leaping from waves, which has been already explained; and fish in general are cleverly depicted by the porcelain decorators swimming among water plants. The fish has always been a favourite motive in China, and in ancient art it appears to have symbolised power and rank. The double fish is one of the Buddhist emblems, and also symbolises conjugal felicity. The tortoise has already been mentioned among the emblems of longevity.

Birds are drawn with wonderful skill and spirit by Chinese artists, and they provide a frequent motive both for the painter and figure modeller. The crane is the companion of Shou Lao and a symbol of long life; a pair of mandarin ducks suggest conjugal affection; egrets among lotus plants, geese, and wild duck in marshy landscapes also pleased the Chinese fancy. The magpie is an emblem of happiness, and two magpies foretell a happy meeting; the cock is the bird of fame, and he is often associated with the peony, which is the *fu kuei* flower, to suggest the phrase *kung ming* (fame), *fu kuei* (riches and honours!). There are other birds which are associated with special trees and flowers; the pheasant is often seen perched on a rock beside the peony and magnolia; partridges and quails go with millet; swallows with the willow; sparrows on the prunus, and so on. A comprehensive group represents the "hundred birds" paying court to the phœnix.

The bat is a symbol of happiness from its name *fu* having the same sound as *fu* (happiness). Among insects, the cicada (at one time regarded as a symbol of life renewed after death) is a very ancient motive; and the praying mantis who catches the cicada is an emblem of courage and perseverance.[511] Fighting crickets are the fighting cocks of China, and supply a sporting motive for the decorator; and butterflies frequently occur with floral designs or in the decoration known as the Hundred Butterflies, which covers the entire surface of the vessel with butterflies and insects.

Flower painting is another forte of the Chinese decorator, and some of the most beautiful porcelain designs are floral. Conventional flowers appear in scrolls, and running designs, especially the lotus and peony scrolls and the scrolls of "fairy flowers," the *pao hsiang hua* of the Ming blue and white. But the most attractive designs are the more naturalistic pictures of flowering plants and shrubs, or of floral bouquets in baskets or vases. The flowers on Chinese porcelain are supple, free, and graceful; and, though true enough to nature to be easily identified, are never of the stiff copy-book order which the European porcelain painter affected at one unhappy period. A long list of the Chinese porcelain flowers given by Bushell includes the orchid (*lan*), rose, jasmine, olea fragrans, pyrus japonica, gardenia, syringa, several kinds of peony, magnolia (*yü lan*), iris, hydrangea, hibiscus, begonia, pink and water fairy flower (*narcissus tazetta*). Many more no doubt can be identified, for the Chinese are great cultivators as they are great lovers of flowers. In fact, the word *hua* 華 flowery is synonymous with Chinese, and *chung hua* 中華 is China. Plate 126 is an example of the Hundred Flower design, known by the French name *mille fleurs*, in which the ground of the vase is a mass of naturalistic flowers so that the porcelain looks like a bouquet.

There are special flowers for the months[512]:—(1) Peach (*t'ao*) for February, (2) Tree Peony (*mu tan*) for March, (3) Double Cherry (*ying t'ao*) for April, (4) Magnolia (*yü lan*) for May, (5) Pomegranate (*shih liu*) for June, (6) Lotus (*lien hua*) for July, (7) Pear (*hai t'ang*) for August, (8) Mallow (*ch'iu k'uei*) for September, (9) Chrysanthemum (*chü*) for October, (10) Gardenia (*chih hua*) for November, (11) Poppy (*ying su*) for December, (12) Prunus (*mei hua*) for January. From these are selected four to represent the seasons—*mu-tan* peony for spring, lotus for summer, chrysanthemum for autumn, and prunus for winter—which supply charming motives for panel decoration or for the sides of quadrangular vases.

The chrysanthemum besides is associated with its admirer T'ao Yüan-ming, and the lotus with Chou Mao-shu and the poet Li T'ai-po. But as a rule the floral designs carry some hidden meaning, the flowers being grouped so as to suggest some felicitous phrase by a play on their names.[513] The peony we have seen to be the *fu kuei* (riches and honours) flower; the chrysanthemum, as Dr. Laufer has suggested, being the flower of the ninth (*chiu*) month, may connote longevity through the word *chiu* (long-enduring); the prunus (*mei hua*) carries the obvious suggestion of *mei* (beautiful), and instances might easily be multiplied.

Among the trees, the cassia suggests literary honours, the willow longevity, as also the pine, bamboo and plum, who are called the "three friends,"[514] faithful even in the "winter of our discontent." Among the fruits the gourd is an emblem both of long life and of fertility, and the three fruits (*san kuo*)—

peach, pomegranate and finger citron—symbolise the Three Abundances of Years, Sons and Happiness. The orange is a symbol of good luck, and no doubt the others which occur less frequently contain similar suggestions.

Landscape (*shan shui*) is one of the four main divisions of Chinese pictorial art, and it is well represented in porcelain decoration. The Sung and Ming masters provided designs which were freely copied, and views of the beauty spots of China and of the celebrated parks and pleasure grounds were frequently used. It is one of these landscapes which the English potters borrowed for the familiar "willow pattern" design, and the sentimental tale which some fanciful writer has attached to the pattern is a mere afterthought. Figure subjects and landscapes are combined in many designs, such as the meeting of sages, romantic incidents, besides the more homely motives of field work, fishing, rustics returning from the plough mounted on their oxen, and the like. The four seasons, too, are represented in landscape with appropriate accessories, such as blossoming peach trees in a mountain scene for spring, a lake scene with lotus gatherers for summer, a swollen river and autumn tints for autumn, and a snowstorm for winter.

A great variety of symbols and emblematical devices appear in the porcelain decoration of all periods, whether interwoven with the designs, grouped in panels, or placed under the base in lieu of a mark. Bushell[515] classifies the most familiar of them under the following headings:—

1. Symbols of Ancient Chinese Lore: *Pa-kua* and *Yin-yang* (see p. 290); *Pa yin* (eight musical instruments); *Shih êrh chang* (twelve ornaments embroidered upon sacrificial robes).

2. Buddhist symbols: *Pa chi hsiang* (eight emblems of happy augury). *Ch'i pao* (seven paraphernalia of the *chakravartin* or universal sovereign).

3. Taoist symbols: *Pa an hsien* (attributes of the Eight Immortals).

4. The Hundred Antiques (*Po ku*). *Pa pao* (the Eight Precious Objects).

The *pa-kua* (eight trigrams) and the *Yin-yang* symbol of the duality of Nature have been described. The eight musical instruments are: (1) *Ch'ing*, the sounding stone, a sort of gong usually in form of a mason's square. It forms a rebus for *ch'ing* (good luck). (2) *Chung*, the bell. (3) *Ch'in*, the lute. (4) *Ti*, the flute. (5) *Chu*, the box, with a metal hammer inside. (6) *Ku*, the drum. (7) *Shêng*, the reed organ. (8) *Hsüan*, the ocarina, a cone with six holes.

The twelve *chang* or ancient embroidery ornaments are: (1) *Jih*, the Sun, a disc in which is a three-legged bird, and sometimes, the character *jih* 日. (2) *Yüeh*, the moon; a disc with hare, toad and cassia tree, and sometimes the character *yüeh* 月. (3) *Hsing ch'ên*, the stars: represented by three stars connected by straight lines. (4) *Shan*, mountains. (5) *Lung*, dragons. (6) *Hua ch'ung*, the "flowery creature," the pheasant. (7) *Tsung yi*, the temple vessels: one with a tiger design and the other with a monkey. (8) *Tsao*, aquatic grass. (9) *Huo*, fire. (10) *Fên mi*, grains of rice. (11) *Fu*, an axe. (12) *Fu*, a symbol of distinction[516] (see vol. i., p. 227).

The Eight Happy Omens (*pa chi hsiang*) were among the signs on the sole of Buddha's foot. They are usually drawn with flowing fillets attached (Fig. 2), and they are as follows: (1) *Lun*, the wheel or chakra, sometimes replaced by the bell (*chung*). (2) *Lo*, the shell. (3) *San*, the State umbrella. (4) *Kai*, the canopy. (5) *Hua*, the (lotus) flower. (6) *P'ing*, the vase. (7) *Yü*, the fish; a pair of them.[517] (8) *Ch'ang*, the angular knot representing the entrails; an emblem of longevity.[518]

Fig. 2.—The Pa chi hsiang

The Seven Gems (*ch'i pao*) are: (1) *Chin lun*, the golden wheel. (2) *Yü nü*, the jade-like girl. (3) *Ma*, the horse. (4) *Hsiang*, the elephant. (5) *Chu ts'ang shên*, divine guardian of the treasury. (6) *Chu ping ch'ên*, general in command of the army. (7) *Ju i chu* the jewels which fulfil every wish; a bundle of jewelled wands bound round with a cord.

The *Pa an hsien*, Attributes of the Eight Immortals, as detailed above (p. 287), are: (1) *Shan*, the fan of Chung-li Ch'üan. (2) *Chien*, the sword of Lü Tung-pin. (3) *Hu lu*, the gourd of Li T'ieh-kuai. (4) *Pan*, the castanets of Ts'ao Kuo-chiu. (5) *Hua lan*, the basket of flowers of Lan Ts'ai-ho. (6) *Yu ku*, the bamboo tube and rods of Chang Kuo Lao. (7) *Ti*, the flute of Han Hsiang Tzŭ. (8) *Lien hua*, the lotus flower of Ho Hsien Ku.

The *Po ku*, or Hundred Antiques, is, as its name implies, a comprehensive group including all manner of symbols and symbolical ornaments, which were frequently grouped together in panel decoration. Bushell[519] describes two typical panels on specimens in the Walters collection. One contained the apparatus of the scholar and painter, viz. books on tables, brushes in vases, water pots and scroll pictures, all enveloped with waving fillets mingled with tasselled wands and double diamonds, which are symbols of literary success. The other contained a tall vase with peonies; a low vase with peacock feather, an emblem of high rank; a lion-shaped censer on a four-legged stand, the incense smoke from which rises in form of a pair of storks; a set of incense-burning implements, a bundle of scroll pictures, a *ju-i* sceptre, a musical stone, a sword, and a paper weight.

A favourite set of *Po-ku* emblems is the *Pa pao* (Fig. 3) or Eight Precious Objects: (1) *Chu*, the pearl, which grants every wish. (2) *Ch'ien*, the "cash," a copper coin used to symbolise wealth. (3) Lozenge, or picture (*hua*). (4) *Fang shêng*, the open lozenge, symbol of victory.[520] (5) *Ch'ing*, the musical stone. (6) *Shu*, a pair of books. (7) *Chüeh*, a pair of horn-like objects. (8) *Ai yeh*, the leaf of the artemisia, fragrant plant of good omen and a preventative of disease.

A branch of coral, a silver ingot, a pencil brush and cake of ink are common emblems; and the swastika occurs both by itself (vol. i., p. 227) or interwoven with the character *shou* (vol. i., p. 227), or even as a fret or diaper pattern. The swastika is a world-wide symbol; in China it is called *wan*, and used as a synonym for *wan* (ten thousand), and as such it is regarded as a symbol of *wan shou* (endless longevity). A lyre wrapped in an embroidered case, a chess- or *gô*-board with round boxes for the white and black pieces, a pair of books, and a pair of scroll pictures symbolise the "four elegant accomplishments," *ch'in*, *ch'i*, *shu*, *hua* (music, chess, writing and painting).

Fig. 3.—The Pa pao

The figurative aspect of Chinese decoration has been repeatedly noticed, and occasional examples of direct play upon words or rebus devices have been given incidentally. The Chinese language is peculiarly suited for punning allusions, one sound having to do duty for many characters; but it is obvious that a fair knowledge of the characters is required for reading these rebus designs. There is, however, a certain number of stock allusions with which the collector can easily make himself familiar. The commonest of these is perhaps the bat (*fu*) which symbolises happiness (also pronounced *fu* in Chinese). The Five Blessings (*wu fu*), which consist of longevity, riches, peacefulness and serenity, love of virtue and an end crowning the life, are suggested by five bats; and a further rebus is formed of red bats among cloud scrolls, reading *hung fu ch'i t'ien*, "great happiness equally heaven" (*t'ien*); *hung* being the sound of the character for "great, vast," as well as for red, and red being, so to speak, the colour of happiness in Chinese eyes.

Other common rebus designs are suggested by such words as *lu* (deer), *lu* (preferment); *yü* (fish), *yü* (abundance); *ch'ing* (sounding stone), *ch'ing* (good luck); *ch'ang* (the intestinal knot), *ch'ang* (long); and the composition of the rebus phrase often includes such ideas as *lien* (lotus), *lien* (connect, combine); *tieh* (butterfly), *tieh* (to double). But almost every sound in the Chinese spoken language represents a considerable number of characters, and it would be possible with a little ingenuity to extract several rebus sentences out of any complicated decoration. It is well to remember, however, that most of the ordinary allusions have reference to some good wish or felicitous phrase bearing on the five blessings, on the three abundances or on literary success.

To quote a few further instances: the design of nine (*chiu*) lions (*shih*) sporting with balls (*chü*) of brocade has been read[521] *chiu shih t'ung chü*, "a family of nine sons living together." An elephant (*hsiang*) carrying a vase (*p'ing*) on its back (*pei*) is read[522] *hsiang pei tai p'ing*, "Peace (p'ing) rules in the north (*pei*)." A tub full of green wheat is read[523] *i t'ung ta ch'ing*, "the whole empire (owns) the great Ch'ing dynasty." Three crabs holding reeds is read[524] *san p'ang hsieh ch'uan lu*, "three generations gaining the first class at the metropolitan examinations." Two pigeons perched on a willow tree is read[525] *êrh pa (k'o) t'eng t'ê*, "at eighteen to be successful in examinations."

A group of three objects consisting of a pencil brush (*pi*), a cake of ink (*ting*) and a *ju-i* sceptre crossed one over the other (Fig. 4), occurs both in the field of the decoration and as a mark under the base. It is a pure rebus, reading *pi ting ju i*, may things be fixed (*ting*) as you wish (*ju i*, lit. according to your idea). Another obvious rebus which occurs as a mark (Fig. 5) consists of two peaches and a bat (double longevity and happiness), and floral designs are very commonly arranged so as to suggest rebus phrases.

Fig. 4

Fig. 5

But the Chinese decorator did not always express himself in riddles. Inscriptions are frequent on all forms of decorative work, as is only natural in a country where calligraphy ranks among the highest branches of art. To the foreign eye Chinese writing will not perhaps appear so ornamental as the beautiful Neshky characters which were freely used for decorative purposes on Persian wares; but for all that, its decorative qualities are undeniable, and to the Chinese who worship the written character it is a most attractive kind of ornament. Sometimes the surface of a vessel is almost entirely occupied by a long inscription treating of the ware or of the decoration which occupies the remaining part; but more often the writing is limited to an epigram or a few lines of verse. The characters as a rule are ranged in columns and read from top to bottom, the columns being taken from left to right; and rhyming verse is written in lines of three, five or seven characters each. The inscriptions are often attested by the name or the seal of the author. The Emperor Ch'ien Lung, a prolific writer of verses, indited many short poems on the motives of porcelain decoration, and these have been copied on subsequent pieces.

As for the style of writing, the ordinary script is the *k'ai shu*, which dates from the Chin dynasty (265–419 A.D.), but there are besides many inscriptions in which the archaic seal characters *chuan tzŭ* are employed, or at least hybrid modern forms of them; and there is the cursive script, known as *ts'ao shu* or grass characters, which is said to have been invented in the first century B.C. The seal and the grass characters are often extremely difficult to translate, and require a special study, which even highly educated Chinese do not profess to have mastered.

Single characters and phrases of auspicious meaning in both seal form and in the ordinary script occur in the decoration and also in the place of the mark. Many instances have already been noted in the chapters dealing with Ming porcelains, such as *fu kuei k'ang ning* (riches, honours, peace and serenity), *ch'ang ming fu kuei* (long life, riches and honours), etc., see vol. i., p. 225. The most frequent of these characters is *shou* (longevity), which is written in a great variety of fanciful forms, mostly of the seal type. The "hundred forms of shou" sometimes constitute the sole decoration of a vase; and as already observed[526] the swastika (*wan*) is sometimes combined with the circular form of the seal character *shou* to make the *wan shou* symbol of ten thousand longevities. *Fu* (happiness) and *lu* (preferment) also occur, though less frequently.

Buddhistic inscriptions are usually in Sanskrit characters, but we find occasional phrases such as *Tien chu en po* 天竺恩波 (propitious waves from India) and *Fo ming ch'ang jih* 佛明常日 (the ever bright Buddha) in ordinary script or seal, one character in each of four medallions; and the sacred name of *O mi t'o fo* 阿彌陀佛, Amida Buddha, similarly applied, would serve as a charm against evil.

In addition to the central designs, there is a number of secondary ornaments which round off the decoration of a piece of porcelain. Chief of these are the border patterns, of which a few favourites may be exemplified. At the head of the list comes the Greek key-fret or meander (see Plate 12, Fig. 1), which, like the swastika, is of world-wide use. On the ancient bronze this pattern was freely used both in borders and as a diaper background, and it is described by Chinese archæologists as the "cloud and thunder pattern." It is sometimes varied by the inclusion of the swastika, in which case it is known as the swastika fret. Another bronze pattern freely borrowed by the porcelain decoration is the border of stiff plantain leaves which appears appropriately on the neck or stem of an upright vase (see Plate 89, Fig. 1).

The border of small "S" shaped scrolls is apparently derived from silkworm cocoons; but the curled scrolls and another scroll pattern with more elaborate curves are intended to suggest clouds. A further development of the cloud pattern is scarcely distinguishable from the *ju-i* head border (see Plate 77, Fig.

2). Indeed the terms, "connected cloud" pattern, *ju-i* cloud pattern, and *ju-i* head pattern, are used almost interchangeably by Chinese archæologists.

Conventional waves are represented by a kind of shaded scale pattern or a diaper of spiral coils, and the more naturalistic "crested wave" border, punctuated by conical rocks, has already been mentioned. There are besides narrow borders of zig-zag pattern with diagonal hatching, and the ordinary diaper designs, in addition to the familiar gadroons and arcaded borders.

The wider borders are usually borrowed from brocade patterns with geometrical or floral ornament, broken by three or four oblong panels containing symbols or sprays of flowers; and when a similar scheme is followed in some of the narrow edgings, the flowers are unhesitatingly cut in half, as though the pattern were just a thin strip taken from a piece of brocade.

A few special borders have been described on the pages dealing with armorial porcelain,[527] among which were the well-known "rat and vine" or "vine and squirrel" pattern (see Plate 119, Fig. 3), reputed to have first appeared on a picture by the Sung artist, Ming Yüan-chang.[528] A rare border formed of red bats side by side occurs on a few plates of fine porcelain which are usually assigned to the K'ang Hsi period, but are probably much later.

On the whole, the Chinese border patterns are comparatively few in number, being in fact a small selection of well-tried designs admirably suited to fill the spaces required and to occupy the positions assigned to them on the different porcelain forms.

As to the sources from which these and the other designs described in this chapter were borrowed by the porcelain decorator, we can only speak in general terms. Ancient bronze vessels, metal mirrors, carved jades, stamped cakes of ink, embroideries, brocades, handkerchiefs, and illustrated books no doubt provided the greater part of them. The purely pictorial subjects would be based on the paintings in silk and paper which the Chinese arrange in four chief categories: (1) figures (*jên wu*),(2) landscape (*shan shui*),(3) nature subjects (*hua niao*, lit. flowers and birds), and (4) miscellaneous designs (*tsa hua*). Selections of desirable designs from various sources were no doubt arranged in pattern books, and issued to the porcelain painters.

CHAPTER XVIII

FORGERIES AND IMITATIONS

With their intense veneration for the antique, it is only natural that the Chinese should excel in imitative work, and a great deal of ingenuity has been quite legitimately exercised by them in this direction. The amateur will sometimes have difficulty in distinguishing the clever copies from the originals, but in most cases the material and the finish of the work frankly belong to a later period, and sometimes all doubt is removed at once by a mark indicating the true period of manufacture. But the collector has to be on his guard against a very different kind of article, the spurious antique and the old piece which has been "improved" by the addition of more elaborate decoration or by an inscription which, if genuine, would give it historic importance. The latter kind of embellishment is specially common on the early potteries of the Han and T'ang periods. Genuine specimens taken from excavated tombs have often been furnished with dates and dedicatory legends cut into the body of the ware and then doctored, to give the appearance of contemporary incisions. But a careful examination of the edges of the channelled lines will show that they have been cut subsequently to the firing of the ware, when the clay was already hard. Had the inscription been cut when the pot was made, it would have been incised in a soft unfired substance, like the writing of a stylus in wax, and the edges of the lines would be forced up and slightly bulging; and if the ware is glazed, some of the glaze will be found in the hollows of the inscription. There are, besides, minor frauds in the nature of repairs. Pieces of old pottery, for instance, are fitted into a broken Han jar; the lost heads and limbs of T'ang figures are replaced from other broken specimens, and defective parts are made up in plaster. Such additions are often carefully concealed by daubs of clay similar to that with which the buried specimen had become encrusted. Further than this, Han and T'ang figures have been recently manufactured in their entirety, and mention has already been made (Vol. I., p. 27) of a factory at Honan Fu, where figures and vases with streaked and mottled glazes, fantastic ewers with phœnix-spouts and wing-like excrescences, and the like, are made with indifferent skill.

The collector of Sung and Yüan wares, too, has many difficulties to surmount. The fine imitations made from the Yung Chêng period onwards, both in pottery and porcelain, fortunately are often marked; but sometimes the mark has been carefully removed by grinding, and the scar made up to look like the natural surface. The imitative wares made in Kuangtung, at Yi-hsing, and in various Japanese factories have been already discussed in the sections concerned; and there is pottery with lavender blue, "old turquoise" and splashed glazes resembling the Chün types, but made at the present day in Honan and elsewhere, which is likely to deceive the beginner. The commonest kind has a buff earthen body which is usually washed with a dull brown clay on the exposed parts. But such obstacles as these add zest to the collector's sport, and they are not really hard to surmount if a careful study be made of the character of authentic specimens. The eye can be easily trained to the peculiarities both of the originals and of the various imitative types, and no one who is prepared to take a little trouble need be afraid of attacking this fascinating part of Chinese ceramics.

The *T'ao lu*[529] quotes an interesting note on the repairing of antique wares: "In the *Chu ming yao* it is stated with regard to old porcelain (*tz'ŭ*), such as (incense-) vessels which are wanting in handles or feet, and vases damaged at the mouth and edge, that men take old porcelain to patch the old, adding a glazing preparation, and giving the piece one firing. When finished it is like an old piece, and all uniform, except that the patched part is dull in colour. But still people prefer these specimens to modern wares. If the process of blowing the glaze on to (the joint of the repair) is used in patching old wares, the patch is still more difficult to trace. As for specimens with flaws (*mao*), I am told that on the Tiger Hill in Su-chou there are menders who have earned the name of *chin* (close-fitters)." The collector knows only too well that there are "close-fitters" in Europe as well as in China.

Apart from the numerous instances in which early Ming marks[530] have been indiscriminately added to later wares, the careful copies and imitations of true Ming types are comparatively few. Among the imitative triumphs of the Yung Chêng potters a few specialties are named, such as blue and white of the Hsüan Tê and the Chia Ching periods, and the enamelled decoration of the Ch'êng Hua and Wan Li, but reference has already been made to these in their respective chapters. The modern Chinese potters make indifferent reproductions of Ming types; and the most dangerous are those of the Japanese, who from the eighteenth century onward seem to have taken the sixteenth century Chinese porcelains as their model. The Chia Ching and Wan Li marks are common on these reproductions, which often catch the tone and spirit of the Ming ware with disquieting exactitude. A well-trained eye and a knowledge of the peculiarities of Japanese workmanship are the only protection against this type of imitation.

The high esteem in which the K'ang Hsi porcelains are now held has naturally invited imitation and fraud. The ordinary modern specimen with a spurious K'ang Hsi mark is, as a rule, feeble and harmless, and even the better class of Chinese and Japanese imitations of the blue and white and enamelled porcelains of this period are, as a rule, so wide of the mark as to deceive only the inexperienced. Many frauds, however, have been perpetrated with French copies of *famille verte*, of *famille rose* "ruby-back" dishes, and of vases with armorial decoration. These are cleverly made, but the expert will see at once that the colours and the drawing lack the true Oriental quality, and that the ware itself is too white and cold. Clever copies of Oriental porcelain, especially of the *famille rose*, have also been made at Herend, in Hungary. But perhaps the most dangerous Continental copies are some of the French-made monochromes of dark blue and lavender colours, with or without crackle, fitted with ormolu mounts in eighteenth century style, which conceal the tell-tale base. Monochromes are, as a rule, the most difficult porcelains to date, and the well-made modern Chinese and Japanese *sang de bœuf*, apple green, and peach bloom are liable to cause trouble, especially when the surface has been carefully rubbed and given the appearance of wear and usage. The expert looks to the truth of the form, the finish of the base, and the character of the clay exposed at the foot rim, and judges if in these points the piece comes up to the proper standard.

But without doubt the most insidious of all the fraudulent wares are those which have been redecorated. I do not refer to the clobbered[531] and retouched polychromes or to the powder blue and mirror black on which the gilding has been renewed, but to the devilish ingenuity which takes a piece of lightly decorated K'ang Hsi porcelain, removes the enamelling, and even the whole glaze if the original ornament has been in underglaze blue, and then proceeds to clothe the denuded surface in a new and resplendent garb of rich enamel. Naturally, it is the most sumptuous style of decoration which is affected in these frauds, such as the prunus tree and birds in a ground of black, green, or yellow enamel on the biscuit; and the drawing, execution and colours are often surprisingly good. The enormous value of this type of vase, if successful, repays the expense and trouble involved in the *truquage*; and the connoisseur who looks at the base for guidance is disarmed because that critical part has been undisturbed, and has all the points of a thoroughbred K'ang Hsi piece. If, however, his suspicion has been aroused by something unconvincing in the design or draughtsmanship, he will probably find upon minute examination some indication of the fraud, some trace of the grinding off of the glaze which the enamels have failed to cover, suspicious passages at the edge of the lip where the old and new surfaces join, or traces of blackening here and there which are rarely absent from a refired piece. But if the work is really successful, and no ingenuity or skill is spared to make it so, his suspicions may not be aroused until too late. Frauds of this kind belong to the most costly types, and concern the wealthy buyers. The poorer collectors have to deal with small deceits, the adding of a *famille verte* border to a bowl or dish, the retouching of defective ornament, the rubbing of modern surfaces to give them fictitious signs of wear, the staining of new wares with tobacco juice, and other devices easily detected by those who are forewarned. Against all these dangers, whether they be from wilful frauds or from innocent imitations, I can only repeat that the collector's sole defence is experience and a well-trained eye.

FOOTNOTES:

[1] See vol. i, p. 153.

[2] *fêng huo*. Bushell renders "blast furnaces."

[3] 爁橫 *lan kuang*, lit. "burn tube." Omitting the radical 火 (*huo*, fire) in both cases, Bushell takes the characters as *lan* (blue) and *huang* (yellow). Possibly Bushell's edition had variant readings.

[4] Bk. vii., fol. 25 recto.

[5] Or, perhaps, "greenish black," taking the two words together.

[6] 脫胎 lit. "omit body." A slightly thicker porcelain is known as *pan t'o t'ai*, or "half bodiless."

[7] 彩錐 *ts'ai chui*. These words seem to have been taken to mean "decorated with an awl"; but they are better translated separately to mean "bright coloured" and "(engraved with) an awl," the suggestion being that *ts'ai* refers to enamelled porcelain.

[8] Bk. ii., fol. 8 verso.

[9] 壓手杯 *Ya shou pei*, lit. "press hand cups."

[10] "Made in the Yung Lo period of the great Ming dynasty."

[11] The reading in the British Museum copy is 白 *pai* (white), which seems to be an error for 四 *ssŭ* (four): taken as it stands, it would mean written in white slip.

[12] 滑 *hua*, lit. "slippery." The meanings include "polished, smooth, ground," etc., from which it will be seen that the word could equally refer to a glazed surface or an unglazed surface which had been polished on the wheel.

[13] This conical form of bowl was by no means new in the Ming period. In fact, we are told in the *T'ao shuo* that it is the *p'ieh* of the Sung dynasty, the old form of tea bowl. See vol. i, p. 175.

[14] There are several others of this type in Continental museums; cf. Zimmermann, op. cit. Plate 23.

[15] *Cat.*, F 6.

[16] Bk. v., fol. 5.

[17] Bk. ii., fol. 8.

[18] *pa pei*, lit. handle cups. This type, as illustrated in Hsiang's Album (op. cit., No. 54) is a shallow cup or tazza on a tall stem which was grasped by the hand.

[19] An example of the figure subjects on Hsüan Tê blue and white is given in the *T'ao shuo*, "teacups decorated with figures armed with light silk fans striking at flying fire-flies"; see Bushell's translation, op. cit., p. 136.

[20] "Citron dishes" are specially mentioned in the *Wên chên hêng ch'ang wu chi* (*T'ao lu*, bk. viii., fol. 4).

[21] *Ch'ang k'ou*, lit. "shed mouth."

[22] Lit. "pot-bellied."

[23] Lit. "cauldron (*fu*) base."

[24] *an hua*, secret decoration (see p. 6).

[25] "Made in the Hsüan Tê period of the great Ming dynasty."

[26] Lit. "orange-peel markings (*chü p'i wên*) rise in the glaze."

[27] i.e. red lines coloured by rubbing ochre into the cracks. See vol. i, p. 99.

[28] *O. C. A.*, p. 371.

[29] Unfortunately the term *pao shih hung* has been loosely applied in modern times to the iron red. See Julien, op. cit., p. 91 note: "Among the colours for porcelain painting which M. Itier brought from China and offered to the Sèvres factory, there is one called *pao shih hung*, which, from M. Salvétat's analysis, is nothing else but oxide of iron with a flux." In other words, it is a material which should have been labelled *fan hung*. This careless terminology has led to much confusion.

[30] *T'ao lu*, bk. v., fol. 7 recto.

[31] The *Ch'ing pi tsang* mentions "designs of flowers, birds, fish and insects, and such like forms" as typical ornaments on the red painted Hsüan porcelain.

[32] The three fruits (*san kuo*) are the peach, pomegranate, and finger citron, which typify the Three Abundances of years, sons and happiness.

[33] *Wu fu*. This may, however, be emblematically rendered by five bats, the bat (*fu*) being a common rebus for *fu* (happiness).

[34] See p. 122.

[35] According to Bushell, *O. C. A.*, p. 130, "cobalt blue, as we learn from the official annals of the Sung dynasty (*Sung shih*, bk. 490, fol. 12), was brought to China by the Arabs under the name of *wu ming yi*." This takes it

back to the tenth century. *Wu ming yi* (nameless rarity) was afterwards used as a general name for cobalt blue, and was applied to the native mineral. The name was sometimes varied to *wu ming tzŭ*. Though we are not expressly told the source of the *su-ni-p'o* blue, it is easily guessed. For the Ming Annals (bk. 325) state that among the objects brought as tribute by envoys from Sumatra were "precious stones, agate, crystal, carbonate of copper, rhinoceros horn, and 回回青 *hui hui ch'ing* (Mohammedan blue)." See W. P. Groeneveldt, *Verhandelingen van het Bataviaasch Genootschap van Kunsten en Wetenschappen*, vol. xxxix., p. 92. These envoys arrived in 1426, 1430, 1433, 1434, and for the last time in 1486. Sumatra was a meeting-place of the traders from East and West, and no doubt the Mohammedan blue was brought thither by Arab merchants. Possibly some of the mineral was brought back by the celebrated eunuch Chêng Ho, who led an expedition to Sumatra in the Yung Lo period. See also p. 30.

[36] See *Cat. B. F. A.*, 1910, L 23; a pilgrim bottle belonging to Mrs. Halsey, inscribed after export to India with the word Alamgir, a name of the famous Aurungzib. Cf. also the fine cylindrical vase in the Victoria and Albert Museum (Case 2), with floral scrolls in this type of blue combined with underglaze red, and the Hsüan Tê mark.

[37] Op. cit., Nos. 9, 31, 37, 39, 48, 69 and 83.

[38] *Hui hu* is a variant for *hui hui* (Mohammedan).

[39] Probably due to over-firing.

[40] On the parallelism between this type of porcelain decoration and cloisonné enamel, see *Burlington Magazine*, September, 1912, p. 320. It is worthy of note that missing parts of these vases, such as neck rim or handles, are often replaced by cloisonné enamel on metal, which is so like the surrounding porcelain that the repairs are often overlooked.

[41] The yellow of this group is usually of a dull, impure tint, but there is a small jar in the Peters Collection in New York on which the yellow is exceptionally pure and brilliant, and almost of lemon colour.

[42] In these cases the porcelain would be first fired without glaze and the colours added when it was in what is called the "biscuit" state. In the blue and white ware, on the other hand, and the bulk of Chinese glazed porcelain, body and glaze were baked together in one firing.

[43] Bushell, *O. C. A.*, p. 152.

[44] Translation of the *T'ao shuo*, op. cit., p. 51.

[45] This is the verdict of the *Po wu yao lan*, and it is repeated in the *T'ao lu*, see Bushell, op. cit., p. 60.

[46] Painted decoration is mentioned in Chiang's Memoir of the Yüan dynasty (see vol. i, p. 160), but without any particulars; and the *Ko ku yao lun* speaks of *wu sê* decoration of a coarse kind at the end of the Yüan period (see vol. i, p. 161). The latter may, of course, refer to the use of coloured glazes.

[47] Op. cit., fig. 77.

[48] The application of these enamels in large washes puts them practically in the category of glazes, but for the sake of clearness it is best to keep the terminology distinct. After all, the difference between a high-fired glaze which is applied to the biscuit and a low-fired enamel applied in the same way is only one of degree, but if we use the term enamel or enamel-glaze for the colours fired in the muffle kiln as distinct from those fired in the porcelain kiln, it will save further explanations.

[49] A late Ming writer quoted in the *T'ao lu* (bk. viii., fol. 18) says, "At the present day Hsüan ware cricket pots are still very greatly treasured. Their price is not less than that of Hsüan Ho pots of the Sung dynasty."

[50] Bushell, op. cit., p. 140.

[51] *Po wu yao lan*, bk. ii., fol. 9 verso.

[52] 憲 *hsien*. The emperor Ch'êng Hua was canonised as Hsien Tsung.

[53] See p. 12.

[54] 淺淡 *ch'ien tan*. The *T'ao shuo*, quoting this passage, uses a variant reading, *ch'ien shên* 深, which Bushell renders "whether light or dark."

[55] *yu hua i*, lit. "have the picture idea."

[56] See Bushell, *O. C. A.*, p. 385.

[57] See Hsiang's Album, op. cit., fig. 38.

[58] Bk. vi., fols. 7–9, and Bushell's translation, op. cit., pp. 141–3.

[59] Op. cit., fig. 55.

[60] *Burlington Magazine*, December, 1912, pp. 153–8.

[61] The author of the *P'u shu t'ing chi* (*Memoirs of the Pavilion for Sunning Books*), quoted in the *T'ao shuo*, loc. cit.

[62] Op. cit., fig. 64.

[63] Bushell (*T'ao shuo*, p. 142) gives the misleading version, "bowls enamelled with jewels" and "jewel-enamelled bowls," omitting in his translation the note in the text which explains their true meaning as *pao shih hung* or ruby red.

[64] 草虫*ts'ao ch'ung* can equally well mean "plants and insects" or "grass insects," i.e. grasshoppers. In fact, Julien translated the phrase in the latter sense.

[65] *Chin hui tui*, lit. brocade ash-heaps.

[66] Not as Bushell (*T'ao shuo*, op. cit., p. 143), "medallions of flower sprays and fruits painted on the four sides"; *ssŭ mien* (lit. four sides) being a common phrase for "on all sides" does not necessarily imply a quadrangular object.

[67] *Shih nü*, strangely rendered by Bushell "a party of young girls."

[68] The dragon boats raced on the rivers and were carried in procession through the streets on the festival of the fifth day of the fifth month. See J. J. M. de Groot, *Annales du Musée Guimet*, vol. xi., p. 346. A design of children playing at dragon boat processions is occasionally seen in later porcelain decoration.

[69] Cf. the favourite design of children under a pine-tree on Japanese Hirado porcelain.

[70] Op. cit., figs. 38, 49, 55, 56, 63, 64, 65, 66 and 76.

[71] 敷色 Bushell has translated it "diffused colours," but *fu* is also used for "applying externally" in the medicinal sense, which seems specially appropriate here.

[72] 填油, lit. "fill up (with) glaze," the colour of the glaze being specified in each case. Cf. *lan ti t'ien hua wu ts'ai* (blue ground filled up with polychrome painting), a phrase used to describe the decoration of the barrel-shaped garden seats of the Hsüan Tê period. See p. 17.

[73] Fig. 63, a cup in form like the chicken cups (*chi kang*).

[74] 其上*ch'i shang*.

[75] Op. cit., Plate ii.

[76] See E. Dillon, *Porcelain*, Plate xviii.

[77] See E. Dillon, *Porcelain*, Plate vii.

[78] See *Cat, B. F. A.*, 1910, H 21, I 7.

[79] 正統

[80] 景泰

[81] 天順.

[82] **弘治**.

[83] Op. cit., No. 42.

[84] **嬌**, delicate, beautiful.

[85] **蒸栗**.

[86] **葵花**.

[87] Vol. ii., p. 277.

[88] See vol. i, p. 154.

[89] See p. 12.

[90] This account is quoted from the *Shih wu kan chu*, published in 1591.

[91] See p. 12.

[92] See Hirth, *China and the Roman Orient*, p. 179.

[93] The converse is equally true, and Chinese porcelain of this kind is frequently classed among Persian wares. Indeed, there are not a few who would argue that these true porcelains of the hard-paste type were actually made in Persia. No evidence has been produced to support this wholly unnecessary theory beyond the facts which I have mentioned in this passage, and the debated specimens which I have had the opportunity to examine were all of a kind which no one trained in Chinese ceramics could possibly mistake for anything but Chinese porcelain.

[94] This peculiarity occurs on a tripod incense vase in the Eumorfopoulos Collection, which in other respects resembles this little group, but it is a peculiarity not confined to the Chêng Tê porcelain, for I have occasionally found it on much later wares.

[95] A somewhat similar effect is seen on the little flask ascribed to the Hsüan Tê period. See p. 14.

[96] Op. cit., Nos. 52 and 80. These are the latest specimens which are given by Hsiang Yüan-p'ien.

[97] *Cat.*, H 8.

[98] A similar vase is in the Victoria and Albert Museum.

[99] **鮮紅土**hsien hung t'u, lit. "the earth for the fresh red," an expression which would naturally refer to the *clay* used in making ware of this particular colour, though Bushell has preferred to take it in reference to the *mineral* used to produce the colour itself. See p. 123.

[100] Bk. ii., fol. 10.

[101] A Ming writer quoted in the *T'ao lu*, bk. viii., fol. 4, adds that these cups were marked under the base 金籙 *chin lu* (golden seal), 大醮 *ta chiao* (great sacrifice), 壇用 *t'an yung* (altar use).

[102] *Ch'ing k'ou*, lit. mouth like a gong or sounding stone.

[103] *Man hsin*, lit. loaf-shaped centre.

[104] *Yüan tsu*, lit. foot with outer border.

[105] An extract from the *I Chih* (quoted in the *T'ao lu*, bk. viii., fol. 14) states that "in the 26th year of Chia Ching, the emperor demanded that vessels should be made with 'fresh red' (*hsien hung*) decoration; they were difficult to make successfully, and Hsü Chên of the Imperial Censorate, memorialised the throne, requesting that red from sulphate of iron (*fan hung*) be used instead." A memorial of similar tenor was sent to the emperor by Hsü Ch'ih in the succeeding reign.

[106] *O. C. A.*, pp. 223–6.

[107] Bk. vi., fols. 9–15. See also Bushell's translation op. cit., pp. 145–51, and *O. C. A.*, loc. cit.

[108] Some idea of the quantity supplied may be gathered from the following items in the list for the year 1546: 300 fish bowls, 1,000 covered jars, 22,000 bowls, 31,000 round dishes (*p'an*), 18,400 wine cups.

[109] See Bushell, *O. C. A.*, p. 226.

[110] There are examples of this work in the British Museum, in which the blue seems to have been sponged on or washed on, and the decoration picked out with a needlepoint, and then the whole covered with a colourless glaze.

[111] *hsiang yün*, lit. felicitous clouds.

[112] 貼金 *t'ieh chin*, lit. stuck-on gold.

[113] *O. C. A.*, p. 221.

[114] 甜白 *t'ien pai*, a phrase frequently used in this sense, though it is not quite obvious how it derives this meaning from its literal sense of "sweet white."

[115] See p. 34. The *fan hung* is an overglaze colour of coral tint, derived from oxide of iron; the *hsien hung* is an underglaze red derived from oxide of copper.

[116] *jang hua*, lit. "abundant or luxuriant ornament." *Embossed* is Bushell's rendering.

[117] See Bushell's translation, op. cit., p. 151.

[118] 結子蓮.

[119] See p. 298.

[120] 靈芝*ling chih*, a species of agaric, at first regarded as an emblem of good luck, and afterwards as a Taoist emblem of immortality.

[121] See Bushell, *O. C. A.*, p. 563.

[122] 獅子*shih tzŭ*. The mythical lion is a fantastic animal with the playful qualities of the Pekingese spaniel, which it resembles in features. In fact the latter is called the lion dog (*shih tzŭ k'ou*), and the former is often loosely named the "dog of Fo (Buddha)," because he is the usual guardian of Buddhist temples and images.

[123] 蒼*ts'ang*, azure or hoary.

[124] Named by Bushell mackerel, carp., marbled perch, and another.

[125] 江下八俊.

[126] 駿*chün*, a fleet horse.

[127] Translation of the *T'ao shuo* (p. 145).

[128] *O. C. A.*, p. 227.

[129] 乾坤六合.

[130] See Laufer, *Jade*, p. 120.

[131] See Mayers, part ii., p. 335.

[132] *hua* 花. Bushell (*T'ao shuo*, p. 146) has rendered this with "flowers and inscriptions, etc." In many cases in these lists it is almost impossible to say whether the word *hua* has the sense of *flowers* or merely *decoration*. The present passage *fu shou k'ang ning hua chung* seems to demand the second interpretation.

[133] This dark blue Chia Ching ware was carefully copied at the Imperial factory in the Yung Chêng period. See p. 203.

[134] See *J. Böttger, Philipp Hainhofer und der Kunstschrank Gustav Adolfs in Upsala*, Stockholm, 1909, Plate 71. The same interesting collection includes a marked Wan Li dish with cloud and stork pattern in underglaze blue, two

cups, and a set of Indian lacquer dishes with centres made of the characteristic Chinese export porcelain described on p. 70.

[135] *Cat B. F. A.*, D 17.

[136] A good example of this colouring is a large bowl with Chia Ching mark in the Kunstgewerbe Museum, Berlin.

[137] See vol. i, p. 225.

[138] Figured in F. Dillon, *Porcelain*, Plate v.

[139] Bk. v., fol. 9 recto.

[140] 催公. *Ts'ui* is a fairly common name. It occurs as a mark on a small figure of an infant in creamy white ware of Ting type in the Eumorfopoulos Collection; but it is highly improbable that this piece has anything to do with the Mr. Ts'ui here in question.

[141] The *Ming ch'ên shih pi chou chai yü t'an*, quoted in the *T'ao lu*, bk. viii., fol. 4, says, "When we come to Chia Ching ware then there are also imitations of both Hsüan Tê and Ch'êng Hua types (they even are said to excel them). But Mr. Ts'ui's ware is honoured in addition, though its price is negligible, being only one-tenth of that of Hsüan and Ch'êng wares."

[142] Bk. iii., fol. 7.

[143] See Bushell, *O. C. A.*, p. 235.

[144] Bk. vi., fol. 16, and Bushell's translation, p. 152.

[145] See *Ming ch'ên shih pi chou chai yü t'an* (quoted in *T'ao lu*, bk. viii., cf. 4 verso): "For Mu Tsung (i.e. Lung Ch'ing) loved sensuality, and therefore orders were given to make this kind of thing; but as a matter of fact 'Spring painting' began in the picture house of Prince Kuang Chüan of the Han dynasty...."

[146] See *T'ao lu*, bk. viii., fols. 10 and 11, quoting from the *Ts'ao t'ien yu chi*.

[147] *T'ang ying lung kang chi*, quoted in the *T'ao lu*, bk. viii., fols. 11 and 12.

[148] Chao was supposed to have displayed superhuman skill in the manufacture of pottery in the Chin dynasty (265–419 A.D.).

[149] Bk. v., fol. 8.

[150] For explanation of these terms, see p. 10.

[151] Bushell's rendering, "cups and saucers," is misleading if not verbally incorrect.

[152] These are Bushell's renderings.

[153] 四鬢頭 *ssŭ hsŭ t'ou*, a phrase which would more usually refer to the beard than the hair of the head. The above rendering is Bushell's.

[154] 頂粧.

[155] 玲瓏.

[156] 昊十九.

[157] 壺隱道人. There is an allusion in this name to the story of Hu Kung, a magician of the third and fourth centuries, who was credited with marvellous healing powers. Every night he disappeared, and it was found at length that he was in the habit of retiring into a hollow gourd which hung from the door post. See A. E. Hippisley, *Catalogue of a Collection of Chinese Porcelains*, Smithsonian Institute, Washington, 1900. Hao's porcelain is also known as *Hu kung yao* (the ware of Mr. Pots).

[158] See *T'ao lu*, bk. v., fol. 10, and bk. viii., fol. 7, and *T'ao shuo*, bk. vi., fol. 26.

[159] 卵幕 *luan mu*, "the curtain inside the egg," which conveys the idea of extreme tenuity better than the most usual expression, "egg shell" porcelain.

[160] Half a *chu*.

[161] 流霞盞.

[162] *Tzŭ chin.* Golden brown with reddish tinge (*tzŭ chin tai chu*), accurately describes one kind of stoneware tea pots made at Yi-hsing (p. 177); but it is not stated whether Hao's imitations were in stoneware or porcelain.

[163] An allusion to the celebrated orchid pavilion at Kuei-chi, in Chêkiang, the meeting place of a coterie of scholars in the fourth century. The scene in which they floated their wine cups on the river has been popularised in pictorial art. See Plate 104 Fig. 1.

[164] 菁田.

[165] The *K'ao p'an yü shih.*

[166] Bk. vi., fol. 16 recto.

[167] See p. 140.

[168] Bk. v., fol. 10 verso, under the heading, *Hsiao nan yao* (Little South Street wares).

[169] 蝦蟆, apparently referring to the size of the vessels and not necessarily implying that they were shaped like a frog. On the other hand,

small water vessels in the form of a frog have been made in China from the Sung period onwards.

[170] 䍌坩.

[171] A similar ewer in Dr. Seligmann's collection is marked with one of the trigrams of the *pa kua*.

[172] *Cat.*, L 24.

[173] *Cat.*, E 19–25.

[174] *Denkmäler Persischer Baukunst*, Plate lii., Text p. 41 and Fig. 44.

[175] The same emperor showed his appreciation for Chinese ceramics by importing a number of Chinese potters into Persia. See p. 30.

[176] It is recorded that the Emperor Wan Li sent presents of large porcelain jars to the Mogul Emperor, and it is likely that similar presents had arrived at the Persian Court.

[177] *Cat.*, Case X, No. 245, and Plate xv.

[178] *Burlington Magazine*, October, 1910, p. 40.

[179] See *Franks Catalogue*, No. 763.

[180] *Burlington Magazine*, March, 1913, p. 310. See also *Hainhofer und der Kunstschrank Gustav Adolfs*, op. cit., Plate 69, where a set of dishes of India lacquer is illustrated, each mounted in the centre with a roundel of this type of porcelain. These dishes are mentioned in a letter dated 1628.

[181] Numbered 1191 and 1192. A number of other painters who have introduced these Chinese porcelains into their work are named by Mr. Perzynski (*Burlington Magazine*, December, 1910, p. 169).

[182] See p. 63.

[183] C 5–7.

[184] *Cat.*, No. 112D.

[185] *Burlington Magazine*, December, 1910, p. 169.

[186] The figures sometimes stand out against a background coloured with washes of green, yellow and aubergine glaze. See Plate 82, Fig. 2.

[187] See p. 43.

[188] See vol. i., p. 218.

[189] See p. 196.

[190] I have seen occasional specimens with the Wan Li mark.

[191] See vol. i., p. 218.

[192] *Cat.*, J 21.

[193] *Cat.*, A 33. In the Lymans Collection in Boston there are several examples of this ware, including specimens with dark and light coffee brown grounds and a jar in blue and white.

[194] A collection of these is in the British Museum, and they include many types of late Ming export porcelains.

[195] *Cat. B. F. A.*, K 37.

[196] A jar with vertical bands of ornament in a misty underglaze red of pale tint in the Eumorfopoulos collection probably belongs to this period. Though technically unsuccessful, the general effect of the bold red-painted design is most attractive.

[197] See vol. i., p. 218.

[198] *Cat.*, J 16.

[199] There is a whole case full of them in the celebrated Dresden collection, a fact which is strongly in favour of a K'ang Hsi origin for the group.

[200] Eight Precious Things. See p. 299.

[201] See vol. i., p. 219.

[202] The fact that the enamellers' shops at Ching-tê Chên to this day are known as *hung tien* (red shops) points to the predominance of this red family in the early history of enamelled decorations.

[203] See p. 67.

[204] See vol. i., p. 218.

[205] See p. 224.

[206] See p. 90.

[207] H 17, exhibited by Mr. G. Eumorfopoulos.

[208] See p. 4.

[209] See p. 94.

[210] Other saucers of this kind have a decoration of radiating floral sprays, and there are bowls of a familiar type with small sprays engraved and filled in with coloured glazes in a ground of green or aubergine purple. Some of these have a rough biscuit suggesting the late Ming period; others of finer finish apparently belong to the K'ang Hsi period. They often have indistinct seal marks, known as "shop marks," in blue.

[211] *Burlington Magazine*, December, 1910, p. 169, and March, 1913, p. 311.

[212] Figured in Monkhouse, op. cit., Fig. 2. The date of the mount is disputed, some authorities placing it at the end of the sixteenth century.

[213] Figured by Perzynski, *Burlington Magazine*, March, 1913. A vase of this style with tulip design in the palace at Charlottenburg has a cyclical date in the decoration, which represents 1639 or 1699 (probably the former) in our chronology.

[214] 白不子 *pai tun tzŭ* white blocks.

[215] A sixteenth-century work. See p. 2.

[216] Many observers positively assert that the grooved foot rim does not occur on pre-K'ang Hsi porcelain. If this is true, it provides a very useful rule for dating; but the rigid application of these rules of thumb is rarely possible, and we can only regard them as useful but not infallible guides.

[217] Quoted in *T'ao lu*, bk. viii., fol. 6.

[218] *fu ti*.

[219] *Man hsin*.

[220] See *T'ao shuo*, bk. iii., fol. 7 verso. "Among other things the porcelain with glaze lustrous and thick like massed lard, and which has millet grains rising like chicken skin and displays palm eyes (*tsung yen*) like orange skin, is prized." The expression "palm eyes" occurring by itself in other contexts has given rise to conflicting opinions, but its use here, qualified by the comparison with orange peel and in contrast with the granular elevations, points clearly to some sort of depressions or pittings which, being characteristic of the classical porcelain, came to be regarded as beauty spots.

[221] e.g. The *P'ing shih*, the *P'ing hua p'u*, and the *Chang wu chih*, all late Ming works. An extract from the second (quoted in the *T'ao lu*, bk. ix., p. 4 verso) tells us that "Chang Tê-ch'ien says all who arrange flowers first must choose vases. For summer and autumn you should use porcelain vases. For the hall and large rooms large vases are fitting; for the study, small ones. Avoid circular arrangement and avoid pairs. Prize the porcelain and disdain gold and silver. Esteem pure elegance. The mouth of the vase should be small and the foot thick. Choose these. They stand firm, and do not emit vapours." Tin linings, we are also told, should be used in winter to prevent the frost cracking the porcelain; and *Chang wu chih* (quoted *ibidem*, fol. 6 verso) speaks of very large Lung-ch'üan and Chün ware vases, two or three feet high, as very suitable for putting old prunus boughs in.

[222] Cobalt, the source of the ceramic blues, is obtained from cobaltiferous ore of manganese, and its quality varies according to the purity of the ore and the care with which it is refined.

[223] *O. C. A.*, p. 263. This very dark blue recalls one of the Chia Ching types noted on page 36.

[224] See p. 10.

[225] But see p. 177.

[226] *Biscuit* is the usual term for a fired porcelain which has not been glazed.

[227] See p. 17.

[228] It has been suggested by Mr. Joseph Burton that the opacity of the colours described in the preceding paragraphs may have been due to the addition of porcelain earth to the glazing material.

[229] See p. 82.

[230] See, however, p. 85.

[231] See p. 2.

[232] The *T'ao lu* (bk. ix., fol. 17 verso) quotes an infallible method for fixing the gold on bowls so that it would never come off; it seems to have consisted of mixing garlic juice with the gold before painting and firing it in the ordinary way.

[233] Loc. cit., and Bushell, *O. C. A.*, p. 268.

[234] See p. 75.

[235] See *T'ao shuo*, bk. iii., fol. 10 verso.

[236] See p. 55.

[237] e.g. The *Chieh tzŭ yüan ma chuan* of the K'ang Hsi period, mentioned by Perzynski, *Burlington Magazine*, March, 1913, p. 310.

[238] Bushell's translation, op. cit., p. 71.

[239] *Ku chin t'u shu chi ch'êng*, section xxxii., bk. 248, section entitled *tz'ŭ ch'i pu hui k'ao*, fol. 13 verso.

[240] 堊土

[241] The supplies of porcelain earth in the immediate district of Jao Chou Fu were exhausted by this time.

[242] The others were the Ch'ing-yün factory at Ssŭ-tu, and the Lan-ch'i factory in the Chien-ning district. The latter district was mentioned in vol. i., p. 130, in connection with the hare's fur bowls of the Sung period.

[243] See vol. i., p. 17.

[244] Tê-hua was formerly included in the Ch'üan-chou Fu, but is now in the Yung-ch'un Chou.

[245] See vol. i., p. 131.

[246] Bk. vii., fol. 13 verso.

[247] Loc. cit.

[248] According to de Groot, *Annales du Musée Guinet*, vol. xi., p. 195.

[249] Brinkley, *China and Japan*, vol. ix., p. 274.

[250] See W. Anderson, *Catalogue of the Japanese and Chinese Paintings in the British Museum*, p. 75.

[251] *O. C. A.*, p. 628.

[252] In the letter dated from Jao Chou, September, 1712, loc. cit.

[253] Incised designs on Fukien wares consist of the ordinary decoration etched in the body of the ware and of inscriptions which have evidently been cut through the glaze before it was fired. The latter often occur on wine cups, and are usually poetical sentiments or aphorisms, e.g. "In business be pure as the wind"; "Amidst the green wine cups we rejoice."

[254] *Japan and China*, vol. ix., p. 273.

[255] *Everyday Life in China, or Scenes in Fukien*, by E. J. Dukes, London, 1885, p. 140. The reference is given by Bushell in his *Oriental Ceramic Art*.

[256] Loc. cit., p. 273.

[257] The *Li t'a k'an k'ao ku ou pien*, a copy of which, published in 1877, is in the British Museum. This book does not inspire confidence, but I give the passage for what it is worth: "When the glaze (of the Chien yao) is white like jade, glossy and lustrous, rich and thick, with a reddish tinge, and the biscuit heavy, the ware is first quality ... Enamelled specimens (*wu ts'ai*) are second rate."

[258] In the Pierpont Morgan collection (vol. i., p. 78), a specimen with a blue mark is described as Fukien porcelain; but I should accept the description with the greatest reserve, white Ching-tê Chên ware being very often wrongly described in this way.

[259] *O. C. A.*, p. 294.

[260] In the second volume of the Pierpont Morgan catalogue—which, unfortunately, had not the benefit of Dr. Bushell's erudition—the late Mr. Laffan extended the term *lang yao* so as to embrace the magnificent three-colour vases with black ground and their kindred masterpieces with green and yellow grounds. It is impossible to justify this extension of the term unless we assume that the pieces in question were all made between the years 1654–1661 and 1665–1668, while Lang T'ing-tso was viceroy of Kiangsi.

[261] *O. C. A.*, p. 302.

[262] Quoted in the Franks *Catalogue*, p. 8.

[263] *O. C. A.*, p. 302 footnote.

[264] See also Hippisley, *Catalogue*, p. 346, where another version is given which makes this Lang actually a Jesuit missionary, a version which Mr. Hippisley afterwards abandoned when research in the Jesuit records failed to discover any evidence for the statement.

[265] See p. 11.

[266] See p. 34.

[267] Op. cit., Section ix. The paragraph in the first letter runs: "Il y en a d'entièrement rouges, et parmi celles-là, les unes sont d'un rouge à l'huile, *yeou li hum*; les autres sont d'un rouge soufflé, *tschoui hum* (*ch'ui hung*), et sont semées de petits points à peu près comme nos mignatures. Quand ces deux sortes d'ouvrages réüssissent dans leur perfection, ce qui est assez difficile, ils sont infiniment estimez et extrêmement chers."

[268] There is a very beautiful glaze effect known as "ashes of roses," which seems to be a partially fired-out *sang de bœuf*. It is a crackled glaze, translucent, and lightly tinged with a copper red which verges on maroon.

[269] The Emperor K'ang Hsi was specially concerned to encourage industry and art, and in 1680 he established a number of factories at Peking for the manufacture of enamels, glass, lacquer, etc. Père d'Entrecolles mentions that he also attempted to set up the manufacture of porcelain in the capital, but though he ordered workmen and materials to be brought from Ching-tê Chên for the purpose, the enterprise failed, possibly, as d'Entrecolles hints, owing to intrigues of the vested interests elsewhere.

[270] Bushell, op. cit., p. 3.

[271] Bk. v., fol. 11.

[272] 澆 lit. watered. This word has been rendered by some translators as "pale"; but probably it has merely the sense of "mixed with the (glaze) water," i.e. a monochrome glaze. The recipe given in the *T'ao lu* (see Julien)

is incomplete, only mentioning "crystals of saltpetre and ferruginous earth (*fer ologiste terreux*)." Another *chiao* which signifies "beautiful, delicate," is applied to the Hung Chih yellow in Hsiang's Album. See vol. ii., p. 28.

[273] Lit. "yellow distribute spots." See, however, p. 190.

[274] See O. C. A., p. 317.

[275] The two letters were published in *Lettres édifiantes et curieuses*. They are reprinted as an appendix to Dr. Bushell's translation of the *T'ao shuo*. They have been well translated by William Burton, in his *Porcelain*, Chap. ix.; Bushell gave a *précis* of them in his O. C. A., Chap, xi., and Stanislas Julien quoted them extensively in his *Porcelaine Chinoise*.

[276] Père d'Entrecolles (second letter, section xii.) points out that the glaze used for the blue and white was considerably softer than that of the ordinary ware, and was fired in the more temperate parts of the kiln. The softening ingredient (which consisted chiefly of the ashes of a certain wood and lime burnt together) was added to the glaze material (*pai yu*) in a proportion of 1 to 7 for the blue and white as against 1 to 13 for the ordinary ware.

[277] On some of the large saucer-shaped dishes of this period the foot rim is unusually broad and channelled with a deep groove.

[278] See Bushell, *T'ao shuo*, op. cit., p. 192. It is tolerably clear that d'Entrecolles in this passage is giving a verbatim rendering of a Chinese description. The "flowers" is, no doubt, *hua*, and might be rendered "decoration" in the general sense, and the "water and the mountains" is, no doubt, *shan shui*, the current phrase for "landscape."

[279] For the shape of the *ju-i* head, see vol. i., p. 227.

[280] "Flaming silver candle lighting up rosy beauty," a Ch'êng Hua design (see p. 25) but often found in K'ang Hsi porcelain, which usually has, by the way, the Ch'êng Hua mark to keep up the associations.

[281] For further notes on design, see chap. xvii.

[282] There is a small collection of these porcelains salved from the sea and presented to the British Museum by H. Adams in 1853; but there is no evidence to show which, if any, were on board the *Haarlem*.

[283] This design was copied on early Worcester blue and white porcelain.

[284] In spite of Bushell's translation of a Ming passage which would lead one to think otherwise; see p. 40.

[285] See vol. i., p. 226.

[286] There are frequent allusions to the European trade in the letters of Père d'Entrecolles. In the first letter (Bushell, *T'ao shuo*, p. 191) a reference is made among moulded porcelains to "celles qui sont d'une figure bisarre, comme les animaux, les grotesques, les Idoles, les bustes que les Europeans ordonnent." On p. 193: "Pour ce qui est des couleurs de la porcelaine, il y en a de toutes les sortes. On n'en voit gueres en Europe que de celle qui est d'un bleu vif sur un fond blanc. Je crois pourtant que nos Marchands y en ont apporté d'autres." On p. 202, to explain the high price of the Chinese porcelain in Europe, we are told that for the porcelain for Europe new models, often very strange and difficult to manufacture, are constantly demanded, and as the porcelain was rejected for the smallest defect, these pieces were left on the potter's hands, and, being un-Chinese in taste, were quite unsaleable. Naturally the potter demanded a high price for the successful pieces to cover his loss on the rejected.

On the other hand, we are told (p. 204) that the mandarins, recognising the inventive genius of the Europeans, sometimes asked him (d'Entrecolles) to procure new and curious designs, in order that they might have novelties to offer to the Emperor. But his converts entreated him not to get these designs, which were often very difficult to execute and led to all manner of ill-treatment of the unfortunate workmen.

On the same page we are told that the European merchants ordered large plaques for inlaying in furniture, but that the potters found it impossible to make any plaque larger than about a foot square. In the second letter (section x.), however, we learn that "this year (1722) they had accepted orders for designs which had hitherto been considered impossible, viz. for urns (*urnes*) 3 feet and more high, with a cover which rose in pyramidal form to an additional foot. They were made in three pieces, so skilfully joined that the seams were not visible, and out of twenty-five made only eight had been successful. These objects were ordered by the Canton merchants, who deal with the Europeans; for in China people are not interested in porcelain which entails such great cost."

[287] This defect is noticed by Père d'Entrecolles, who mentions another remedy used by the Chinese potters. They applied, he tells us in section ii. of the second letter, a preparation of bamboo ashes mixed with glazing material to the edges of the plate before the glazing proper. This was supposed to have the desired effect without impairing the whiteness of the porcelain.

[288] See p. 74.

[289] Second letter, section iv.

[290] See Bushell, O. C. A., p. 320.

[291] See p. 201.

[292] The use of crackle glaze over blue (*porcelaine toute azurée*) is noted by Père d'Entrecolles in his first letter. See Bushell, op. cit., p. 195.

[293] See Bushell, *T'ao shuo*, p. 197.

[294] A somewhat similar but clumsier decoration was the "scratched blue" of the Staffordshire salt glaze made about 1750.

[295] On exceptional examples the red seems to have turned almost black, and in some cases it seems to have penetrated the glaze and turned brown.

[296] A similar combination of coloured glazes was effectively used on the moulded porcelains of the Japanese Hirado factory.

[297] See pp. 48 and 100.

[298] Loc. cit., second letter, section xiv.

[299] Apparently *huang lü huan*, yellow and green (?) circles. But without the Chinese characters it is impossible to say which *huan* is intended. The description seems to apply to the "tiger skin" ware, where yellow, green and aubergine glazes have been applied in large patches. Bushell (*O. C. A.*, p. 331) makes this expression refer to the specimens with engraved designs in colour contrasting with the surrounding ground, such as Fig. 1 of Plate 79; but this does not seem to suit the word *huan*.

[300] Loc. cit., section xiv.

[301] See footnote on p. 89.

[302] The same technique is employed on some of the Japanese Kaga wares.

[303] Apparently derived from manganese.

[304] See p. 80.

[305] Another favourite form is the ovoid beaker (see Plate 101), which is sometimes called the *yen yen* vase, apparently from *yen*, beautiful. But I only have this name on hearsay, and it is perhaps merely a trader's term.

[306] See p. 110.

[307] A lotus-shaped set in the Salting collection numbers thirteen sections.

[308] The underglaze blue almost invariably suffered in the subsequent firings which were necessary for the enamels, and, as we shall see, a different kind of glaze was used on the pure enamelled ware and on the blue and white.

[309] Apart from the cases in which the enamel colours were added to faulty specimens of blue and white to conceal defects.

[310] See p. 85.

[311] Op. cit., section vi. "Il n'y a, dit on, que vingt ans ou environ qu'on a trouvé le secret de peindre avec le *tsoui* ou en violet et de dorer la porcelaine." As far as the gilding is concerned, this statement is many centuries wrong. The *tsoui* is no doubt the *ts'ui*, which is very vaguely described in section xii. (under the name *tsiu*) of the same letter. Here it is stated to have been compounded of a kind of stone, but the description of its treatment clearly shows that the material was really a coloured glass, which is, in fact, the basis of the violet blue enamel.

[312] Bushell, op. cit., p. 193.

[313] Loc. cit., p. 195.

[314] See d'Entrecolles, second letter, section xii.

[315] Burnt lime and wood ashes. See p. 92.

[316] Catalogue of the 1910 exhibition, No. 84.

[317] These seals are usually difficult to decipher, and the one in question might be read *shui shih chü* (water and rock dwelling). This would be a matter of small importance did not the signature read by Bushell as *wan shih chü* occur in the Pierpont Morgan Collection. Other instances in the same collection are *chu chü* (bamboo retreat), *shih chü* (rock retreat), and *chu shih chü* (red rock retreat). The signature *chu chü* also occurs on a dish in the Dresden collection.

[318] See p. 212.

[319] See p. 64.

[320] Cat., vol. i., p. 156.

[321] Similar bottles in the Drucker Collection have the "G" mark.

[322] *Fang tung yang*, "imitating the Eastern Sea" (i.e. Japan).

[323] The first specimens (according to Bushell, *O. C. A.*, p. 309) to reach America came from the collection of the Prince of Yi, whose line was founded by the thirteenth son of the Emperor K'ang Hsi.

[324] The general reader will probably not be much concerned as to whether the peach bloom was produced by oxide of copper or by some other process. Having learnt the outward signs of the glaze, he will take the inner meaning of it for granted. Others, however, will be interested to know that practically all the features of the peach bloom glaze, the pink colour, the green ground and the russet brown spots can be produced by chrome tin fired at a high temperature. I have seen examples of these chrome tin pinks made by Mr.

Mott at Doulton's, which exhibit practically all the peculiarities of the Chinese peach bloom. It does not, of course, follow that the Chinese used the same methods or even had any knowledge of chrome tin. They may have arrived at the same results by entirely different methods, and the peach bloom tints developed on some of the painted underglaze copper reds point to the one which is generally believed to have been used; but the difference between these and the fully developed peach bloom is considerable, and though we have no definite evidence one way or the other, the possibilities of chrome tin cannot be overlooked.

[325] The form of this water pot is known (according to Bushell, *O. C. A.*, p. 318) as the *T'ai-po tsun*, because it was designed after the traditional shape of the wine jar of Li T'ai-po, the celebrated T'ang poet. In its complete state it has a short neck with slightly spreading mouth.

[326] See p. 146.

[327] See p. 64.

[328] i.e. lead glass.

[329] *Chi*, lit. sky-clearing, and *chi ch'ing* might be rendered "blue of the sky after rain."

[330] There are some bowls and bottles in the Dresden collection with glazes of a pale luminous blue which are hard to parallel elsewhere.

[331] Loc. cit., section xvii. In another place (section iii.) we are told how the Chinese surrounded the ware with paper during the blowing operation, so as to catch and save all the precious material which fell wide of the porcelain.

[332] I cannot recall any example of the powder blue crackle which is here described.

[333] See Julien, p. 107.

[334] P. 170.

[335] Second letter, section xvii.

[336] The word "mazarine" has become naturalised in the English language. Goldsmith spoke of "gowns of mazarine blue edged with fur"; and "Ingoldsby" says the sky was "bright mazarine." See R. L. Hobson, *Worcester Porcelain*, p. 101.

[337] See p. 99.

[338] See p. 102.

[339] These glazes generally have the appearance of being in two coats, and in some cases there actually seem to be two layers of crackle.

[340] See p. 125.

[341] i.e. the strong heavy types. Chinese literature speaks of thinner and more refined celadons of the Sung period, but few of these have come down to our day.

[342] Père d'Entrecolles fully describes these spurious celadons. See vol. i., p. 83.

[343] Second letter, section vii.

[344] The *T'ao lu* (see Julien, p. 213) gives this recipe for the kind of celadon known as *Tung ch'ing*, and a similar prescription with a small percentage of blue added for the variety known as *Lung-ch'üan*.

[345] See Bushell, O. C. A., p. 316.

[346] See p. 147.

[347] There are some fine examples of orange yellow monochrome in the Peters Collection in New York. The colour was also used with success in the Ch'ien Lung period, the mark of which reign occurs on a good example in the Peters Collection.

[348] Bushell, *O. C. A.*, Plates xxv. and lxxxiii.

[349] See Monkhouse, op. cit., fig. 22. The crackle on the mustard yellow glaze is usually small, but there is a fine specimen in the Peters Collection with large even crackle. Sometimes this yellow has a greenish tinge, and in a few instances it is combined with crackled green glaze.

[350] Second letter, section vi.

[351] See Père d'Entrecolles, second letter, section xiii.: "L'argent sur le vernis *tse kin (tzŭ chin)* a beaucoup d'éclat."

[352] See p. 145.

[353] The blue of the cobalt is sometimes clearly visible in the fracture of the glaze; and in other cases the black has a decided tinge of brown.

[354] d'Entrecolles, loc. cit., section viii.: "Le noir éclatant ou le noir de miroir appellé *ou kim*" *(wu chin).*

[355] d'Entrecolles declares that it was the result of many experiments, apparently in his own time. See p. 194.

[356] Second letter, section xi.

[357] See M. Seymour de Ricci in the introduction to the *Catalogue of a Collection of Mounted Porcelain belonging to E. M. Hodgkins, Paris,* 1911, where much interesting information has been collected on the subject of French

mounts and their designers. He quotes also from the *Livre-journal de Lazare Duvaux marchand-bijoutier ordinaire du Roy* (1748–1758), which includes a list of objects mounted for Madame de Pompadour and others, giving the nature of the wares and the cost of the work.

[358] Persian, Indian, and occasionally even Chinese metal mounts are found on porcelain; and Mr. S. E. Kennedy has a fine enamelled vase of the K'ang Hsi period with spirited dragon handles of old Chinese bronze.

[359] White was also used in the worship of the Year Star (Jupiter). Other colours which have a ritual significance are *yellow*, used in the Ancestral Temple by the Emperor, and on the altars of the god of Agriculture and of the goddess of Silk; *blue*, in the Temple of Heaven and in the Temple of Land and Grain; and *red*, in the worship of the Sun.

[360] Brinkley has aptly described it as "snow-white oil."

[361] Cf. Père d'Entrecolles, second letter, section xviii.: "(The designs) are first outlined with a graving-tool on the body of the vase, and afterwards lightly channelled around to give them relief. After this they are glazed."

[362] See d'Entrecolles, loc. cit., sections iv. and v. After describing the preparation of the steatite (*hua shih*) by mixing it with water, he continues: "Then they dip a brush in the mixture and trace various designs on the porcelain, and when they are dry the glaze is applied. When the ware is fired, these designs emerge in a white which differs from that of the body. It is as though a faint mist had spread over the surface. The white from *hoa che* (*hua shih* or *steatite*) is called ivory white, *siam ya pe* (*hsiang ya pai*)." In the next section he describes another material used for white painting under the glaze. This is *shih kao*, which has been identified with fibrous gypsum.

[363] See p. 74.

[364] First letter, Bushell, op. cit., p. 195.

[365] *O. C. A.*, p. 533.

[366] *Ku chin t'u shu*, section xxxii., vol. 248, fol. 15. In this way, we are told, were produced (1) the thousandfold millet crackle and (2) the drab-brown (*ho*) cups. The colour of the latter was obtained by rubbing on a decoction of old tea leaves. The former is a name given to a glaze broken into "numerous small points."

[367] See Bushell, *T'ao shuo*, loc. cit., p. 195.

[368] The *Tao lu* (see Julien, p. 214) informs us that the *sui ch'i yu* (crackle ware glaze) was made from briquettes formed of the natural rock of San-pao-p'êng. If highly refined this material produced small crackle; if less carefully refined, coarse crackle. In reference to *sui ch'i* in an earlier part of

the same work, we are told that the Sung potters mixed *hua shih* with the glaze to produce crackle. *Hua shih* is a material of the nature of steatite, and Bushell (*O. C. A.*, p. 447) states that the Chinese potters mix powdered steatite with the glaze to make it crackle. It is, then, highly probable that the "white pebbles" of Père d'Entrecolles and the rock of San-pao-p'êng are the same material and of a steatitic nature.

[369] 年希堯. Another name of this official, *Yen kung*, is mentioned in the *T'ao lu*, bk. v., fol. 11 verso.

[370] Situated at the junction of the Grand Canal and the Yangtze.

[371] Loc. cit.

[372] Silvering the entire surface (*mo yin*), as opposed to merely decorating with painted designs in silver (*miao yin*), appears to have been a novelty introduced by T'ang Ying.

[373] i.e. porcelain services painted with European coats of arms.

[374] See p. 215.

[375] See p. 225, Nos. 41 and 42.

[376] Cf. p. 25, where "high-flaming silver candle lighting up rosy beauty" is explained in this sense among the Ch'êng Hua designs.

[377] See p. 13.

[378] See p. 225, No. 45.

[379] See p. 224, Nos. 19 and 20.

[380] A beautiful example of a "stem-cup" in the Eumorfopoulos Collection, with three fishes on the exterior in underglaze red of brilliant quality and the Hsüan Tê mark inside the bowl, probably belongs to this class.

[381] See p. 148.

[382] See p. 225, No. 30.

[383] See p. 224, No. 26.

[384] See *Catalogue* 300–303. "On each is a miniature group of the Seven Worthies of the Bamboo Grove with an attendant bringing a jar of wine and flowers. The porcelain is so thin that the design, with all the details of colour, can be distinctly perceived from the inside." It is only right to say that their learned possessor has catalogued them as genuine examples of the Ch'êng Hua period.

[385] See p. 224, No. 25.

[386] See p. 201.

[387] See p. 224, No. 27.

[388] See p. 225, No. 36.

[389] *T'ao shuo*, bk. i., fol. 15 verso.

[390] See p. 225, No. 49. *Fo-lang, fa-lang, fu-lang,* and *fa-lan* are used indiscriminately by the Chinese in the sense of enamels on metal.

[391] In the *T'ao lu*, under the heading *Yang tz'ŭ*. It is a curious paradox that the Chinese called *famille rose* porcelain *yang ts'ai* (foreign colours) and the Canton enamels *yang tz'ŭ* (foreign porcelain). See *Burlington Magazine*, December, 1912, "Note on Canton Enamels."

[392] See pp. 224–226, Nos. 29, 37, 38, 49, 51, 53, and 54.

[393] Apart from the rose pinks which are derived from purple of cassius, i.e. precipitate of gold, and the opaque white derived from arsenic, the colouring agents of the *famille rose* enamels are essentially the same as those of the *famille verte*. The colours themselves were brought to Ching-tê Chên in the form of lumps of coloured glass prepared at the Shantung glass works. These lumps were ground to a fine powder and mixed with a little white lead, and in some cases with sand (apparently potash was also used in some cases to modify the tones), and the powder was worked up for the painter's use with turpentine, weak glue, or even with water. Cobaltiferous ore of manganese, oxide of copper, iron peroxide, and antimony were still the main colouring agents. The first produced the various shades of blue, violet, purple, and black; the second, the various greens; the third, coral or brick red; and the fourth, yellow of various shades. A little iron in the yellow gave the colour an orange tone.

The modifications of the green are more numerous. The pure binoxide of copper produced the shade used for distant mountains (*shan lü*), which could be converted into turquoise by the admixture of white. The ordinary leaf green was darkened by strengthening the lead element in the flux and made bluer by the introduction of potash in the mixture. Combined with yellow it gave an opaque yellowish green colour known as *ku lü* (ancient green); and a very pale greenish white, the "moon white" of the enameller, was made by a tinge of green added to the arsenious white.

The carmine and crimson rose tints derived from the glass tinted with precipitate of gold, which was known as *yen chih hung* (rouge red), were modified with white to produce the *fên hung* or pale pink; and the same carmine was combined with white and deep blue to make the amaranth or blue lotus (*ch'ing lien*) colour.

The ordinary brick red (the *ta hung* or *mo hung*) was derived from peroxide of iron mixed with a little glue to make it adhere, but depending on the glaze for any vitrification it could obtain. The addition of a plumbo-alcaline flux produced the more brilliant and glossy red of coral tint known as *tsao'rh hung* (jujube red).

The dry, dull black derived from cobaltiferous manganese was converted into a glossy enamel by mixing with green. This is the *famille rose* black as distinct from the black of the *famille verte*, which was formed by a layer of green washed over a layer of dull black on the porcelain itself.

There are, besides, numerous other shades, such as lavender, French grey, etc., obtained by cunning mixtures, and all these enamels were capable of use as monochromes in place of coloured glazes as well as for brushwork.

[394] Bushell, *Chinese Art*, vol. ii., fig. 61.

[395] *Histoire de la porcelaine*, pt. viii., fig. 3.

[396] These marks were discussed by Bushell in the *Burlington Magazine*, August and September, 1906. They are figured on vol. i., pp. 219 and 223.

[397] Quoted from a letter written to Sir Wollaston Franks by Mr. Arthur B. French, who visited Ching-tê Chên in 1882.

[398] Officially the reign of K'ang Hsi dates from 1662–1722, but he actually succeeded to the throne on the death of Shun Chih in 1661, so that his reign completed the cycle of sixty years in 1721.

[399] As Bushell has done in *Chinese Art*, vol. ii., p. 42.

[400] See "Note on Canton Enamels," *Burlington Magazine*, December, 1912.

[401] See p. 225, No. 40.

[402] Op. cit., second letter, section xx.

[403] Nos. 39 and 55–57.

[404] *Miao* is used in the sense of to "draw" a picture or design.

[405] Bushell, *O. C. A.*, p. 400, explains how the studio name was formed by the common device of splitting up Hu 胡 into its component parts *ku* 古 and *yüeh* 月.

[406] From the Hippisley collection, *Catalogue*, p. 408.

[407] *Catalogue of Hippisley Collection*, p. 347.

[408] *Chinese Art*, vol. ii., fig. 74.

[409] See p. 224, Nos. 15–17.

[410] A recipe given in the *T'ao lu* (bk. iii., fol. 12 verso) for the *lu chün* glaze speaks of "crystals of nitre, rock crystal, and (?) cobaltiferous manganese (*liao*) mixed with ordinary glaze." But apart from the uncertain rendering of *liao* (which Bushell takes as *ch'ing liao*, i.e. the material used for blue painting), it is difficult to see how this composition, including the ordinary porcelain glaze, can have been fired in the muffle kiln.

[411] In the jujube red the iron oxide is mixed with the plumbo-alcaline flux of the enameller, whereas in the *mo hung* it is simply made to adhere to the porcelain by means of glue, and depends for the silicates, which give it a vitreous appearance, on the glaze beneath it.

[412] *O. C. A.*, p. 360.

[413] See p. 224, No. 18.

[414] See p. 225, No. 44.

[415] Op. cit., p. 67.

[416] *Catalogue*, K. 18.

[417] *Catalogue*, vol. i., p. 38. The colour has already been discussed in a note on p. 68 of vol. i. of this book.

[418] See vol. i., p. 68.

[419] See Bushell, *O. C. A.*, p. 368

[420] The Chinese is *kua yu* 掛釉, lit. hanging, suspended or applied glaze. The Yi-hsing stoneware was not usually glazed; hence the force of the epithet *kua* applied.

[421] The gold-flecked turquoise has yet to be identified.

[422] Bushell says this is the sapphire blue (*pao shih lan*) of the period.

[423] 抹 mo, lit. "rubbed." Bushell (*O. C. A.*, p. 383) explains the term *mo hung* as "applied to the process of painting the coral red monochrome derived from iron over the glaze with an ordinary brush."

[424] Bushell takes this to be the lemon yellow enamel which was first used at this time.

[425] See p. 37.

[426] 有通川紅釉繪畫者有青葉紅花者 *yu t'ung yung hung yu hui hua chê, yu ch'ing yeh hung hua chê*. Bushell (*O. C. A.*, p. 386) gives a slightly different application of this passage, but the meaning seems to be obviously that given above.

[427] This note is given by Bushell, apparently from the Chinese edition which he used; but it does not appear in the British Museum copy. It is, however, attached to the list as quoted in the *T'ao lu*.

[428] As already explained, *miao chin* refers to gilt designs painted with a brush, and *mo chin* to gilding covering the entire surface.

[429] *O. C. A.*, p. 50.

[430] 唐英

[431] Translated by Bushell, *O. C. A.*, p. 398.

[432] Bk. v., fol. 12.

[433] 又新製, *yu hsin shih*, lit. "also he newly made." This is undoubtedly the sense given by the Chinese original, and Julien renders it "il avait nouvellement mis en œuvre." Bushell, on the other hand, translates: "He also made porcelain decorated with the various coloured glazes *newly invented*," a reading which makes the word *chih* do duty twice over, and leaves it doubtful whether T'ang was the inventor of these types of decoration or merely the user of them. Both the grammar and the balance of the sentences in the original are against this colourless rendering.

[434] See p. 192.

[435] *La Porcelaine Chinoise*, p. 216.

[436] See p. 225. "In the new copies of the Western style of painting in enamels (*hsi yang fa lang hua fa*), the landscapes and figure scenes, the flowering plants and birds are without exception of supernatural beauty."

[437] See p. 209.

[438] P. 397.

[439] An interesting series of these bird's egg glazes appearing, as they often do, on tiny vases was exhibited by his Excellency the Chinese Minister at the Whitechapel Art Gallery in November, 1913.

[440] There is a very old superstition in China that cracked or broken pottery is the abode of evil spirits. The modern collector abhors the cracked or damaged specimen for other reasons, and it is certain that such things would not be admitted to the Imperial collections. Many rare and interesting pieces which have come to Europe in the past will be found on examination to be more or less defective, and it is probable that we owe their presence chiefly to this circumstance.

[441] See Bushell's translation, op. cit., p. 6.

[442] The *T'ao shuo* was published in 1774.

[443] See vol. i., p. 119.

[444] See Julien, op. cit., p. 101, under the heading *lung kang yao* (kilns for the dragon jars).

[445] The Chinese foot as at present standardised is about two inches longer than the English foot, and the Chinese inch is one-tenth of it.

[446] See p. 58.

[447] There are four examples of the large size of fish bowl in the Pierpont Morgan Collection, but they are of late Ming date.

[448] Possibly the tint named in the *T'ao shuo* (Bushell, op. cit., p. 5). "They are coloured wax yellow, tea green, gold brown, or the tint of old Lama books," in reference to incense burners of this period.

[449] Nos. 8, 9 and 11. See Bushell, *T'ao shuo*, op. cit., pp. 16–19.

[450] See p. 140.

[451] A plaque in the Bushell Collection with *famille verte* painting has also a remarkably lustrous appearance, which I can only ascribe to excessive iridescence.

[452] See Bushell's translation, op. cit. p. 20.

[453] Figured by L. Binyon, *Painting in the Far East*, first edition, Plate XIX. There is a fine vase of late Ming blue and white porcelain with this design in the Dresden collection.

[454] This green enamel is sometimes netted over with lines suggesting crackle studded with prunus blossoms. Possibly this is intended to recall both in colour and pattern the "plum blossom" crackle of the Sung Kuan yao; see vol. i., p. 61.

[455] *Shên tê t'ang* and *ch'ing wei t'ang*. See vol. i., p. 220.

[456] See Burton and Hobson, Marks on *Pottery* and *Porcelain*, p. 151.

[457] Op. cit., pp. 116–175.

[458] *T'ao shuo*, op. cit., pp. 7–30 and O. C. A., ch. xv.

[459] The Lowestoft factory started about 1752, but its earlier productions were almost entirely blue and white, often copied, like most of the contemporary blue and white from Chinese export wares.

[460] A curious instance of imitation of European ornament is a small bowl which I recently saw with openwork sides and medallions, apparently moulded from a glass cameo made by Tassie at the end of the eighteenth

century; and there is a puzzle jug with openwork neck, copied from the well known Delft-ware model, in the Metropolitan Museum, New York.

[461] Rotterdam was captured by the Spaniards in 1572; but those who are interested in the anachronism of Chinese marks will observe that these plates have the date mark of the Ch'êng Hua period (1465–1487).

[462] See vol. i., p. 226.

[463] Op. cit., p. 207.

[464] An interesting example of an early eighteenth century service with European designs is the "trumpeter service," of which several specimens may be seen in the Salting Collection. It has a design of trumpeters, or perhaps heralds, reserved in a black enamelled ground.

[465] One of these pieces, for instance, is a plate with arms of Sir John Lambert, who was created a baronet in 1711 and died in 1722. It has enamels of the transition kind.

[466] P. 209.

[467] The willow pattern is merely an English adaptation of the conventional Chinese landscape and river scene which occurs frequently on the export blue and white porcelain of the eighteenth century. That it represents any particular story is extremely improbable.

[468] Frank Falkner, *The Wood Family of Burslem*, p. 67.

[469] Another *chambrelan* who flourished about the same time and who worked in the same style was C. F. de Wolfsbourg.

[470] *O. C. A.,* p. 464.

[471] "The mountains are high, the rivers long."

[472] See vol. i., p. 220.

[473] *Catalogue*, No. 367.

[474] Vol. i., p. 220.

[475] Hippisley Collection, *Catalogue*, No. 169.

[476] *O. C. A.,* p. 469.

[477] This extravagant idea has been long ago exploded, and need not be rediscussed. See, however, Julien *Porcelaine Chinoise*, p. xix., and Medhurst, *Transactions of the China Branch of the Royal Asiatic Society*, Hong Kong, 1853.

[478] *O. C. A.,* p. 470.

[479] Bk. 93, fols. 13–15.

[480] *O. C. A.*, pp. 474–83.

[481] Bushell applies the phrase *pan tzǔ* to the bowls and renders it "of ring-like outline."

[482] Bushell renders *ju-i* in the general sense, "with words of happy augury"; it is, however, applied to ornaments of *ju-i* staffs and to borders of *ju-i* heads.

[483] See vol. i., p. 225.

[484] Bk. i., fols. 1 and 2; see Bushell, op. cit., pp. 3–6.

[485] This is a variety of the key pattern or Greek fret, which is of world-wide distribution.

[486] A less usual variety has the ovoid body actually surmounted by a beaker

[487] See Bushell, *O. C. A.*, p. 797.

[488] See Bushell's translation, op. cit., p. 4.

[489] See Bushell, *O. C. A.,* p. 489.

[490] Among others is the "tantalus cup," with a small tube in the bottom concealed by a figure of a man or smiling boy. When the water in the cup reaches the top of the tube it runs away from the base.

[491] Loc. cit., p. 204.

[492] The cup with handle was made in the tea services for the European market, but the handle is not, as has been sometimes asserted, a European addition to the cup. Cups with handles were made in China as early as the T'ang dynasty (see Plate 11, Fig. 2); but for both wine and tea drinking the Chinese seem to have preferred the handleless variety.

[493] When the names are known the incidents can usually be found in such works of reference as Mayers' *Chinese Reader's Manual*, Giles's *Chinese Biographical Dictionary*, and Anderson's Catalogue of Chinese and Japanese Pictures.

[494] Told in the *Shui Hu Chuan*; see *O. C. A.*, p. 570, a note in Bushell's excellent chapter on Chinese decorative motives, of which free use has been made here.

[495] A not uncommon subject is the meeting of a young horseman with a beautiful lady in a chariot, and it has been suggested that this may be the meeting of Ming Huang and Yang Kuei-fei; but the identification is quite conjectural.

[496] Another game, *hsiang ch'i* (elephant checkers), is far nearer to our chess.

[497] A group of five old men similarly employed represents the *wu lao* (the five old ones), the spirits of the five planets.

[498] Chang Kuo Lao, the Taoist Immortal, is also regarded as one of the gods of Literature; see p. 287.

[499] Vajrapani is one of the gods of the Four Quarters of the Heaven, who are guardians of Buddha. They are represented as ferocious looking warriors, sometimes stamping on prostrate demon-figures. As such they occur among the T'ang tomb statuettes, but they are not often represented on the later porcelains.

[500] The Kanzan and Jitoku of Japanese lore.

[501] See *Catalogue of the Pierpont Morgan Collection*, vol. i., p. 156.

[502] Indeed it is likely that the modern *ju-i* head derives from the fungus. The *ju-i* 如意 means "as you wish" or "according (*ju*) to your idea (*i*)," and the sceptre, which is made in all manner of materials such as wood, porcelain, lacquer, cloisonné enamel, etc., is a suitable gift for wedding or birthday. Its form is a slightly curved staff about 12 to 15 inches long, with a fungus-shaped head bent over like a hook. On the origin of the *ju-i*, see Laufer, *Jade*, p. 335.

[503] The Japanese Mt. Horai.

[504] See Hippisley, *Catalogue*, op. cit., p. 392.

[505] The Buddhist pearl or jewel, which grants every wish.

[506] See a rare silver cup depicting this legend, figured in the *Burlington Magazine*, December, 1912.

[507] See W. Perceval Yetts, *Symbolism in Chinese Art*, read before the China Society, January 8th, 1912, p. 3.

[508] Hippisley (op. cit., p. 368), speaking of the various dragons, says that "the distinction is not at present rigidly maintained, and the five-clawed dragon is met with embroidered on officers' uniforms."

[509] A dual creature, the *fêng* being the male and the huang the female.

[510] See Laufer, *Jade*, pl. 43.

[511] See Laufer, *Jade*, p. 266.

[512] See Bushell, *Chinese Art*, vol. i., p. 111.

[513] See p. 300.

[514] They also symbolise the three friends, Confucius, Buddha, and Lao-tzŭ.

[515] *O. C. A.*, p. 106.

[516] It is also used as a synonym for "embroidered," and when it occurs as a mark on porcelain, it suggests the idea "richly decorated."

[517] Also a symbol of conjugal felicity; and a rebus for *yü*, fertility or abundance.

[518] Having the same sound as *ch'ang* (long).

[519] *O. C. A.*, p. 119.

[520] A pair of open lozenges interlaced are read as a rebus *t'ung hsin fang shêng* (union gives success); see Bushell, *O. C. A.*, p. 120.

[521] Bushell, *O. C. A.*, p. 521.

[522] See Hippisley, *Catalogue* No. 381.

[523] *Ibid.*

[524] *Ibid.*, No. 388.

[525] *Ibid.*

[526] See p. 299.

[527] See p. 258.

[528] See Anderson, op. cit., No. 747.

[529] Bk. viii., fol. 4, quoting the *Shih ch'ing jihcha*.

[530] See chap. xvii. of vol. i., which deals with marks.

[531] See p. 261.

www.ingramcontent.com/pod-product-compliance
Ingram Content Group UK Ltd.
Pitfield, Milton Keynes, MK11 3LW, UK
UKHW031827270325
456796UK00002B/260